AMANA

THE COMMUNITY OF TRUE INSPIRATION

BY

BERTHA M. H. SHAMBAUGH

A village kinderschule (children's school) in the 1890s

A Penfield Press facsimile of the 1908 edition of *Amana: The Community of True Inspiration* by Bertha M. H. Shambaugh. This book is published in cooperation with the Museum of Amana History and the State Historical Society of Iowa.

About This Book

This facsimile of *Amana: Community of True Inspiration* is an exact reproduction of the original 1908 book with one exception. In that edition, only one photograph appeared. This edition features photographs taken by a young Bertha M. Horack in the 1890s—the first documentary photographs ever taken in the Amanas.

Until 1932, the rules of the religious communal system of the Amana Colonies did not permit the taking or display of photographs. The future Mrs. Shambaugh was so loved and respected by the Amana people that they posed for her without concern, even among the elders, for that rule.

Mrs. Shambaugh was charmed by the way of life she discovered in the Amana Colonies. The Community of True Inspiration became her own inspired guidance as she faithfully recorded its story for future generations.

We thank those who have contributed to this edition. They include Lanny Haldy, director of the Museum of Amana History; Mary Bennett, archivist, Christie Dailey, director of publications, and Nancy Kraft, library and archives, all of the State Historical Society of Iowa; John Zug, editor of Penfield Press; and Ruth Julin of Julin Printing Company, who has made this book a reality.

Joan Liffring-Zug, publisher
Penfield Press

About the cover: Blue is a traditional color of the old Amanas

Printed on archival paper

Library of Congress catalog number 88-60159

ISBN paper edition 0-941016-47-1
ISBN cloth edition 0-941016-51-X

Bertha Shambaugh in church costume of the Amana women.

When Bertha M. Horack Shambaugh (1871-1953) died at age 82, the Amana church elders and Amana Society directors in a rare joint statement said: "Mrs. Shambaugh's writings about Amana, its history and its people and its Faith, prove and substantiate her love and her deep concern and interest. . .The sincerity of her thoughts and words. . .often approach a poetical charm and quality which has never been equaled or duplicated in any other article or manuscript about Amana."

Bertha Horack was in her teens when her family vacationed for a week at an Amana hotel. This and other family outings to the Amanas began her lifelong friendship with the Amana people.

In 1897 she married Benjamin F. Shambaugh, professor of political science and director of the State Historical Society of Iowa. Mrs. Shambaugh, talented in drawing and painting, soon was making maps and charts, editing, reading proofs and preparing indexes for publications of the Historical Society. Entertaining was the favorite Shambaugh pastime. Hamlin Garland, Thornton Wilder and Jane Addams were among their dinner guests.

Mrs. Shambaugh's father, an attorney, was born in Czechoslovakia. Of her mother, Katharine Horack, Mrs. Shambaugh said: "Anything that I have done in the past and all I hope to do in the future is due to her inspiring guidance."

To My Mother

Whose Beautiful Life

Will Be an Ever Present Inspiration

To Her Children

AUTHOR'S PREFACE

In the pages of this book the Community of True Inspiration has been treated from three points of view, namely: the history of the Community; the life and the social institutions of Amana; and the religious beliefs and customs of the Inspirationists.

The early history of the Community as given in Part I is brief, since the beginnings belong to European rather than to American history. Indeed, a separate volume might well be devoted to the history of the Inspirationists in Europe. For such an undertaking there are in the *Archiv* at Middle Amana thousands of pages of manuscript material hitherto unused either by European or American students.

The descriptive account of Amana, presented in Part II, portrays the life and social institutions of the Community and is intended as a contribution to the contemporary history of the Commonwealth of Iowa.

Since the meaning of Amana is to be found in the fact that the *real* Amana is Amana the Church — Amana the Community of True Inspiration — special attention is given in Part III to the religious beliefs and customs of the Inspirationists.

Through numerous quotations (and in some instances extended extracts) from the sources, the author has hoped to reveal the spirit of this remarkable Community and explain in a measure the *Weltanschauung* of the Inspirationist in his own words. This was found to be especially difficult since the sources are wholly in the German language, as a glance at the *Notes and References* will indicate. Furthermore, much of the vocabulary used in the sources is more or less obsolete or provincial. The sentence construction is often loose and incomplete. In the historical narratives, as well as in the religious literature, the phraseology of the Bible is frequently used or imitated. Throughout the testimonies there is considerable tautology; and the language describing religious experiences is naturally vague and indefinite. And so, some of the spirit (and no little of the thought) has doubtless been lost in the translations; but by adhering rather closely to a policy of literal translation it is hoped that much has been preserved in the English version. In this connection the author desires to acknowledge the valuable assistance rendered by Mr. Josef Wiehr (Instructor in German at

The State University of Iowa) by whom many of the religious documents, which are published in English for the first time in this book, were translated.

It would be difficult to make adequate or individual acknowledgement of the assistance which has come from members of the Community and without which this volume would have been impossible. In a real sense the whole Community, whose hospitality the author has so often enjoyed, have contributed to its pages. But more especially is the author indebted to the many members whose personal acquaintance she has made and whose friendship she has cherished during the past eighteen years. Names, dates, and statistical facts may be obtained from books, reports, and blanks; but the spirit of a community and the *Weltanschauung* of its people are more adequately transmitted through personal contact and years of social intercourse.

BERTHA M. H. SHAMBAUGH

IOWA CITY IOWA
MAY 1908

1745.

Habe ich dis schreibbuch zu meinem
gebrauch genomen, u. mein haus
rechnungen u. nothwendigkeiten alle
darein schreiben, u. den Anfang
heute gemacht.

Hbg d. 8. Januarius 1745.

Johan Friedrich
Keck.

CONTENTS

PART II

A DESCRIPTIVE ACCOUNT OF AMANA

PART III

THE RELIGION OF THE INSPIRATIONISTS

PLATES

INTRODUCTORY

In one of the garden spots of Iowa there is a charming little valley from which the surrounding hills recede like the steps of a Greek theater. Through this valley the historic Iowa River flows peacefully to the eastward. A closer view reveals seven old-fashioned villages nestling among the trees or sleeping on the hillsides. About these seven villages stretch twenty-six thousand goodly acres clothed with fields of corn, pastures, meadows, vineyards, and seas of waving grain. Beyond and above, surrounding the little valley, are richly timbered hills, forming as though by design a frame for this quaint picture of Amana — the home of the Community of True Inspiration.

A bit of Europe in America, a voice out of the past on the world's western frontier, this unique Community stands as the nearest approach in our day to the Utopian's dream of a community of men and women living together in peace, plenty, and happiness, away from the world and its many distractions. But the communism of Amana is not a dream: it is a fact—an established order of life.

Of more significance, however, than the fact of communism at Amana is the deeper truth that, while standing at the head of successful communistic societies, the rise and development of the Community of True Inspiration were in no way inspired by the social philosophy of the eighteenth and nineteenth centuries. Indeed, communism is only incidental to the life and thought of this Community: its chief concern is spiritual. Born of religious enthusiasm and disciplined by persecution, it has ever remained primarily a Church. And so the *real* Amana is Amana the Church — Amana the Community of True Inspiration.

In language, in manners, in dress, in traditions, as well as in religious and economic institutions, the Community of True Inspiration is foreign to its surroundings — so much so that the visitor is at once impressed with the fact that here is something *different* from the surrounding world. In the eighteenth century the Inspirationists paid the penalty in the Old World for their non-conformity to established customs by imprisonment and exile. In the twentieth century they are objects of curiosity to their neighbors and the subject of no little speculation. The Inspirationist is by nature and by discipline given to attending quietly to his own business; and much impertinent inquiry on the part of visitors has intensified this reticence. But Amana has no secrets to hide from the world. Full liberty to worship God in their own way and to be let alone are all that the men and women of this Community have ever asked of their neighbors. And the stranger who comes with "honest intentions," sympathy, and a fair degree of common politeness finds at Amana a naive frankness, a whole-souled heartiness, and a hospitality that for genuineness are rarely excelled in the outside world.

There is much in the life of the people of Amana that seems plain and monotonous to the outside world. And yet we are compelled to acknowledge frankly that theirs is in many respects a more rational and ideal life than that which is found in our average country village. It is more genuine and uniform. There are no "company manners", and fewer "white lies." There is less extravagance; no living beyond one's means; no keeping up of "appearances"; and fewer attempts to pass for more than one is worth.

But of more fundamental concern than plain living is the fact that the Community of True Inspiration has throughout its history been dominated by an ideal and a determined purpose to realize that ideal. To this end they persevered, suffered, and sacrificed for nearly two hundred years. And finally, that their ideal of a simple religious life might prevail, they substituted a system of brotherly coöperation for one of selfish competition. For over half a century the Community has enjoyed material prosperity under this system of communism, being one of the few communistic societies which have shown steady and continuous increase in membership and in property.

It is apparent, however, that that isolation from the world for which the Community of True Inspiration has so earnestly striven and which it has so jealously guarded for six generations becomes less and less easy to preserve. Railroads, telephones, and daily newspapers have at last brought the Community and the world so close together that, despite the earnest efforts of the First Brethren, marked changes are taking place in the customs of the people and in their attitude toward life.

Whether the spirit of brotherly love and devotion to the ideals of the *Urgrosseltern* will be strong enough in this day and generation to counteract successfully the "ways of the world" can not be foreseen. But whatever lies hidden in the future for the Community of True Inspiration, the history of mankind is the richer for their example of loyal devotion to religious inspiration and plain living.

PART I

A HISTORY OF THE COMMUNITY OF TRUE INSPIRATION

itchen gardens, Amana—1890s

[Facsimile of the title-page of a volume published in the early years of the New Spiritual Economy]

J. J. J.

Buß=Weck= und Warnungs=
Stimme/

Welche der Geist der wahren

INSPIRATION

In dem
Dietzischen/Zweybrückischen/Elsaß und in
der Schweitz insonderheit erschallen lassen/
Im Jahr 1716. und 1717.

Durch

Johann Adam Gruber/

Begleitet von

Sigmund Heinrich Gleim/ und Blasius Daniel
Mackinet;

Nebst

Vorausgesetzter Beschreibung

Eines

Vor dieser und anderer Aussendung auf der Ronnäburg in dem
Büdingischen gehaltenen

Liebes=Mahles.

Gedruckt im Jahr 1718.

I

THE NEW SPIRITUAL ECONOMY

As a religious movement the Community of True Inspiration traces its origin to the German Mystics and Pietists of the sixteenth and seventeenth centuries.[1] Its rise was one of the numerous protests against the dogmatism and formality that had grown up in the Lutheran Church. As a distinct religious sect the Community dates from the year 1714 with the writings and teachings of Eberhard Ludwig Gruber and Johann Friedrich Rock, who are regarded as its real founders.[2]

Gruber was a Lutheran clergyman who had incurred the displeasure of the church by denouncing the forms that had crept into its organization and polity; while Rock was the son of a Lutheran clergyman whose father's faith had "ceased to satisfy the yearnings of the soul." In their search for truth these "heroes of faith" found each other, and together they studied the Pietism of Spener;[3] together they meditated upon the mysteries of religion; and together they formulated and improved the doctrines of the early Mystics and Pietists — particularly of that little branch of the Pietists which arose during the last quarter of the seventeenth century and whose followers are said to have "prophesied like the prophets of old" and were called the "Inspirationists."

Gruber and Rock believed profoundly in the Inspiration of the Bible; but they also believed in present-day Inspiration. "Does not the same God live to-day?" they argued, "and is it not reasonable to believe that He will inspire His followers now as then? There is no reason to believe that God has in any way changed His methods of communication, and as He revealed hidden things through visions, dreams, and by revelations in olden times He will lead His people to-day by the words of His Inspiration if they but listen to His voice."[4]

In the Community of True Inspiration as founded by Gruber and Rock (or in the "New Spiritual Economy" as it is called in the early records) divine guidance came through individuals who were regarded as especially endowed by the Lord with the "miraculous gift of Inspiration" and who were called *Werkzeuge.* Through these *Werkzeuge* (instruments) the Lord testified and spoke directly to His children, the *Werkzeug* being "solely a passive instrument in the hands of the Lord."[5] This is still the unique fundamental doctrine of the Community of True Inspiration, although there has been no *Werkzeug* since the death of Barbara Heinemann in 1883.

From the time of Rock and Gruber the *Werkzeug* has usually been accompanied by a *Schreiber* (Scribe) who faithfully recorded all that was said by the *Werkzeug* while under the influence of the Spirit of Inspiration. Indeed, a large portion of the thousands of pages of manuscript archives preserved by the Community consists of the recorded words or testimonies *(Zeugnisse* or *Bezeugnisse* or *Bezeugungen)* of the *Werkzeuge.* Published according to "the dictation of the Lord and the decision of the Brethren" in volumes of convenient size and distributed among the faithful, these *Zeugnisse* or *Bezeugungen* are regarded as of equal authority and of almost equal importance with the Bible. In his *Kennzeichen der Göttlichkeit der Wahren Inspiration,* Eberhard Ludwig Gruber defines the "new word and testimony" thus:

> Its truths are in common with the written word of the prophets and the apostles . . . . It aspires for no preference; on the contrary it gives the preference to the word of the witnesses first chosen [prophets and apostles] just after the likeness of two sons and brothers, in which case the oldest son as the first-born has the preference before the younger son who was born after him, though they are both equal and children begotten of one and the same father.

And later in the same essay he says:

> But both the old and the new revelation, of which we here speak, are of divine origin and the testimonies of one and the same Spirit of God and of Jesus Christ, just as the sons mentioned above are equally children of one and the same father though there exists through the natural birth a slight difference between them.

Gruber, who was an ardent student, wrote much regarding false and true Inspiration; for it was the belief of Gruber and Rock and their followers that there was false as well as true Inspiration. In other words they held that many persons who considered themselves inspired instruments were not such in fact. From the very beginning of the Community it was customary to appoint a committee to examine those who spoke by Inspiration; and the early *Jahrbücher* or *Bezeugungen des Geistes des Herrn* record many instances where the aspiring *Werkzeug* was condemned as false, denied the privilege of prophesying, "and thereupon underwent, indeed, sincere submission and humiliation."[6] In his *Bericht von der Inspirations-Sache,* Gruber describes his own sensations on coming in contact with a false spirit in these words:

> This strange thing happened. If perchance a false spirit was among them [the congregation] and wished to assail me in disguise, or if an insincere member wished to distinguish himself at our meeting in prayer or in some other manner, then I was befallen by an extraordinary shaking of the head and shivering of the mouth; and it

[Facsimile of the title-page of a volume on true and false Inspiration wherein the name of Eberhard Ludwig Gruber is concealed in the line which reads: *E*inem *L*ichts-*G*enossen]

J. J. J.

Nöthiges und Nutzliches Gespräch

Von

der Wahren und Falschen

INSPIRATION:

auffgesetzt

Von

Einem Lichts-Genossen.

Hoseä 12/10.

Ich rede zu den Propheten/ und Ich bins/ der so viel Weissagung gibt / und durch die Propheten mich anzeige.

Matth. 16/3.

Ihr Heuchler! des Himmels Gestalt könnet ihr urtheilen; könnet ihr dann nicht auch die Zeichen dieser Zeit urtheilen?

Cap. 21/16.

Ja/ habt ihr nie gelesen: Auß dem Mund der Unmündigen und Säuglingen hastu Lob zugerichtet.

Luc. 19/40.

Ich sage euch/ wo diese werden schweigen/ so werden die Steine schreyen.

Zum Druck übergeben

1716.

has been proven a hundred times that such was not without significance, but indeed a true warning, whatever he who is unskilled and inexperienced in these matters may deem of it according to his academic precepts and literal conclusions of reason.

II

THE SPREAD OF THE FAITH : PERSECUTION

Gruber and Rock, and others in the tiny band who were acknowledged to have the spirit and gift of Revelation and Inspiration, "went about preaching and testifying as they were directed by the Lord."[7] They made extensive travels through Germany, Switzerland, Holland, and other European countries, establishing many small congregations of followers. Under the date of June 29, 1716, there are recorded in *Inspirations-Historie* the following questions which were asked by Gruber of those who wished to share the "treasure and blessing" of True Inspiration:

(1) Whether he intends to behave as a true member of the Community of Jesus Christ towards the members and also in respect to the public prayer meetings and the arrangement of the same?

(2) Whether he be ready to suffer all inward and external pain and to risk cheerfully through the mercy of God everything, even body and soul?

(3) Whether he had obtained divine conviction with regard to the work and word of Inspiration; and whether he for his purification and sanctification would submit to the same?

(4) Whether he was in a state of reconciliation, or in some disagreement with some Brother or Sister; also if he had aught to say against anyone, or if anyone had aught to say against him?[8]

The numbers in these congregations of the New Spiritual Economy were not large during the ministration of Gruber and Rock; but the religious fervor they aroused was nevertheless rather disconcerting to the established church.

The boldness with which these independent religionists attacked "the utter hollowness and formality" of the church of state and denounced the "godless and immoral lives" of many of the clergy naturally brought them into conflict with the established church and the orthodox clergy.[9] Their cause soon encountered the opposition of the government, for the Inspirationists declined to perform military duty or to take the legal oath. "We cannot", they said, "serve the state as soldiers, because a Christian cannot murder his enemy, much less his friend."

Their refusal to take the oath was based on the fifth chapter of *Matthew,* especially upon the two passages: "But I say unto you, Swear not at all;" and, "Let your communication be, Yea, yea; Nay, nay; for whatsoever is more than these cometh of evil." In their literal adherence to this scriptural injunction, they suffered cruel humiliation and even persecution just as the Quakers in

England and the pioneers of a score of other religious communities have in their turn suffered for the iniquity of "being different."

There is, moreover, an account written in the year 1717, of the arrest of Johann Adam Gruber and his companions for refusing to take the oath, which shows their aversion to "obeying the commands of the flesh which are contrary to divine law."

> Before the city gate the executioner untied us in the presence of the sheriff. The latter held in his hand a parchment with the oath written upon it and bade us raise three fingers and to repeat. We replied that we should not swear. He urged us forcibly with many threats. The Brother [H. S. Gleim] repeated again that we should not swear; we should give a promise with hand-shake *(Handgelöbniss)* and our word should be as good as an oath, yet he would leave to me the freedom to do as I pleased. I affirmed then likewise I should not swear since our Saviour had forbidden it. [10]

The displeasure of the governments of some of the smaller German states was further aroused by the refusal of the Inspirationists to send their children to the public schools which were conducted by the Lutheran clergy. They were perfectly willing to support the state schools, or to pay the fines imposed by the government for non-conformity with the law; but they wished to train their children in their own way and in their own simple faith. This disregard of the dictates of both church and state brought upon them the wrath of both institutions. They were persecuted and prosecuted; they were fined, pilloried, flogged, imprisoned, legislated against, and stripped of their possessions. And to the shame of the German Lutheran Church of the eighteenth century it is recorded that in Zürich, under the auspices of the Lutheran clergy and by order of the city council, their pamphlets were publicly burned by the executioner, their members pilloried, then flogged through the principal streets, each person receiving sixty-two lashes, while the clergy of the established church followed and joined with the mob in yelling its approval when the streets were colored with their blood.[11] But in spite of the edicts of city councils, in spite of public humiliation and torture, the congregations of Inspirationists continued to multiply.

As persecution increased the Inspirationists naturally sought refuge under governments where the largest liberty was allowed. Perhaps the most liberal government in Germany during the eighteenth century was that of Hessen; and here the followers of Gruber and Rock came in great numbers.[12]

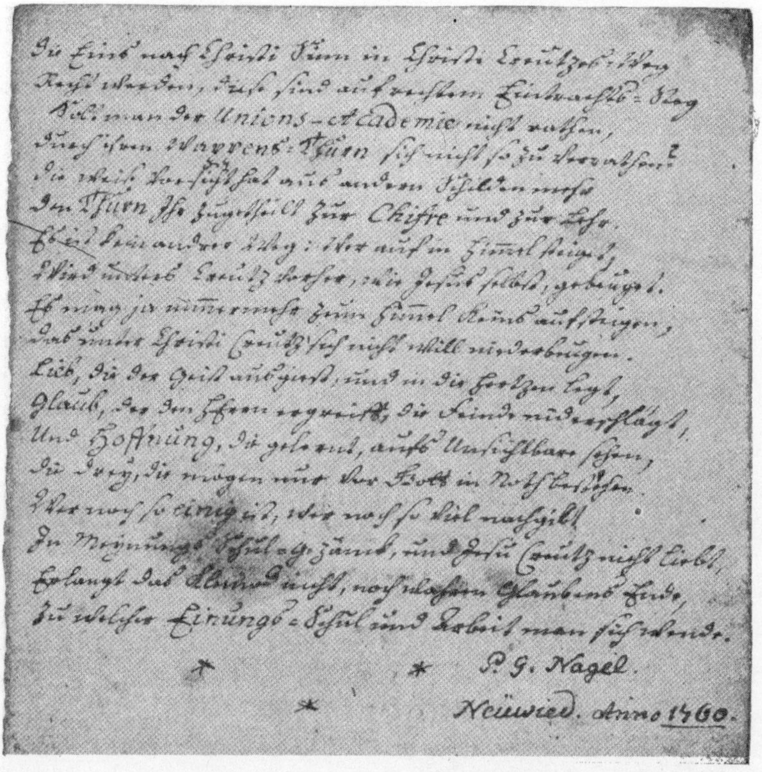

P. G. Nagel.

Neüwied. Anno 1760.

FAC SIMILE (WITHOUT REDUCTION) OF THE HAND-WRITING AND AUTOGRAPH OF THE *Schreiber*, PAUL GIESBERT NAGEL, A PROMINENT SPIRITUAL LEADER IN THE COMMUNITY DURING THE DECLINE

The millrace—1890s

III

DEATH OF GRUBER AND ROCK: THE DECLINE

In the accounts for the year 1728 it is recorded that on December 11, "after a blessed period of two times seven years spent in the service of this Brotherhood and Community into which the Lord through His holy Inspiration had led him," the time came to pass "when it pleased the Lord to recall His faithful worker and servant E. L. Gruber from this life and to transplant him into a blissful eternity."[13] Twenty-one, or "three times seven" years later, on the second day of March occurred the death of Johann Friedrich Rock; and with the record of his death is given this characteristic biographical sketch with its seventeenth century accent of the mystic seven:

The time of his pilgrimage on earth was 10 times 7 or 70 years, 3 months and 3 days. In the year 1707, when he was 4 times 7 years old, he emigrated with Br. E. L. Gruber from his native country. In the year 1714, when he counted 5 times 7 years, there came to him the gift of the Spirit and of Prophecy and he made until 1742, in 4 times 7 years, over 100 lesser and great journeys in this service. In the year 1728, when he was 7 times 7 years old he lost his faithful Brother, E. L. Gruber, and in 1742, when he counted 9 times 7, or 63 years, he ceased to travel into distant countries and spent the remaining 7 years largely at home.[14]

With the death of Rock the gift of Inspiration is said to have ceased among his people. The Communities began to decline. In the account of the year 1780, Christian Metz in his *Historische Beschreibung der Wahren Inspirations-Gemeinschaft* relates that, "after the death of the beloved sainted Brother Joh. Fried. Rock, well-founded Brethren endowed with divine mercy who were still living witnesses of the great blessings of Inspiration carried on the work of the Lord in the Communities. One by one these faithful witnesses and Elders went into eternity and were followed by less gifted and less blessed Brethren and Elders who as much as possible filled the widening gap."[15] In lieu of a *Werkzeug* they read and reread the writings and testimonies of Rock and Gruber. The movement, however, was on the wane.[16] "At the beginning of the nineteenth century but few of the once large congregations remained; even these few had fallen back into the ways of the common world more or less, preferring an easy-going way to the trials and tribulations suffered by their fathers."[17]

The historian, Gottlieb Scheuner, in his account of the Decline, laments that "the majority of the old Elders did not wish to be disturbed in their own lukewarm manner and form of worship to

[Facsimile of the first page of a pamphlet containing "two testimonies of the Spirit of True Inspiration"]

J. J. J.

Zwey

Zeugnisse des Geistes der Wahren Inspiration.

Anno 1716.

Ronneburg den 11. Augusti.

In der Versammlung der Brüder geschahe folgende Gebets-Bezeugung, durch Antrieb des Geistes des HErrn, von Br. Johann Adam Gruber.

JEHOVAH!

DIr, Dir gebühret Sieg und Uberwindung, Macht, Ehre und

A Stär-

which they had become accustomed.''[18] Indeed, ''they did not really possess the deep foundation and experience in divine things; although they still preserved the old rules of the Community as to assembling and common discussions.'' Another cause of the spiritual decline of the Communities was their peaceful external state. ''They had no longer to endure the religious struggles and trials for freedom of conscience and most of them now thought and strove more for material prosperity and success than for divine things.''

A third cause for the spiritual decline is found ''in the circumstance that the last decades of the previous [the eighteenth] and the first decades of the present [the nineteenth] century were hard and trialsome times for nearly all Europe because of great wars, destructions, and devastations, so that at times all commerce and intercourse as likewise journeying and correspondence were checked, whence a stop and stagnation resulted in everything. The places and neighborhoods where the Communities were had also to suffer much under the general oppression.'' What can be said of the work of grace during the following years ''consists only of a few fragments and brief remarks.''[18]

IV

MICHAEL KRAUSERT AND THE REAWAKENING

The Decline continued until the year 1817 — almost three quarters of a century — when, we are told, "a new and greater period dawned for the Community. The old workers had long ago foretold that the good work would not die out, that there would come a time when new teachers would arise and with new life and vigor proclaim the old doctrines. For years the prospect for the fulfilment of these prophecies had been dark and gloomy and many had begun to doubt their truth. But the time had now arrived, the revival came, and with it new life and zeal were awakened." [19]

Michael Krausert was the "first *Werkzeug* whom the Lord employed for the now commencing revival." He was a tailor journey-man of Strassburg "who sought and searched everywhere to find what would satisfy the longings of his heart." [20] In the course of his travels "the testimonies of Br. Rock fell into his hands, and in these he found the key to the concealed yearnings of his soul which thereby was now led into this channel. The Lord took him more and more into His inner training, bestowed His mercy upon him, and made him a *Werkzeug* of Inspiration.''[21] On September 11, 1817, he gave his first testimony to the Community at Ronneburg in the form of a summons for the new revival. It reads in part thus:

> Oh Ronneburg! Ronneburg! Where are thy former champions, the old defenders of the faith? They are no longer to be found, and effeminates dwell in the citadel. Well, then, do ye not desire to become strong? The eternal power is offered to you.[22]

Thus a new era was ushered in at Ronneburg and the other Communities; and the ''souls that had been longing for a revival rejoiced and recognized in the event the beginning of that new awakening and bestowal of mercy for which they were yearning.'' There were, however, some ''*selbstständige und eigenmächtige*'' Elders who ''despised and rejected this new summons of the Lord, saying that they had had enough of testimonies.''[23] But those ''who bore within themselves a longing for renewal'', those ''whose hearts and eyes the Lord could open that they might see the light and comprehend and seize upon the new mercy'', gathered about the new *Werkzeug* of Inspiration. And ''thus began the 'great power' and the 'new day' which the Lord had promised.''[24]

A few months later Barbara Heinemann, ''*eine ganz geringe und ungelehrte Magd*'' (a humble and unlearned servant maid) of Leitersweiler, Alsace, and Christian Metz, a carpenter of Ronneburg (a grandson of Jakob Metz who joined the Community just a century before) "came to a spiritual awakening, were endowed with the miraculous gift of Inspiration, and prepared for the service of the Lord and the Community. Thus the work of the Lord made good headway; and there followed a most blessed time abounding in mercy."[25]

With all his religious fervor Krausert seems to have lacked the courage to face the persecutions that threatened the revival of the unorthodox doctrines of the Inspirationists; and it is recorded that "at the arrest and subsequent examination at Bergzabern he showed fear of men and resulting weakness."[26] There were also internal troubles; and when "the old hostile Elders seemed to assume a threatening attitude, Krausert became timid and undecided and ran, so to speak, before he was chased. Through such fear of men and reluctance for suffering he lost his inner firmness in the mercy of the Lord, went gradually astray from the divine guidance", and "soon fell back into the world."[27] In truth when "he did not again find himself" he was through the Council of the Brethren (*Bruderrathsbeschluss)* severed from the Community.[28] And thus for a time "the tie of love joined by the Lord himself was torn, and the beautiful and blessed spiritual harmony existing at first had been destroyed to the great grief of the Lord and of all faithful souls, especially of those who through Krausert had been led into the steep paths of spiritual life.'' But in spite of his extremely human frailties Michael Krausert is given full credit in the Community records for the important part he played in the Reawakening.[29]

After the fall of Krausert the spiritual affairs of the Community were under the guidance of Christian Metz and Barbara Heinemann, who carried on the work in much the same way that Rock and Gruber had done a century before. They came to be regarded as the true founders and recognized as the leaders of what was now called the ''New Community.''[30]

V

THE STORY OF BARBARA HEINEMANN

The story of Barbara Heinemann is one of the most interesting chapters in the history of the Community of True Inspiration. She was born outside of the influence of the New Spiritual Economy, and "had, moreover, grown up almost completely without education and culture." Her parents were so poor that at the early age of eight she was sent to a neighboring factory to earn a pittance at spinning wool. Later she earned her living as a servant; but, like the Maid of Orleans, she dreamed dreams and saw visions. "The grace of God acted so powerfully upon my heart", says Barbara Heinemann in her *Kurze Erzählung von den Erweckungs-Umständen,* "that I often felt strange and mysterious impulses from within to do this or that which I at first resisted although in vain."[31]

It was in an effort to interpret these dreams and visions, these "continual inward promptings", that she sought out the little group of devout Pietists of whom she had been told. The Community had always used great caution in taking in new members and there was considerable hesitation before Barbara Heinemann was admitted to the meetings. "But the Lord had taken her into His immediate training and preparation . . . . and brought it to pass in a strange manner that she became acquainted with M. Krausert . . . . and she at once was called through him as a *Werkzeug* of the Lord and was also immediately ordered [by the Lord] to go along on a journey."

It was in Bergzabern (the Palatinate) on Christmas Day in the year 1818, at the age of twenty-three, that "the Lord aroused and quickened her from within so powerfully and vigorously that she, without knowing what was taking place within her, was led into and carried on in the immediate ways and rulings of the Spirit." Thus Barbara Heinemann became the "Lord's instrument and the receptacle of his mercy." "Thereupon", relates Barbara Heinemann, "I was released from my worldly service as servant girl, since the Lord, as announced through Brother Krausert, desired to take me into His service and to use me as His handmaid." [32] And this was done, writes Gottlieb Scheuner, "much to the wonder and surprise, but also for the assurance and strengthening of the faith, of all those who had previously known her." [33]

Barbara Heinemann at once set about to learn to read. The Bible was her text-book; and great was her joy when she could follow the Holy Scriptures. They made a profound impression upon her mind — so much so that the language of both her early and later testimonies is almost wholly that of the Bible, particularly of the Old Testament.

She also learned to write; but this was ever a labored process, and so most of her testimonies were given orally and written down by Scribes.[34] In her account of her first inner promptings Barbara Heinemann describes the difficulty of recording the same due to her inability to write. "I felt a compulsion to do something", she says, "without knowing what or why. Finally I was bidden from within: 'Write'. When I told her [the friend she was visiting] this, and said at the same time that I could not write, she replied I should at least try it; perchance I might have the necessary knowledge, and she gave me paper, pen, and ink. I sat down and I wrote single letters and syllables, as best I could, for I had never before written, according to the words craving for utterance and which were to be written. When I had finished they were, however, not able to read it or even find and discern its meaning. The Sister helped me then in improving upon it and to write the words which I still remembered more correctly. I did so with her assistance, as well as possible, and now we succeeded in getting at the meaning; and behold it was a message [*Einsprache*] dealing with a tree of many branches, leaves, blossoms, and fruits which I however did not yet comprehend. I now felt relieved and knew that the will of God had thereby been fulfilled."[35]

One gathers from the records that Barbara Heinemann had from the beginning more or less difficulty with the leading Elders of the Community, who, it is evident, never lost sight of the fact that she was "*eine ganz geringe und ungelehrte Magd.*" Indeed, so violent was the opposition at one time that she was "declared false and banished to her native place." And we are told that it was some time after her reinstatement, and after she had been "strengthened and endowed anew by the Lord with special spiritual power", that "the great wild monster called Dissension" was driven away and the "true harmony of Spirit" restored among the congregations.[36]

In Christian Metz's *Historische Beschreibung der Wahren Inspirations-Gemeinschaft* it is related under the date of August, 1822, that the "Enemy" tempted Barbara Heinemann with a desire to marry George Landmann, a young school-teacher in Bischweiler; but "the Lord showed to the *Bruderrath* and also to her own conscience that this step was against His holy will, and accordingly they did not marry, but did repent concerning it, and the Lord's grace was once more given her."

But from a later account by Gottlieb Scheuner we learn that in the course of the summer of 1823, about four years from the time she first became inspired, "Sister B. Heinemann became wearied of travelling the narrow path and she now, after repeated *Fassung und Findung,* really carried out her former intention of marrying Brother G. Landmann and thereby lost her divine calling [37] . . . . But the preserving grace of God did not desert her entirely, for the Lord had it reserved to Himself at His own time again to reach out to her His hand and to raise her from her fall." And so, after a lapse of twenty-six years, "the Lord again sent her a ray of His light and bestowed His mercy upon her." [38] Within a short time the Community removed to Iowa, where Barbara Heinemann * remained an *Inspirations-Werkzeug* until the time of her death in 1883, a period of thirty-four years. [39]

* To avoid possible confusion the maiden name Barbara Heinemann is used throughout in the text and notes of this book.

VI

CHRISTIAN METZ : STRUGGLE FOR INDEPENDENCE : EXILE

After the marriage of Barbara Heinemann in 1823 the spiritual management of the Community rested mainly with Christian Metz, [40] who was, perhaps, the most remarkable personage ever connected with the Community of True Inspiration. Unlike Barbara Heinemann he was born within the influence of the Community. The name Metz is of frequent occurrence in the history of the Inspirationists from the time of Rock and Gruber. The grandfather of Christian Metz, referred to by Gottlieb Scheuner as "the often mentioned brother Jakob Metz, of Himbach", was banished from Alsace for his nonconformity to the established church in 1716, and at Himbach became one of the "principal members" of the meeting established there by Rock and Gruber.

Christian Metz was born at Neuwied on December 30, 1794, and at the age of seven came with his parents to Ronneburg, the rallying ground of the Inspirationists. "When the first summons went forth to the Community at Ronneburg through M. Krausert", it is recorded that "he [Christian Metz] experienced a thorough revival . . . . and was soon after also endowed with the miraculous gift of Inspiration."[41]

From the "fall" of Krausert until after the establishment of the new home in the State of Iowa, Christian Metz was not only the spiritual head of the Community but also (as the records clearly show) the leader in its temporal affairs. A successful organizer and a man of much executive ability, he was withal a man of the deepest piety; and so there are in *Inspirations-Historie* many loving tributes to the so "*hoch begabte und begnadigte*" Br. Christian Metz through whom "the weightiest and greatest things were wrought and accomplished in the Community." Even to this day the spell of the influence of Christian Metz is felt at Amana.

He is described by the members of the Community as a man of commanding presence and of great personal magnetism, who challenged admiration, respect, and even homage wherever he went. Worldly men and "unbelievers" who still remember the "gifted Brother" speak of him as "a rare soul", "a remarkable personage", "a wonderful man." The attitude of the Community toward this "specially endowed Brother" while deferential was entirely free from what they so deplore in the Shakers' "divine reverence and canonization of Ann Lee."

Christian Metz felt deeply the responsibility of his office, and his sincerity in "the great work of God's mercy" is beyond question. "Often I had to feel God's earnestness concerning my own unworthiness", he laments in his *Tagebuch,* "nay, I should have wished to hide my mouth in the dust, instead of speaking to the others and teaching them. But I had, in spite of God's judgment over my own shortcomings, to continue in the faith in order that the will of the Lord be done and that I and the others might be brought to genuine repentance and atonement."[42] The testimonies of Christian Metz are couched in beautiful language and are altogether on a higher plane than those of Barbara Heinemann — particularly those given after the return of her gift of Inspiration in America.[43]

When Barbara Heinemann and Christian Metz took up their religious work a century had elapsed since Gruber and Rock were endowed with the "gift of the Spirit and of Prophecy." In the meantime the penalties for independent thinking had been modified to some extent; but it was still dangerous in most of the provinces of Germany to follow the dictates of one's own conscience when those dictates were opposed in any way to the decrees of the government. Barbara Heinemann and Christian Metz, along with "the converted souls who had united into small prayer-meetings and were much in earnest and zealous in the work'', were repeatedly arrested. It is recorded that in February, 1820, ''the mob several times threw stones in the windows where the Community had assembled for prayer, and the members moreover were attacked and insulted on the streets and elsewhere.''[44]

The old troublesome questions of military duty and taking the oath again came to the front; while the investigations of the political authorities revealed the fact that the Inspirationists were teaching their children their own peculiar faith instead of sending them to the public schools to be grounded in orthodox Lutheranism. Numerous appeals to the authorities were made for the privilege of separate schools, in response to which the decision of the *Hohe Ministerium der geistlichen Angelegenheiten,* given in March, 1825, in regard to ''the new Separatists in Schwarzenau'', is a type of the replies received by the various Communities. It is summed up in five points as follows:

(1) That the privileges of a tolerated religious society could not be granted to them, and that they consequently could not be permitted to keep their own teachers for the instruction of their children.

(2) That they would be punished to the full extent of the law, if they should refuse to fulfil the common duties of citizens of the state.

(3) That they must pay taxes and contributions for the support of church and school like all other citizens.

(4) That the children should be baptized by compulsion through the court if their parents refused to have this done voluntarily.

(5) That the children of school age should be compelled to attend the public schools and participate in the religious instruction given by the pastor.[45]

In February of the following year this same congregation (of Schwarzenau) was ordered by the authorities to leave the country within six months; and the annalist records:

In spite of the repeated explanations and presentations of the Brethren why they had separated themselves from the state church, namely, because they had through God's grace recognized and found something better, and had been forced to this step for conscience sake and that they therefore could not again return, and that they moreover were and would remain loyal citizens and subjects and that they merely desired to worship God according to the dictates of their conscience, they again and again received the reply that the church offered and taught everything that was necessary and beneficial for salvation, and thus came at last the positive decision: "Either back into the fold of the church, or out of the country."[46]

It is, moreover, recorded at the time of this decision that a "strange apparition was seen in the sky as a real miracle of God to strengthen the faith of the souls of the Community." During a testimony in which the Lord expressed a wish that the Community might "persevere in the faith" the *Werkzeug,* Barbara Heinemann, pointed to the heavens, first to the right and then to the left, and exclaimed: "Oh what great joy and glory do I behold there. But what woe and terrifying judgment do I see yonder hovering over the tower of Babel." And as the *Werkzeug* pointed upward with her hands "several Sisters looked at the sky, and there they beheld, as announced, in the heavens to the right, above the house of Brother ——— in which the assembly was held and where the *Werkzeuge* stayed a bright cloud and in it an exceedingly bright star surrounded by many little stars. But to the left where the [Lutheran] church, school, and parsonage stood there was a very black threatening cloud to be seen."[47]

With the alternative of "either back into the fold of the church, or out of the country" the growing congregations of Inspirationists, repeating the history of their forefathers a century before, flocked to the more tolerant province of Hessen; and in the *Jahrbuch* for 1830 it is recorded that on October 31st "the Lord sent a message to the Grand Duke of Hessen-Darmstadt as a promise of grace and blessing because he had given protection to the Community in his country." And elsewhere it is recorded "that when the Brethren A——— B——— and Chr. Metz two days afterward delivered the message to the Grand Duke through his *valet de chambre*, he sent them reply after a while that he had read it and thanked them very much."

VII

MARIENBORN : HERRNHAAG : ARMENBURG ENGELTHAL

In Hessen the far-sighted Christian Metz, whose phenomenal gift of organization was always abreast his religious enthusiasm, conceived the idea of leasing some large estate in common and of making it a refuge for the faithful, where each would be given "an opportunity to earn his living according to his calling or inclination." After much investigation and negotiation "it came about through the mediation of the Landrath of Büdingen that a part of the cloister at Marienborn was given in rent by the noble family of Meerholz, which was very convenient for the Community since it lay near Ronneburg"—the home of the principal Elders. "But there arose some hesitancy because the Lord had formerly pronounced his curse upon this place, at the time when the Herrnhuter had their doings there.[48] This obstacle however was removed through a testimony in which the Lord said: 'I will be with you under the present circumstances, know and learn ye that my hand can make something out of nothing and nothing out of something.

I can bless and curse; I can change a curse into a blessing and a blessing into a curse.' "[49]

To Marienborn flocked the weary and heavy-laden Inspirationists until the cloister and all the adjoining buildings were full to overflowing. It was a strange turn of fortune's wheel that converted this mediaeval cloister into a refuge for the humble band of peasant Inspirationists. They came believing that this new home was the fulfilment of the prophecy of Christian Metz that "the Lord would soon collect and gather in His faithful servants."

Another abode with the adjoining estate, called Herrnhaag, was likewise leased to house the long oppressed Community at Edenkoben; and the account of the transaction is given in these words:

The Brethren had negotiated more than six months with the noble family of Meerholz to rent if possible the remaining portion of the castle at Marienborn for the Community of Edenkoben. But the affair was delayed from month to month since the owners asked too large a price and could not be induced to give in. All at once the Lord made the hearts of the noble family of Büdingen willing to rent the Herrnhaag to the Community, which place in Brother Rock's time had been built by the Herrnhuter but had been vacant for more than seventy years. The Lord gave to this, through His word on March first (1828), His consent and the Brethren were ordered to accept this as an opportunity coming from the Lord and to break off negotiations with the others since they did not wish to deal justly and fairly. So it was now fulfilled as previously announced through the word that it would be a place which they often had seen but not yet recognized as the one. This lease proved materially much more profitable for the Community than the other. Thus the great anxiety and trouble was suddenly changed into joy. But much more work and many expenses resulted before they could occupy the place, for many things were out of order which had to be fixed and repaired. [50]

Owing to the growing hostility of the government toward the Community at Ronneburg—the place where "the Lord had so long had his dwelling and where he had bestowed so many blessings"—it was found necessary for the third time in its history (once in 1725 and again in 1742) for the Community to move away from Ronneburg.

Through the efforts of Christian Metz the old cloister at Arnsburg was leased in 1832. The Community had hoped to rent only a portion of this estate, but "the Count would lease only the entire cloister with all the land and the mill belonging to it. . . . This appeared to the Brethren an impossibility because the Community was too small and too poor to undertake it, and doubts and cares arose again. But the Lord had His hidden hand in this for He saw into the future and knew what He had determined in His will. He now came also to the assistance of the *Werkzeug,* who was in great trouble and perplexity, and gave directions to risk this great undertaking in faith." And so the contract for the lease of Arnsburg was concluded in the month of March, and the Community at Ronneburg began to move thither.

The name of the cloister, it appears, was "not pleasing to the Lord"; and there is recorded in the *Jahrbuch* for 1832, under the date of April 28, the following "loving word" through Christian Metz in which the name was changed and in which the "Lord promised quiet and peace to the place and bade the evil spirits who had dwelt there to depart":

> Child of man, your companions desire to know where I shall establish my dwelling for them. Listen then: I have chosen Arnsburg, which indeed did not receive this name from me, but now, when you take possession of it, you shall call it otherwise, namely, *die Armenburg* [the castle of the poor]. Abide then by this word, though the enemy may attack from without or also from within. [51]

Two years later "the arrival of a large number of souls whom the Lord had called to the Community from other countries, especially from Switzerland", resulted again in a scarcity of habitations and land, for all the spare room at Armenburg had been occupied by those who had previously arrived at different times. But we learn from the *Jahrbücher* that "the Lord had already decided in His holy counsel what to do, and likewise had already announced that He would establish still a further Community. This work was now to be achieved and negotiations were already under way" which finally resulted in the renting of the old stone walled convent of Engelthal, together with a large rural estate, in September, 1834. "Concerning this affair the Lord testified at the Haag on the seventeenth day of September and He gave His approval."[52]

The four estates leased by the Inspirationists were within a radius of a few miles[53] and under one common management. Indeed it is here that we discover the beginnings of the communistic life which the Inspirationists afterwards adopted as a community system. Communism was, in fact, a natural development of the mode of life which these people had been forced to adopt. Under a common roof there were rich and poor, educated and uneducated, professional men, merchants, manufacturers, artisans, farmers, and laborers — brave souls who were generously and gloriously sacrificing individual for the common welfare, and who, after the manner of religious independents in all ages, were willing to suffer any hardships if only they might worship God in their own chosen way.

At each Community in a large room school was conducted and religious services were held. Here the members gathered to plan the work that was to make it possible for them to continue to live in accordance with what they considered the precepts of true Christianity. The rich gave freely of their means, and the merchants of their business ability, and the artisans and farmers of their labor. It was not long before the Community attained a degree of prosperity which promised the free, simple, quiet, and peaceful life foretold in the early prophecies and for which its members had been striving so many years.

But the fulfilment of this gracious promise was reserved for another time. Revolution was abroad in Europe, and non-conformity to established customs was as of old considered a highly dangerous tendency by the ruling classes. And so one by one the cherished liberties regarding military duty, the rights of citizenship, [54] the legal oath, and separate schools were taken away. Gladly did they pay the fines imposed for every absence from the public school "for conscience sake", which "amounted to a considerable sum each term for those families which had several children"; but "at last no longer were they at liberty to obey this unjust and excessive demand."

Time after time they petitioned the government for exemption from the legal oath; and even "the word of the Lord" was ignored by the ruling powers. "The book of the law", reads one of these divine messages, "which was given to us in the days when the word became flesh is unalterable. All other commands and laws which are given are not acknowledged by the true worshippers of God and by those having the right faith if they are contrary to the divine law. Now it does read: Thou shalt not swear. In the same spirit of the living God I speak unto you to-day. My children, my communities shall by all means not do it, they shall not swear an oath. Behold they have three times humbly entreated you [the government] to spare them in accordance with the duties of their conscience, and you have not done it."[55]

Rents were growing more and more exorbitant and land was too high to buy. The very elements seemed against the Inspirationists; since owing to excessive heat and drouth there was nothing for the faithful band to gather at harvest time.

FAC SIMILÆ (WITHOUT REDUCTION) OF A DESCRIPTION AND AUTOGRAPH SIGNATURE OF CHRISTIAN METZ, THE *Werkzeug* THROUGH WHOM THE COMMUNITY OF TRUE INSPIRATION WAS LED TO AMERICA. TAKEN FROM THE PASSPORT OF CHRISTIAN METZ

Beschreibung.

Alter fünfzig Jahr

Größe,
in hessischem dec. Maaß:

Zoll: sechszig zwei

Strich: –

Haare braun

Stirn nieder

Augenbraunen braun

Augen braun

Nase mittel

Mund klein

Bart braun

Kinn breit

Angesicht oval

Gesichtsfarbe [illegible] blaß

Besondere Kennzeichen:

0

Unterschrift des Reisenden:

Christian Metz

Two views of the dredge boat on the 7-mile millrace from the Iowa River to Amana. Oxen were used in digging the canal.

VIII

THE HIDDEN PROPHECY : AMERICA

It was during this period of depression that "the Lord revealed through his instrument, Christian Metz, that he would lead them out of this land of adversity, to one where they and their children could live in peace and liberty." There was, in truth, as far back as May 20, 1826, "a hidden prophecy" regarding emigration to America, which reads as follows:

> I proceed in mysterious ways, says thy God, and my foot is seldom seen openly. I found my dwelling in the depths and my path leads through great waters. I prepare for Me a place in the wilderness and establish for Me a dwelling, where there was none. [56]

When the *Werkzeug* and the Elders became convinced that it was "God's holy purpose and will" that they "should bring about a great change in the Communities" there were many meetings and much serious discussion. [57] At length there came a testimony from the Lord which reads:

> Your goal and your way shall lead towards the west to the land which still is open to you and your faith. I am with you and shall lead you over the sea. Hold Me, call upon Me through your prayer when the storm or

temptation arises. . . . Four may then prepare themselves.[58]

Thereupon those who were to go were appointed by the Lord "with full power to act for all the members and to purchase land where they deemed best."[59]

On August 27, 1842, the faithful members of the Communities gathered at Armenburg[60] to celebrate the *Liebesmahl,* the most solemn and important religious ceremony of the Inspirationists — a ceremony inherited from their earliest history.[61] After a touching farewell the committee on whose success the future happiness of more than a thousand souls rested turned their faces westward. "We commend ourselves to your perpetual brotherly loving remembrance and to your prayer before the Lord", said Christian Metz in a farewell letter, "for in so great a journey fraught with dangers one needs the assistance of God most urgently, and this help may ever be obtained by earnest prayer. To be sure, the Lord has promised us His mighty assistance and on this I rely in inner and outer things."[62]

The voyage to America, made at the time of the autumnal equinox, was one of many hardships and privations. It was almost forty days before the harbor of New York was reached on October 26, 1842. Nor did their hardships come to an end upon reaching land. For three months these conscientious men, ever mindful of the responsibilities that rested with them, suffered the winter wind and cold of the lake region while they examined tracts of land, dealt with unscrupulous land companies, and weighed the advantages of various situations. Finally, after a "long and anxious period of waiting", during which the "Brothers often conversed on and meditated over how things should be and go after the purchase shall have been made and the members of the Community shall have come over", they purchased the Seneca Indian Reservation — a tract of five thousand acres near Buffalo in Erie County in the State of New York.

IX

EBENEZER: HITHERTO HATH THE LORD HELPED US

So eager were the members in Germany to help in the upbuilding of the new home in the promised land that within four months of the purchase of the Reservation the first village of the Community was laid out and peopled.[63] This village they called Ebenezer — suggested, it is said, by the passage in *Samuel*[64] which reads: "Then Samuel took a stone, and set it between Mizpeh and Shen, and called the name of it Eben-ezer,[65] saying 'Hitherto hath the Lord helped us.'" According to their own records the name was given to the new home before the final purchase was made. The account reads:

In this gloomy and uncertain time of waiting [for the decision of the land agents] the Lord sent a most encouraging and uplifting outflow of His mercy on December 7, 1842, in a song through Brother Christian Metz, in which He gave a positive affirmation and promise with regard to the land[66] and even called the new place by name . . .

Ebenezer you shall call it
Hitherto our Lord has helped us
He was with us on our journey
And from many perils saved us
His path and way are wonderful
And the end makes clear the start.[67]

In less than a year from the founding of Ebenezer two more villages were laid out on either side of the first, called Upper Ebenezer and Lower Ebenezer — the first village being called thereafter Middle Ebenezer. Later another village, New Ebenezer, was laid out. And when a family of "Pennsylvania Dutch" joined the Community from Canada, thus bringing to the Community a fine tract of Canadian timber land, two villages were located on the Canada side of the river and were named Canada Ebenezer and Kenneberg, respectively. Each village had its store, its school, and its church. There were sawmills, woolen mills, flour mills, and numerous other branches of industry, giving employment to all according to their talents and inclination.

The Community adopted a "provisional constitution, which was to be valid at least for the start and establishment of the Community in this country [America]",[68] and was formally organized under the name of "Ebenezer Society" in 1843. The provisional constitution, which was rather a lengthy document of thirty-five paragraphs, was "approved by the Lord" on February 20, 1843. It included a resolution providing that all land and all improvements, everything with the exception of clothing and household goods, should be held in common. The prosperous members were to advance the money to cover all expenses and were to receive a proportionate share of the whole (in the form of a mortgage) as security.

The provisions of the Constitution of the Ebenezer Society are nearly the same as those which in 1859 were incorporated into the Constitution of the Amana Society. It is worthy of note, however, that the management of the Ebenezer Society was vested in a Select Council of thirteen Elders; while the title of the Ebenezer lands was vested in sixteen members who, as joint tenants, held it in trust for the members of the Community. It was also provided that the interest of any one of the Trustees (who were specifically named) should terminate at death or upon withdrawal or upon the request of two-thirds of the Trustees. Vacancies were filled by the Trustees out of the number of Elders in the Community. When the removal of the Community to Iowa had been determined upon, joint ownership was conveyed by the Trustees to Brothers G. A. Weber, Wm. Moerschel, and Henry Meyer, who in turn gave their power of attorney to Brothers Fr. Moerschel and John P. Trautmann. This was done in order to facilitate business in connection with the sale of the Ebenezer estate.

During the time of the planting and building of the new home, the Community of True Inspiration is said to have been especially blessed with the

"Lord's holy word and counsel"; and He "gave precepts, directions, and explanations concerning the external and internal affairs of that time."[69]

X

COMMUNISM THROUGH REVELATION

At the time of the purchase of the New York land the Inspirationists were not especially socialistic or communistic in their ideas. Indeed, the intention of the Community was to live simply as a Christian congregation or church. The well-to-do Brethren and members, "according to the direction of the Lord and the insight and decision of all the united Brethren of the Community", were to make contributions in money to cover the expenses; and the Community proposed to hold the land and houses thus purchased in common for two years, each member's contribution to the purchase money being secured by a proportionate share in the real estate and drawing a reasonable rate of interest. This arrangement, however, was soon found to be impracticable since the members were unequal in age, strength, experience, and enterprise. Some were old and feeble; and many were so poor that they found it difficult to save money enough to pay for their land.

Christian Metz and the First Brethren presently saw that sheer necessity would soon compel the people to scatter, and that the whole enterprise would fail unless it was established upon a different foundation. Besides, "the Lord had gradually announced more and more clearly that it was His intention and pleasure, nay His most holy will that everything should be and remain in common."[70]

In the words of Gottlieb Scheuner, "it was therefore necessary to draw up and adopt a permanent constitution for the Community, on the one hand for the convenience and instruction of the members in regard to their mutual relations and duties and on the other hand for the protection and security of the Community against false and deserting Brothers as also against hostile attacks from without. While now several Brothers were engaged in the task of drawing up a constitution and while they met here and there great difficulties, especially since the draft was to be translated into English and through an attorney at Buffalo submitted to the legislature of the State for approval, the Lord in His mercy gave instruction and guidance in this affair."[71]

It is, moreover, evident that the subject of absolute communism caused considerable dissension among the Brethren, and many "were waiting for a division and desired that it should be made." There are numerous references by the Elders to the manifest intention of the Lord in the doctrine of the apostles set forth in the *Acts* in which the primitive Christian church is described as follows: "And all that believed were together, and had all things common; and sold their possessions and goods, and parted them to all men as every man had need."[72]

In the midst of the discussion "a very important revelation occurred again at Mittel Ebenezer on October 23, 1850, in which the Lord expressed his grief and displeasure over the discontent of many members with regard to common possession." And on the nineteenth day of March in the year 1854 the "Lord testified most emphatically and earnestly to put to shame those who would not believe and trust in the Lord and the Brethren. He announced that it was not His holy will and never should be that communism should be abolished, and He pronounced His curse upon all those who would attempt it, but gave a most gracious promise to those who would faithfully preserve it." This important testimony reads in part:

As truly as I live, says the Lord, it is at no time my will to dissolve the ties of the Community in such manner or to suffer its dissolution, neither through artful devices or skill and diplomacy nor cunning or power of men; nay, the faith which has love and the bond of peace for its essence and foundation shall continue to exist. And there shall come eternal disgrace, shame and disfavor upon those who cause it, their children shall suffer want and be without blessing in time and eternity. Their material possessions shall melt away and the divine treasure they have disavowed; therefore the Lord is against them.[73]

And thereupon the discontented Brethren "did repent concerning it" and signed the amendment to the Constitution providing for the adoption of absolute communism. This amendment, moreover, was incorporated in the new Constitution, which was later adopted in the State of Iowa, and has ever since been one of the fundamental principles of the Community.

From this sketch of their early history it will be seen that the original and basic purpose of the Community of True Inspiration was to worship God according to their peculiar faith in freedom, and for the better advancement of that end to live in a neighborhood. The adoption of communism was a necessity born of a combination of peculiar circumstances and was not the result of any understanding or interpretation of the social theories of Jesus, as has been the case with so many religious communities. Furthermore, it is a step the Community never regretted, for it has solved the problem of furnishing remunerative labor to an ever increasing membership and at the same time has given to each member the requisite leisure to attend the eleven or twelve weekly religious services of the Community and "to think upon the things that are of the Lord."

"I greatly desire", said Christian Metz in a letter written in the autumn of 1856, "that the Community become a more complete and pure sacrifice to God that He may take delight in us." [74]

XI

MATERIAL PROSPERITY

More than eight hundred members of the Community came to Ebenezer from Germany. And yet many remained in Germany — some because they had property interests which held them to the Old World, and some because they found it hard to break home ties. The majority of those who came to America were of the artisan and peasant class. They were men and women of force and moral earnestness — as "Separatists" and "Comeouters" have been in all the ages. In the genial atmosphere of free America they developed remarkable talents for organization and government which had been suppressed for generations by intolerance and persecution in the Fatherland.

The Seneca Indian Reservation in New York did not prove to be that haven of peace for which the German Inspirationists had hoped. They bought the land with the understanding that the Seneca tribe was to leave at once; but with the appearance of the first dwellings of the newcomers the Indians not only showed a decided disinclination to leave the Reservation but were extremely hostile. For three years the Inspirationists suffered the thieving and the threats of the Indians, and it was only after the Society had invoked the assistance of the authorities at Washington that the last of the Seneca tribe could be induced to leave for the New Reservation which had been assigned to them when they sold their claim to the Ebenezer land.[75]

Materially, however, the Society prospered in its new home. The members were all comfortably housed and were well pleased with their communistic life which had developed a spirit of self-denial and of brotherly love, of mutual protection and helpfulness, and had enabled them in an astonishingly short period of time to gratify every want of the body with a simple and wholesome abundance. The mills and factories had established a reputation in the commercial world; while the newly broken fields yielded abundant harvests.

The original purchase was large enough for the comfortable accommodation of the eight hundred members who came from Germany; but the Society continued to grow to such an extent that in 1854 it became apparent that more land would have to be acquired. The rapid growth of the city of Buffalo, which was but five miles away, had caused such an advance in the price of available real estate in the neighborhood that additional land in any appreciable quantities was out of the question.

In addition to the lack of available land another more serious problem from the standpoint of the Community now daily confronted the First Brethren. The thriving city of Buffalo with its worldly influences and attractions was too easily accessible to the young people for the peace of mind of the Elders who considered the salvation of the soul of paramount importance in this world. They were profoundly convinced that in order "to cultivate humility, obedience to God's will, faithfulness and love to Christ" (and to that end preserve in its simplicity their divinely ordained brotherhood), it was best, as far as possible, to keep apart from the world with its strifes, temptations, and anxieties. "Have no intercourse with worldly minded men", wrote Eberhard Ludwig Gruber in 1715, "that you be not tempted and led away."[76]

XII

WESTWARD

In the *Jahrbuch* for 1854 it is recorded that "when Brother Christian Metz took up the matter of the future of the Community to learn the will of the Lord his heart received the impression that the Community should be moved . . . and on August 31, 1854, followed a second message of the Lord in which the change was announced more plainly since it declared 'You shall direct your eyes toward a distant goal in the West to find and obtain there a start and entrance or a settlement.'"[77] This proposition caused "much discussion, considering, hesitating, speculation, and adjusting"; but soon "weighty and urgent" testimonies occurred through Christian Metz which declared that "many opportunities already have passed by unused because of this hesitancy" and directed them (the Elders) to appoint "four men to find a new home in the far West."

Thereupon a committee of four, of which Christian Metz was one, was appointed by Inspiration. With no very definite plans these men started for the West. The Territory of Kansas had been opened up to settlement and land seekers were flocking thither in search of claims; and so the committee naturally followed the current of migration to Kansas, where they spent a month in traveling across the country, inspecting each new tract of land recommended for their consideration by eloquent land agents. They were, however, unable to come to a decision, and returned to Ebenezer much discouraged by the failure of their commission.

The circumstance of the miscarriage of their original plans was not, however, enough to weaken the purpose of these dauntless pioneers. Greater seclusion and cheaper and more abundant lands were what they wanted, and these they still hoped to obtain. After a few weeks of earnest discussion over possible locations, a new committee, consisting of two of the First Brethren, was appointed to go to the new State of Iowa and there inspect the large tracts of United States government lands.

The present location of the Community in Iowa was described in such glowing terms by this committee that immediately a third committee of four members was dispatched to make a purchase. And so without further delay a tract of nearly eighteen thousand acres was secured in the new Commonwealth of Iowa. The Community showed its sagacity by buying at the outset the scattered farms — even at a high figure when necessary — in order to secure a contiguous tract of land; for thereby they were spared the tribulations of the Icarian Community whose original tract of land in Texas consisted of thirty-two half sections scattered through two townships.

The new site was a well selected and valuable tract of land — one of the garden spots of the fertile State of Iowa. Through it ran the Iowa River bordered with the wonderful black soil of its wide valley. On one side were the bluffs and the uplands covered with a luxuriant growth of timber — with an apparently limitless supply of fuel and building material. There were a few quarries of sandstone and limestone along the river; while the clay in the hills was unexcelled for the manufacture of brick. On the other side of the river stretched the rolling prairie land. To the Inspirationists, who had been obliged to cut heavy timber and remove stones and boulders from the Ebenezer land before it could be tilled, the long green stretches of virgin prairie "ready for the plow" seemed the most wonderful feature of the splendid new domain on which all the hopes of the future were centered.

But it takes more than a beautiful location to make a successful community: it takes moral earnestness and untiring industry. These the Inspirationists brought with them to their new home. Then, too, the Ebenezer experiment had added twelve years experience in pioneering. Unlike Etienne Cabet's French tailors and shoemakers of the Icarian Community in Texas, the Inspirationists knew how to turn the matted sod of the prairie. Bountiful harvests rewarded their industry and skill.

With a will they set to work to cut the timber and quarry the stone and build anew houses, shops, mills, factories, churches, and schoolhouses. They planted orchards and vineyards, and purchased flocks and herds. They revived the old industries and started new ones. There was some sickness incident to pioneering, but withal they felt that in this new home to which "the Lord had directed them" the fulfilment of all the early prophecies was at hand. Bodily ills are more easily healed than spiritual ones; and so, in spite of the malaria and the ague the Inspirationists flourished in their new home.

In the removal from New York to Iowa the Community showed the same prudence and ability with which its members have always conducted their business affairs. More communities have died for want of common sense than for want of capital. With the Inspirationists common sense has been the very cement in the foundation of their institutions. On such a foundation the superstructure of religious enthusiasm and communistic zeal can rest securely. This extreme sanity, however, has been so rare a thing in communistic endeavors — particularly in religious communities — that it may be said to be the distinguishing feature of the Community of True Inspiration.

There was no rush to the country so gloriously described by the Iowa fore-guards, though no one can doubt the eagerness with which every member looked forward to the upbuilding of the new home. The removal from Ebenezer extended over a period of ten years. During this time the *Werkzeug,* Christian Metz, made "in the name of God eight journeys to Ebenezer." [78]

While one detail of members prepared the new home in Iowa, the other looked to the profitable selling of the old estate in New York. As they found purchasers for the latter, they sent families to the former. To their business credit it is recorded that they were able to dispose of the whole of the eight thousand acre tract in the State of New York with all the improvements without the loss of a single dollar, notwithstanding such a sale presented great difficulties — for the six communistic villages and their peculiar arrangement of buildings, with mills, factories, and workshops had peculiarities which detracted from their value for individual uses. Much of the Ebenezer land had been surveyed and laid out in lots; and when disposed of it was sold piece by piece, a task which required much time and patience.

"The vacated houses are occupied by the children of the world", wrote one of the Brethren when the sale of the New York land was about completed, "and the tumult is getting worse and worse. . . . It appears that Mittel Ebenezer is turned into a desolate place, and it is high time for us to depart. Ebenezer has started to become the meeting ground of the world, and it will soon become a wilderness after we have all departed. One must suffer and endure much to preserve peace. But Jacob, too, had to stoop before Esau, and if God grants us His mercy for this, then it is not difficult."[79]

The first village on the Iowa purchase was laid out during the summer of 1855 on a sloping hillside north of the Iowa River.

XIII

AMANA : GLAUB TREU

"The time had now come", writes the Community historian, Gottlieb Scheuner, "when the new settlement in Iowa was to receive a name. When the Community emigrated from Germany and settled near Buffalo in the State of New York, the Lord called that place Ebenezer, that is, 'Hitherto the Lord hath helped us.' Now He again led them out from there to a new place which as the work proceeded was to be called *'Bleibe treu'* [remain faithful]. This had been laid into the heart of the *Werkzeug,* Chr. Metz, who later poured it forth in a song beginning thus:

'Bleibtreu soll der Name sein
Dort in Iowa der Gemein.' [80]

"The new home of the Community was then to be called *'Bleibtreu'*. But since it was diffcult to express this word or name in English, it was proposed to write instead the Biblical name *'Amana',* which signifies *'glaub treu'* [believe faithfully] and had thus a very similar meaning. To this the Lord gave His approval in an important song which was poured forth through Christian

Metz on September 23, 1855.[81] Thus the new place was henceforth called Amana.''[82]

By the year 1862 — two years before the last of the members came to Iowa — five more villages were laid out within a radius of six miles from Amana. They were named, in accordance with their locations, West Amana, South Amana, High Amana, East Amana, and Middle Amana; but in referring to the various villages the members of the Community habitually use the adjectives alone.

Up to this time (1861) the nearest railroad station had been Iowa City, which was twenty miles distant; but in 1861 the Mississippi and Missouri Railroad was completed as far as Homestead, a small town south of the Community's territory. All goods from the East would now be unloaded there, and it would also form the shipping point for the neighboring farming population. The Community saw the necessity of owning this railroad station, and so the entire village of Homestead was purchased.

The purchase of Homestead caused the Brethren much worry and anxiety because of the danger of ''the place remaining the meeting ground of hostile spirits.'' Since it was evident that it was the ''will and the pleasure of the Lord that the outsiders at Homestead should be bought out and that they should be removed'', it was finally agreed by the

Great Council of the Brethren that the purchase should be made. Then, too, when Sister Barbara Heinemann, the *Werkzeug*, was requested to express her opinion, "she fell into Inspiration and the Lord in His mercy gave His affirmation" as follows:

> How can I establish my dwelling at that place [Homestead] when you own it only in part. Better order must be established, for there are indeed still dwelling at that place those who rob earthly treasures as well as treasures of the soul, and therefore I cannot enter. But labor further in patience as best you can and as opportunity offers itself. However, let no chance pass by or you will not succeed and the place will remain the meeting ground and abode of robbers and hostile spirits. [83]

In the system of village life, which has been the great conservator of the Community's purity and simplicity, the Inspirationists have shown their farsightedness. The villages are near enough to one another to facilitate superintendence and to preserve a feeling of unity. At the same time they are far enough apart to maintain simplicity of living, which would probably be impossible with the same number of people congregated in one place. By this means the Community, while taking advantage of every progressive step in the methods of agriculture and the processes of manufacture, [84] has been able to sustain in its social, political, and religious life an insular position.

On July 27, 1867, six years after the establishment of the last of the seven Iowa villages and two years after the completion of the Ebenezer sale and the removal of the last detail of the Community to the new home in the West, Christian Metz, the "important, highly endowed, and specially favored *Werkzeug* of the Lord . . . . who in the whole external and internal leadership of the Community had to bear the bulk of the burden and care", and "through whom the weightiest and greatest things were wrought and accomplished" was after "fifty years of effort and labor recalled from the field of his endeavor" at the age of seventy-two years, six months, and twenty-four days.[85]

Half a century — the most eventful years of the Community's inspiring history — spans the interval between the "bestowal of God's mercy" on Michael Krausert at the time of the Reawakening and the "blessed departure and release" of Christian Metz in 1867. During that period the Community was at no time without a *Werkzeug*; great undertakings and changes occurred; and material progress unparalleled in communistic history was theirs.

In the gathering of the congregations in Hessen, in the preparation for the emigration of the Community to America, in the establishment of the "dwelling in the wilderness where there was none", and in the final removal to the new home in the State of Iowa, the one voice that oftenest revealed what "from the first had been ordained in the hidden counsel of God" was that of Christian Metz. From the year 1823 to the time of his death, a period of 5 times 9 or 45 years, there came from him to the Community through *Aus- und Einsprachen des Geistes des Herrn* three thousand six hundred and fifty-four testimonies, besides many beautiful "outpourings of the Spirit" in song and rhyme. There were many Brothers who gave to the service freely of their means, their business insight and experience, and even the labor of their hands; but without the sustained enthusiasm and phenomenal spiritual leadership of Christian Metz there would in all probability never have been so remarkable a fulfilment of the gracious promises recorded in the early *Jahrbücher*.

XIV

THE AMANA SOCIETY

By the time the sale of the Ebenezer land had been completed, the Community's territory in Iowa consisted of twenty-six thousand acres which is approximately the amount owned at the present time. With the exception of some seventeen hundred acres in the adjoining county of Johnson, all of the land lies within the boundaries of Iowa County. Furthermore, the larger part of this area falls within the civil township of Amana which was established in 1858.

In a recent suit in the Supreme Court of Iowa (*State of Iowa v. Amana Society,* 132 Iowa 304) it was pointed out that the Community owned and controlled "an entire political division of the State"; and the Attorney General argued that this was "contrary to public policy", since "it [the Amana Society] may obtain control of many political divisions" and finally gain control over the entire State. But this argument is dismissed by the court with the remark that "the fate of other similar enterprises during the past century, such as Brook Farm, the Phalanxes, and other experiments of the followers of Fourier, Owen and others, indicate that the peril is not at all imminent. So long as selfishness is the controlling passion of the human heart, the individual in all probability will be safe as against the encroachments of communism. At any rate, it will be time enough to obviate the danger, when, if ever, it is seriously threatened, with appropriate legislation."

Two steps of great importance were taken by the Community soon after its removal to Iowa. One was its incorporation under the laws of the State as the "Amana Society"; and the other was the adoption of a new Constitution.

It was under the general law of the State, entitled "An act for the incorporation of benevolent, charitable, religious and scientific societies", that the Community of True Inspiration became a legal corporation in December, 1859. At intervals of twenty years (1880 and 1900) the Amana Society has been reincorporated under the provisions of the Code relative to corporations which are established for other than pecuniary profit.

Having secured a legal status as a corporation under the laws of the State, and having associated themselves anew under the corporate name of "Amana Society", the members of the Community proceeded in December, 1859, to the adoption of a new Constitution and By-laws. As a matter of fact there were no radical changes made in this new draft of the fundamental law. Indeed, the old Ebenezer Constitution which, it will be remembered, was drawn up "according to the known will of God", was simply remodeled to harmonize with new conditions; and after receiving the signatures of "all members of lawful age male and female" went into force with the beginning of the year 1860 (See below Appendix).

The Amana Constitution is a simple document of ten short articles. Unlike some of its contemporaries, it is neither a "Declaration of Mental Independence" nor the outlines of a scheme of a "World-wide Socialistic Brotherhood." On the contrary, it provides simply and briefly a civil organization for a religious society. Furthermore, it is worthy of comment that, unlike Owen's New Harmony Society which adopted seven constitutions in two years, the Amana Society still lives under the provisions of the instrument which went into effect on the first day of January, 1860, and which has received the signature of every member of the Society since its adoption in December, 1859. Prepared with characteristic German caution and thoroughness, it is likely to remain the fundamental law of the Society.

Nearly all of the peace-loving brotherhoods of America that have fled to the wilderness to escape the vexations of the world have at some time during their history been dragged into court and made to defend, if not their right to existence as a Society, at least their particular mode of living. And it is interesting to note that almost without exception the courts have sustained the communities. The Shaker Societies have, perhaps, suffered most from actions brought by former members for their distributive share of the property or for compensation for services rendered while members of the Society. The plucky little Society of Zoar was several times called upon to establish its legal status by resort to the highest judicial tribunal of the State of Ohio. In each case the action was brought by some member who had been expelled from the organization or had been deprived of supposed rights, or by "world heirs" of members who sought to obtain their distributive share of the Zoar property. And the Harmony Society in its turn had to prove through the Supreme Court of Pennsylvania that its association was not "contrary to public policy." The decision of the court in each case, after elaborate and often long drawn-out trials, was in favor of the society and against the contestants. Some of these communities, due to the vicissitudes of fortune, are reduced to mere remnants; but they will be gratefully remembered by communists in the future for their efforts in settling through courts of last resort important legal principles.[86]

The recent case of *State of Iowa v. Amana Society* is unique in the history of communistic societies in that action was brought not by a member or ex-member, nor even by a "world heir", but by a "resident and taxpayer of Iowa County" who attempted to prove that the Society as a religious organization had exceeded its corporate power in holding much real property and in establishing and conducting various "purely secular industries" and had therefore "forfeited its corporate franchise." The decision handed down by the Judge of the District Court in which the case was first brought was in favor of the Amana Society. After reviewing the history of the organization, its object and ideals, its industrial activity and material prosperity the Judge said:

We therefore reach the conclusion that no abuse of corporate power has been shown. Under the peculiar organization, aims, and purposes of the Society, to deny it the privilege of engaging in secular occupations for certain purposes would be tantamount to denying it existence. If the theory of the State obtains we would have the absurd position of authorizing corporations to exist and denying them the means of subsistence. But it is said, let them organize a corporation for pecuniary profit. This would require the abandonment of principles which are the basis of their religious belief and faith and the promulgation of which is the primary purpose of the Society. If they have a right to believe in community of property as a religious doctrine and to organize in order to live in conformity to that doctrine, any employment devoted to their support would be accomplishing the purpose of the Society's existence.

The case was appealed to the Supreme Court, where the decision of the District Court was affirmed in November, 1906. The court held that "a religious society, organized under Chapter 2 Title 9 of the Code, seeking to effectuate its ideals of religious life through the common ownership and management of the property of its members, may so acquire and hold real property and establish and conduct various industries, and so long as its enterprises are extended and conducted simply to meet the needs of its members and maintain them in a manner consistent with their religious faith to which its total income and accumulation of property is devoted will not be dissolved and its privileges forfeited on the ground that it has exceeded its corporate power."

There was solemn rejoicing at Amana when the decision of the Supreme Court was announced; and especially did the older members, those who had shared in "the great and weighty inner and outer cares and burdens of the Community", feel that "the Lord had permitted this to happen" for the purpose of strengthening the faith of the Community as well as to establish "once for all" their legal status.

XV

THE REALIZATION

Materially all of the fondest hopes of the little band of Inspirationists in Germany struggling to pay the rent of their first estate have been realized. The membership, numbering eight hundred when the Community migrated to New York and twelve hundred when the removal to Iowa took place, has increased to eighteen hundred at the present day. Bountiful harvests have rewarded their untiring industry; the products of their mills and factories have found a market from Maine to California; and in the books of the Auditor of Iowa County, their real and personal property was listed in 1908 at $1,843,720.00.

Communistic societies are like individuals. Many have been able to stand adversity, but only the steadiest minded are able to stand prosperity. The Amana Society belongs to the extremely small class of the latter. In spite of the continued prosperity of the last half century, the "solidarity" of the Community is still intact. The element of self-interest demanding individual gain and good is still kept in abeyance by the spirit of brotherly love.

After the death of Christian Metz "the blessed continuance of the work of grace" was carried on by Barbara Heinemann (who retained her gift to the time of her death at the age of eighty-eight), and by the Elders in whom the "Lord manifested himself so strongly and powerfully during the last illness of Brother Christian Metz."[87] Since the death of Barbara Heinemann in 1883 no *Werkzeug* has been called in the Community of True Inspiration; but as in the period following the death of Rock "well founded Brethren endowed with divine mercy who are still living witnesses of the great blessing of Inspiration carry on the work of the Lord in the Community."

How long the coming generation will "fill the widening gap" with no *Werkzeug* for their spiritual guidance and with the breaking of the link in "the passing into eternity" of "these faithful witnesses and Elders" which bind them to the past with its inspiring history "is ordained only in the hidden counsel of God."

PART II

A DESCRIPTIVE ACCOUNT OF AMANA

Village architecture—1890s

Top: View of South Amana *Below: Village homes*

I

THE LAND AND THE VILLAGES

Whether the choice of the Iowa home of the Community of True Inspiration was due to "a blessed decision through the word" or to the human wisdom and foresight of the gifted Christian Metz and his associates, it is perhaps true that a better place for the working out of an ideal could scarcely anywhere have been selected. For, in addition to the rare natural beauties of the location, the Amana domain includes some of the richest bottom-land and the most fertile upland in all Iowa — including that variety of surface and soil requisite for meadows, grain fields, pastures, and vineyards, in addition to an abundant supply of water. Besides, there are the well timbered hills which have furnished most of the building materials and all of the fuel for the entire Community for over half a century without any present indication of ever being completely stripped.

The Amana estate, which includes twenty-six thousand acres (inclusive of timber and swamp lands), is divided approximately into (1) village and factory sites, five hundred acres; (2) vegetable gardens, one hundred acres; (3) timber land, ten thousand acres; (4) cultivated fields, seven thousand acres; and (5) grazing land, four thousand acres. In a recent suit in the district court the Inspirationists were accused of being land monopolists. A glance at the figures, however, reveals the absurdity of such a statement, since the average number of acres per individual is less than fifteen. The Amana Society has in truth been singularly free from "land mania" — which the founder of the Oneida Society declares might be written as an epitaph on half the tombstones in the communistic graveyard.[88]

The picturesqueness of the Amana estate is enhanced by a mill-race — a canal seven miles long which furnishes the water power for the mills and factories. This mill-race is now old enough to be fringed with pickerel weed and dwarf willows bent by the weight of wild grape-vines. Here and there the race is spanned by quaint wooden bridges. Halfway between two of the villages the mill-race expands into a lake which covers about two hundred acres and is bordered at places, to the width of sixty feet, with the American lotus or yellow nelumbo. It is worth a journey of many miles to see this little sheet of water in the month of July, when the lotus lifts hundreds of great buff blossoms above the water.[89]

The seven villages into which the Community is grouped are known as Amana or "Old Amana" (the Capital), Middle Amana, East Amana, West Amana, South Amana, High Amana, and Homestead. They lie from a mile and a half to four miles apart; but all are within a radius of six miles from Old Amana. They are connected with one another, as well as with most of the important towns and cities of the State, by telephone.

Each village consists of a cluster of from forty to one hundred houses, arranged in the manner of the German *Dorf* with one long straggling street and several irregular offshoots. Indeed, so striking is the resemblance of the Amana village to the German *Dorf* that the visitor almost feels that he is in the Fatherland. At one end are the village barns and sheds; at the other, the factories and workshops; and on either side lie the orchards, the vineyards, and the gardens.

Each village has its own church and school, its bakery, its dairy, its wine-cellar, its post-office, and its general store. In each there is a sawmill for the working up of hard wood for the frame houses, which are for the most part built of hard lumber on the principle that the best is the cheapest. The lumber is obtained largely from the Society's own timber land. At the three railway stations [90] there are grain-houses and lumber-yards. The establishment of hotels, in no way a part of the original village plan, has been made necessary by the hundreds of strangers who visit the Community every year.

Each village has its water-works and fire-engine; and every able-bodied man in the Community is a member of the fire department. Although the loss by fire during the past twenty-five years has been between eighty and one hundred thousand dollars, the Society still deems it a matter of economy to rebuild rather than pay insurance premiums. The water-supply is furnished in the main by deep artesian wells. There is one well at Amana, sixteen hundred feet deep, that yields warm sulphurized water which is used in the dye-works; while another at Homestead, furnishing the water-supply for the village, is twenty-one hundred feet deep.

There are no hospitals in Amana; but the Community enjoys the best of medical service.[91] Defectives (the insane, blind, feeble-minded, and deaf-mutes) are for the most part sent to the State institutions for treatment. The milder cases are, however, cared for in the homes of the Community.

The Community houses are two (rarely three) story structures of frame, brick, or a peculiar brown sandstone which is found in the vicinity. At Ebenezer, the frame houses were painted; but the Society has since decided that it is more economical to rebuild when occasion requires than to attempt to preserve the wood with paint. The predominance of weather-stained buildings gives to the villages a dull and monotonous aspect. The style of architecture (or it would be more accurate to say the lack of style) is the same throughout the entire Community — plain, square structures, with gable roofs.

Happily the severe aspect of the houses is softened in the summer time by a singular arrangement of vines which partly cover dwelling-house, school, church, and hotel alike. These vines are usually trained over a frame work, or trellis, a few inches from the building itself so as to prevent any injury to the wall and at the same time afford an adequate support for the vines. For these vines are not simply the ornamental ivies ordinarily used for such decoration, but grape-vines which serve the double purpose of protection and decoration in the summer-time and yield an abundant harvest in the fall. Here and there where the householder has a tendency to worldliness a trumpet vine or a climbing rose may be seen climbing a trellis in company with the grape.

There is in the *Jahrbuch* for 1880 a testimony by Barbara Heinemann, given three years before her death, in which the planting of ornamental trees is severely denounced by the Lord. "Wilt thou then'', it reads, ''prove that it is a beautiful custom to plant trees not bearing fruit? Know then that the pleasures of the eye and of the flesh and the over-bearing manner are a mark of worldliness, and that the spirit of the world has created in you the desire for such a beginning. Alas, away with this idolatry . . . See ye to it then that all trees not bearing fruit be removed from the house, for they belong to the pleasure of the eye. You indeed have the opportunity to plant a fruit-tree instead, in which the Lord and all sensible people take pleasure.''

How it came to pass that the planting of flowers escaped condemnation as ''a pleasure to the eye'' is more than the ''worldly minded'' can explain. We only know that it is so and are thankful. For all the pent up love for the beautiful in the Community of True Inspiration for six generations seems to find expression in the cultivation of flowers, which are found in great profusion everywhere — around each dwelling, in front of the church, and even in the hotel and school yards. Indeed, the Amana village from June to October is one huge German garden all aglow with quaint old-fashioned flowers. There are great rows of four-o'clocks and lady-slippers, borders of candy-tuft and six-weeks-stock; gorgeous masses of zenias, marigolds, and geraniums; great pansy beds and rose gardens —

all laid out with great precision and cared for with such devotion and such genuine pleasure that the visitor too rejoices. And sometimes he who with great sincerity has admired the flowers carries home a huge bouquet containing no less than thirty-seven varieties of the garden's choicest bloom.

Although isolation from the world was one of the Community's prime purposes in seeking a home in the then frontier Commonwealth of Iowa, it is a fact that the very quaintness of the people and their villages has conspired to bring the world to Amana by attracting scores of visitors from the neighboring towns and country.

Indeed, the experience of the Community of True Inspiration in Iowa has been the same as that of any other people who have sought seclusion from the world. For "when you and some of your friends go off by yourselves to lead a perfect life, and hang up a sign reading 'Please pass on and leave us alone' some stranger will invite himself in to ask why you put up a sign like that. Then he will invite a friend or two from town to go with him and see what a queer lot you are, and the company will insist on being fed and kept over night, and in the goodness of your heart you will take them in and be done for. A hotel being started in this fashion, other strangers will come strolling in from various places to stare and gibe, and the first thing you know strangers will be all over the place, peeping in at your windows, staring at you through insolent lorgnettes and remarking rudely as you try to steal through your own streets to your own post-office.''[92]

The average number of visitors in Old Amana alone is twelve hundred annually. Some come for the outing; and some, interested in political and social science, come for purposes of ''investigation'' — much to the annoyance of the Inspirationists. ''Vas you one of dem newspaper fellers what wants to know everytings?'' inquired a member of the Zoar Society. ''No'', was the dignified reply, ''I am a college professor.'' ''Oh well'', retorted the Zoarite, ''dot vas the same ting and joost as bad.''[93]

By far the greater number of Amana's visitors come out of sheer curiosity, to find out if possible (in the words of Mr. Skinner) ''what there is so durned private goin' on here.'' And so, there is little wonder that the stranger with the pencil or the camera has not always been welcomed with outstretched hands and that the scientific inquirer has usually received in response to his many questions the simple but emphatic, ''I don' know.'' Trained for nearly seven generations to ''have no intercourse with worldly minded men'', the Inspirationists until comparatively recently have been exceedingly reticent with reference to the business and religious affairs of the Community. And naturally this reticence has at times given rise to absurd speculations regarding the nature of the Society and its inner workings. In justice it should be remarked that much impertinent inquiry has been borne with great patience by the Community of True Inspiration.[94]

There is another class of uninvited guests for which the Community has been forced to make special provision in much the same manner that it has been compelled to establish hotels for its picnicers and excursionists. These are the tramps. "Give to him that asketh thee," said Jesus in his sermon on the mount, "and from him that would borrow of thee turn not thou away." Like all other religious communities, Amana has endeavored to follow this precept of the Master. But like them too it has been most shamefully imposed upon by "victims of misfortune."

The Harmony Society was obliged to set a house apart for the lodging of such individuals, with bed accommodations for twenty men, and make constant provision of coffee and bread for as many "extra boarders." The Shaker Families made regular provision for the "winter Shakers" who came "with empty stomachs and empty trunks" to be cared for until the spring sun was warm enough to make traveling agreeable once more. The Zoar Society found it necessary to build a calaboose for the benefit of those who reached the belligerent stage.[95] And the Inspirationists in their turn have been obliged to erect at the edge of the larger villages what the younger Inspirationists term a "Hobo Hotel." It is heated, and is furnished with such articles as are deemed necessary for the comfort of the "guests", who take their meals on the European plan — first at one kitchen then at another until if skilful they have made the rounds of all the kitchens in the seven villages.

In recent years the tramp problem has become so vexing that the Community has endeavored to make some distinction between the professional tramp and the really unfortunate and worthy wayfarer. One feels, however, that there are still too many "tough customers" systematically fed and cared for at the Amana villages. "Haymaker Shorty", "Captain Jack", "Hobo Charlie", "No Neck", and "King Hobo" should be emphatically requested to discontinue their annual visits.[96]

II

GOVERNMENT

In the Community of True Inspiration that extreme democracy in government and administration which has proved to be one of the chief sources of weakness in so many associative endeavors has not been especially encouraged. Indeed, the political ideal of the Inspirationist is quite the opposite, being that of a strong central authority wisely administered and implicitly obeyed.

The entire conduct of the affairs of the Amana Society rests with a Board of Trustees consisting of thirteen members who are elected annually by popular vote out of the whole number of Elders in the Community.[97] Moreover, the members of the Board of Trustees are the spiritual as well as the temporal leaders of the Community, and as such are known as the "Great Council of the Brethren." Thus there has been effected in the Community an harmonious blending of temporal rule and spiritual authority, which is regarded as the fulfilment of the will of the Lord as revealed through Inspiration.

On October 8 [1844] there came a serious word to the Community through Inspiration as a guidance for the Elders, directing how they should establish better order and unite themselves, instead of permitting self-willed quarrels, giving offence and a bad example to the members. The bitter spirit of natural men should not and must not rule in the Community; but they should all be subjected to and governed by the Divine guidance and through this means the external management and arrangement was to be accomplished in a calm manner. Some of the leading men of each place should form a Council, and the others should be obedient to them. [98]

The present system of electing the members of the Great Council of the Brethren by popular vote out of the whole number of Elders, that is, out of the "specially endowed Brethren", was inaugurated after the incorporation of the Community as Ebenezer Society. "In order to follow out the directions of the Lord to the best of our ability", says the historian, Gottlieb Scheuner, in speaking of this system, "we have sought and found a way to carry out the election of Trustees in such manner that we do not conflict with the laws of this country to which we owe obedience and at the same time suffer no harm through the intermingling of anything which is contrary to the principles of our faith and our rules of salvation. In the world there rules the spirit of the world, the spirit of unbelief, the spirit of self-will, and under its influence and sway the elections of the world are conducted amidst the feud and strife of the several parties struggling for diverse selfish ends — each endeavoring to gain power and control. But not so in the Community of the faithful which has one common goal — the glory of God and the salvation of men — and in which the spirit of Jesus Christ shall alone rule and wield the scepter." [99]

The Trustees elect annually on the second Tuesday of the month of December out of their own number a President, a Vice President, and a Secretary. The incumbents are usually reëlected; for rotation in office has never been a part of the Amana theory of government.

There has always been a strong religious sentiment against allowing personal ambition to play much if any part in the government of the Community. To disregard any of the duties entrusted to a member of the Community is to "break the sacred covenant which the Brethren have made with the Lord and with one another." The office-holder is expected to accept office not for its honors or its perquisites, but as a sacred responsibility. To be sure there have been lapses from this ideal from time to time; for now and then "a First Elder has too much regard for his own profit whereby he causes much strife"; or a leading Brother "stands in his overbearingness too high." [100]

In his study of *American Communities,* William A. Hinds reaches the conclusion that the "best way to manage a community is to perfect the machinery of government and let a few smart men run it.'' This has literally been the policy of the Community of True Inspiration; and it is worthy of remark that, despite the opportunity and the temptations which this system would seem to offer for the exercise of arbitrary and despotic power, the officers have generally performed their duties in the spirit of ''whoever will be chief among you let him be your servant.''

The Amana spirit in administration is nowhere better exemplified than in the life and services of the great leader, Christian Metz. His *Tagebuch* is full of earnest prayers for wisdom, for strength, and for divine guidance in the management of the affairs of the Community. Only once in his long period of service did he utter a complaint of the double burden of business manager and spiritual leader which he was called upon to bear. On that occasion after speaking of his own unworthiness and his longing to do ''the great work of God's grace'', he adds:

> On the second Christmas day the members of the second class gathered and I again went into violent inner labor before grace came upon me, in which respect my Brethren [of the Great Council] and the members are too often at fault, since they do not leave me an hour of quiet self-collection, and overrun me until the very hour of the meeting so that one indeed may pray for true patience. [101]

The leaders to-day are men whose good sense and shrewd intelligence would be recognized in any sphere of life.[102] Nor is it an easy matter to manage the affairs of eighteen hundred persons scattered in seven villages; for the members of a community (albeit a religious one) are essentially human. They are just as fond of their own way as are their brothers of the world. Personal ambition can not always be kept in the background. Some will "strive for particular gifts and envy the one or the other." Some "lend their ears to suspicion and prejudice and take offence where there is none."[103] Differences of opinion as to the general policy of the Community arise; discontent and petty jealousies appear; and there are "occasional bickerings as it should be among near relatives."[104] In his *Tagebuch* Christian Metz, who during his lifetime "had to bear the bulk of the burden and care of the Community", laments that "there are many presumptuous members in our Communities who are always aspiring for something. The one wants to be an Elder, and the other even a *Werkzeug;* and the cause of it all is self-love and a false desire of the soul."[105]

To maintain peace and harmony and at the same time to promote the interests of the Society requires something of the ability of the statesman and the general. Men of such parts the Amana Society is fortunate enough to have; and the growth and prosperity of the organization in its western home is in a large measure due to the force, patience, sagacity, broadmindedness and withal the faithful service of competent leaders.

The Board of Trustees, or Great Council of the Brethren, whose meetings are held alternately in the different villages on the first Tuesday of each month, directs not only all the internal affairs of the Society, but determines as well its business relations with the world. In short, in it the members of the Society vest "all the powers, right of action, and privileges granted to corporations by the laws of the State of Iowa." [106]

The *Werkzeug*, when the Community was fortunate enough to have one, was usually consulted by the Great Council to learn if possible the will of the Lord in important matters before announcing their decision. In truth the *Werkzeug*, "being solely a passive instrument in the hand of the Lord", was regarded as the real head of the organization. "You must stand to him [the Werkzeug]", reads an old testimony, "in strict subjection and obedience . . . . Let not a word affirmed by him be acted against." As late as December 2, 1879, it is recorded that in a matter that had caused the Great Council of the Brethren much worry and anxiety, Sister Barbara Heinemann was requested to express her opinion and "she fell into Inspiration and the Lord in His mercy then gave further directions to the Council."

The Lord says Yes and Amen! Do then thus as you have agreed, and endeavor that the burden does not wholly and solely remain upon your shoulders, if possible. If it however cannot be brought about, be ready none the less, though it should be somewhat difficult; it is a small matter for Me to help you on and through, so let all apprehensions and prejudices be dropped for this is in accordance with the divine guidance, and take heed that you lose not on account of the money for I know that it is a necessary evil. And let there be no delay, for this too had to come about that they objected and caused opposition. It will be for your benefit and you will comprehend it, when it will come about that in your neighborhood there will be no place of business [market]. To this adhere.[107]

In the month of June in each year the Trustees exhibit to the voting members of the Society (who comprise, according to the By-laws, all male members who have signed the Constitution, all widows, and such female members as are thirty years of age and are not represented through some male member) a full statement of "the real and personal estate of the Society." In matters of great importance special meetings of the whole Society may be called. But in general the Society has avoided the mistake (common enough in many contemporary communities) of too many mass meetings. It took five upheavals of the Icarian Community to teach the lesson of leaving routine administration to committees instead of discussing every detail in frequent meetings of the assembly.

The Amana Society aims to keep its members informed on the general condition of affairs; but there is a decided tendency to reduce unnecessary discussion to the minimum by "leaving such things to those that best understand them." This policy has been of the greatest significance, since it has saved the Society from the mistakes and follies that have brought ruin to so many democratic communities in which every man feels in duty bound to air his views. A survivor of one of the Fourier experiments being asked the cause of the downfall of his Phalanx replied: "Talk, talk; too much damn talk." At Amana, on the other hand, there is, perhaps, too much silence.

The Board of Trustees is the high court of appeals in cases of disagreements, dissension, and complaints within the Society. When the "bitter spirit of natural men" has not been properly "subjected" and difficulties between Brethren arise, the matter is brought before the village Elders for adjustment. From their decision either party may appeal to the Great Council, or Board of Trustees, where the matter is finally and most emphatically closed with their decision. "Obey them that have the rule over you'', said Paul in his Epistle to the Hebrews, ''and submit yourselves: for they watch for your souls, as they that must give account, that they may do it with joy, and not with grief: for that is unprofitable for you.'' [108] This has ever been the chief of the governing principles of the Community of True Inspiration. ''See to it'', reads the *Kinder-Stimme,* ''that you practice an entirely voluntary obedience and submission to the superiors set over you by God in all things.'' And again it is written: ''Obey the counsel of your superiors without reasoning'', and ''do not offend God through your sinful self-willed deeds nor offend Him in your superiors.'' [109]

The business of the Community of a legal character is transacted at Marengo, the seat of Iowa County. Owing to the nature of the organization there are no lawyers in the Community of True Inspiration. However, in suits with outside parties the Society does not hesitate to employ counsel.

Each village is governed by a group of from seven to nineteen Elders — not necessarily old men, but men who are deemed to be of deep piety and spirituality. At the same time the Community profoundly believes that ''Days should speak and multitude of years should teach wisdom.'' [110] Formerly the Elders were named or appointed by Inspiration, ''through the Spirit'', with the approval and consent of the already existing Elders. "I bid thee to sit thyself with the Elders", reads one of these summons of the Lord, "for the time has come when thou hast been made ready to assist in the work of the Lord. For such the Lord selects only those who in affairs temporal and spiritual prove faithful to the common grace." "And thou", reads another, "shalt assist the *übelhörende* when it is necessary, and shalt help in the holding of the general meeting . . . . Art thou willing? Will you pledge your faith and will you share in the burden of the Community that you may be co-workers and watchers over the malice of Belial and that in spirit you may come down to the feet of your master, for the servant can not be greater than the master?" [111]

At present, there being no *Werkzeug,* the Elders are appointed by the Great Council in this manner:—The resident Trustee of each village recommends to the Great Council, of which he is a member, a list of Elders from the most spiritual of the members of his village. After careful consideration of these lists the Great Council appoints the Elders for each village according to spiritual rank. And "through fervent prayer" it is hoped that the "Lord will grant to them, his mercy, strength, insight, and discrimination". [112]

The governing board of each village is known as the *Bruderrath*, and is composed of the resident Trustee and a number of the leading Elders of the village, who call into conference the foremen of the different branches of industry and such other members of the Community as may on occasion be of assistance in arranging the village work. It is this *Bruderrath* that appoints the foremen for the different industries and departments of labor and assigns to each individual his apportioned task. To them each individual desiring more money, more house-room, an extra holiday, or lighter work must appeal; for these allotments are as occasion requires "revised and fixed anew."

By that nice adjustment of functions that necessarily grows up in such a community, the highest authority in the village in matters spiritual is the Head Elder; in matters temporal, the resident Trustee. And although the Trustee is a member of the Great Council itself, which is the spiritual head of the Community, in the village church the Head Elder outranks the Trustee.

Each village keeps its own books and manages its own affairs in accordance with the resolutions of the Great Council; but all accounts are finally sent to the headquarters at Old Amana where they are inspected and the balance of profit or loss is discovered. It is presumed that the labor of each village produces a profit; but whether it does or not makes no difference in the supplies allotted to the village or members thereof. The system of government is thus a sort of federation wherein each village maintains a certain sphere of independence in local administration, but is under the general control and supervision of a governing central authority — the Board of Trustees, or Great Council of the Brethren.

The Amana system of government has been criticised as "an aristocracy of Elders" and as tending to produce too great distinctions between the governing and governed classes. Theoretically it is best, no doubt, so to conduct a community that every one shall feel, not only that he is personally interested in the general welfare but that he contributes to its management according to the measure of his ability. In the Amana Community questions relating to business or general policy are always discussed and settled among the leaders, the rank and file being consulted only at the option of the leaders. However this system may fall short of the democratic ideal, its advantages and working possibilities have been demonstrated by the Community of True Inspiration.

III

MEMBERSHIP

In accordance with the Constitution each member of the Community of True Inspiration "is in duty bound to give his or her personal and real property to the Trustees for the common fund" at the time of his or her acceptance as a member and before signing the Constitution. And "for such payments into the common fund each member is entitled to a credit thereof in the books of the Society and to a receipt signed by the President and Secretary of the Board of Trustees, and is moreover secured for such payments by the pledge of the common property of the Society."[113] These contributions to the common fund of the Society have varied from $50,000 (the largest sum paid into the treasury by any one member) to the bare working capacity of the ordinary laborer.

"Every member of the Society is", according to Article VI of the Constitution, "besides the free board, dwelling, support, and care secured to him in old age, sickness and infirmity, further entitled out of the common fund to an annual sum of maintenance for him or herself, children, and relations in the Society; and these annual allowances shall be fixed by the Trustees for each member single or in families according to justice and equity, and shall be from time to time revised and fixed anew." At the same time the "members of this corporation in consideration of the enjoyment of these blessings in the bond of our Communion, do hereby release, grant and quit-claim to the said corporation, for ourselves, our children, heirs and administrators all claims for wages and interest of the capital paid into the common fund, also all claims for any part of the income and profits and of any share in the estate and property of the Society separate from the whole and common stock."

The annual sum of maintenance varies with "justice and equity" from twenty-five to fifty dollars, or in some cases even more — the variation causing at times no little jealousy and discontent. This allowance, made in the form of a credit at the village store and guarded by a pass-book and a day of judgment at the close of the year, is not likely to be spent in riotous living. Recently coupon books for five dollars and ten dollars have been issued and are now used by the members for smaller purchases. This simplifies the bookkeeping and adds, no doubt, very greatly to the peace of mind of those members who do not always use the proper amount of discretion (from the Inspirationist's point of view) in the spending of their allowance.

Some years ago a talented Brother appealed to one of the First Brethren for a larger sum of maintenance on the ground that the service rendered by him was of unusual value to the Community and that his position required a larger personal expenditure than that of the average Brother. The reply of the First Brother is an admirable illustration of the spirit of the Community. He sat by an open window overlooking a meadow where Eduard, a half-witted shepherd, was tending his flock of sheep. "Dost thou see Eduard yonder in the meadow?" asked the First Brother. "Yes Brother." "Doth he not perform the task allotted to him faithfully and to the utmost extent of his ability?" "Yes, Brother." "Go thou then, my dear Brother, and do likewise. Be thankful that the Almighty God hath endowed thee with greater gifts, for therein thou hast already received a fuller allowance. Go render unto the Community thy best service and offer up a prayer to the Heavenly Father for His special kindness and gracious gifts to thee."

Through generations of admonition and practice the Inspirationists have learned thoroughly the fundamental principle of frugality. But, if by chance an erring Brother in this family of eighteen hundred souls should so far forget himself as to spend "his means for that he hath no need", his Brothers and Sisters will not let the offence pass by unnoticed. The chances are that the unwise Brother will soon mend his ways, since public opinion at Amana, as in the outside world, exercises a censorship that is more potent than all the laws which human wisdom can devise.

"Such members as may recede from the Society, either by their own choice or by expulsion, shall be entitled to receive back the moneys paid by them into the common fund and to interest thereon at the rate not exceeding five per cent per annum from the time of the adjustment of their accounts until the repayment of their credits." [114] Although this system would not seem to be particularly attractive to the American spirit of commercialism, there are among the members of the Amana Society to-day native-born Americans who grew to manhood and womanhood in the "tumult of the world" before joining the Society.

It is not surprising to learn that persons sojourning for a while at other communities and religious societies (particularly the Separatist Society of Zoar and the Harmony Society of Economy) should later have joined the Community of True Inspiration. One of the most capable business leaders that the Amana Society has ever had — a man who "had travelled much, had a good command of the English language and knew the laws of the country", who conducted "the difficult affair with the Ogden Company and the Indians", and who assisted so efficiently in the sale of the Ebenezer property — was led to them from the Zoar Society "by the hand of God at a time when he was imperatively needed."[115] In origin, language, manner of living, and in Christian ideals these organizations had so much in common that Zoarites and Harmonists who could adopt the "modern inspiration" tenet of the Inspirationists would have felt very much at home in the Community.[116] A number of former Catholics have subscribed to the faith and joined the Society — among them a Catholic priest who, wearied with the pomp and ceremony of the Church of Rome, sought refuge in the Community of True Inspiration. But by far the largest accessions to membership have been from Germany.

There is a homogeneity among the eighteen hundred members of the Community of True Inspiration not commonly found in coöperative or communistic societies. This has, no doubt, had much to do with its perpetuity. A common origin, a common religion, and a common tongue have given to the Community what the Icarians were fond of calling "solidarity."

The records of the Society show that at an earlier period there were sometimes paid out of the common treasury the expenses of poor families who recommended themselves to the Society by letter and whom the leaders (usually the *Werkzeuge*, through the "gift of Prophecy") declared to be worthy. Through "a serious and decisive word of the Lord" the Society has even assumed the debts of desirable persons who wished to become members. Occasionally "a pharisaical spirit" would agree to abide by "the divine ordinances and the ruling of the Community" until his wife and children were brought from Europe at the expense of the Community "when he would denounce the divine ruling of the Community entirely and declare that he did not believe in the divine nature of Inspiration." Such an one would of course be straightway "excommunicated."[117] But despite the excellent opportunity such impositions have been remarkably few.

It is moreover an interesting fact that of a considerable number of new members who came to the Community some years after the removal to Iowa not a few were more interested in socialistic ideas and propaganda than they were zealous devotees of the tenets of True Inspiration. And so there has been a discordant note in the Community which at times has caused the First Brethren no little uneasiness and trouble. At the same time these new-comers have been dealt with sympathetically and patiently by the old-line members, who doubtless understand that it must be extremely difficult to maintain the true spirit of the Community when one lacks the advantages of Pietist ancestry,

Community education and training, and family traditions interwoven with the history of the Community. Guided by the light of experience the Society has wisely adopted the policy of rejecting the scores of applications for membership which are annually made by letter.

The exceptional person who after careful consideration is permitted to become a candidate for membership in the Society enters on a period of probation, signing an obligation to labor faithfully, to conduct himself according to the regulations of the Society, and to demand no wages. If at the close of this period of probation he gives "proof of being fully in accord with the religious doctrine of the Society" and appears in every other way to be a proper person he deeds over to the Society all his worldly goods (if he has any), takes part in the "Renewing of the Covenant", listens to the reading of, then signs, the Constitution, and is admitted to full membership with all the rights and privileges thereto pertaining. The period of probation was, during the reign of the *Werkzeuge*, sometimes shortened and sometimes dispensed with altogether by "the direct word of the Lord." [118]

Moreover, the records show that formerly new members were expected to make a public confession of sins before being taken into fellowship, and were sorely punished by the Lord for not telling the whole truth.[119]

It is worth noting that the growth of the Amana Society during the last quarter of a century has been mainly from within, notwithstanding some of the young people on whom the hopes of the Community were centered have been drawn from the "pathway of the Lord" by the gayeties and pleasures of the "sinful world."

Generations of training in strict obedience and submission to the will of the Lord and the decision of the Brethren have not altogether eliminated the "spirit of the enemy", and there are times when "the sprouting wings of manhood must unfold for a moment in the breeze of insubordination." But the First Brethren are usually patient, hold their peace, and "think up some good job for the boy", knowing full well that the youth grows more conservative as he grows older and comes to feel the sobering effect of responsibility. Their "experienceful" lives have taught them that restive Brothers who at twenty show their independence by wearing "store clothes" and a colored necktie to meetings, will at thirty of their own initiative be wearing "Colony trousers." It is a significant fact that sixty per cent of the young people who having "in the hatred of restriction" chosen the lot of the world have returned to the tranquil well-ordered life of the Community.

As a rule the Amana youth's ambition is some day to be counted a member of the Community, and perhaps to work as foreman in the shop or factory. He hopes to be (and his dear mother prays he may be) good enough to one day be an Elder or even a member of the Great Council of the Brethren. The importance of being well fitted both intellectually and spiritually (particularly the latter) for his place in the Community is constantly kept before him.

And the little Amana maid — what is her ambition? Is it to cook in the kitchen-house one week and wash dishes the next? Is it perchance to marry and have a home of her own? But Barbara Heinemann, *eine ganz geringe und ungelehrte Magd*, was called as a *Werkzeug* of the Lord. And so, who knows what dreams the little Amana maid may have as she sits on the front bench in the prayer-meeting with the ponderous *Psalter-Spiel* in her lap. Whatever they may be, she and her brother on becoming of age sign the Constitution and are taken into full membership.

The signing of the Constitution and By-Laws in the "Great Book" of the Society takes place with ceremony enough to impress properly the young people with the importance of the step they are taking. The resident Trustee sends word of their coming to headquarters; and so the young people when they arrive are met by the President and Secretary of the Great Council and two or three other Brethren. After the young people have in turn expressed their desire to become full members of the Community, the Constitution is read aloud, the significance of the organization is reviewed, and great emphasis is laid upon the responsibility each member assumes on the signing of the Constitution and the desirability of preserving the organization in its pristine purity. When the signatures have been affixed to the Constitution as engrossed in the Great Book all the rights and privileges of full membership are bestowed upon the candidates.

Members guilty of voluntary disobedience, those who rebel against authority or refuse to fulfill duties, were, during the lifetime of the *Werkzeuge*, rebuked in general meeting by a "severe testimony of the Lord" and sometimes expelled. Indeed, the Community has always exhibited great courage in following the scriptural admonition: "And if thy right eye offend thee, pluck it out, and cast it from thee: for it is profitable for thee that one of thy members should perish, and not that thy whole body should be cast into hell."[120] At the time of the removal of the Community to America one of the leading Elders who had been left in charge of affairs in Germany wrote the following to Christian Metz:

Many will have to undergo a deep pruning, which of necessity shall and must be undertaken and which will be very painful; and a few will become food for the flames, unless the Lord performs a special act of grace.[121]

And the following entry made in the *Jahrbuch* very soon after the laying out of Ebenezer shows that "in accordance with the divine guidance and the vote of the Great Council of the Brethren" the pruning process was inaugurated:

The Lord had already at the beginning of the year sent a decisive message with regard to this [the misdemeanors of one of the Brethren] and after he [the erring Brother] had arrived it was once more confirmed, that he not only was removed from his office and duty as Elder, but that he furthermore must settle and dwell without the Community.

At the present time the Great Council settles all questions of discipline; and from their decision there is no appeal in the Community. There is no case on record where an expelled member has resorted to law for reinstatement. In the recorded testimonies of the *Werkzeuge* there are many lamentations of the Lord over "Brothers with false aims and purposes" who were "discontented with regard to common possessions" and "disinclined to share the great and weighty inner and outer cares and burdens of the Community." But "for all such the way stands open", and they are "at liberty to separate and take their own."

Individual accomplishment counts for naught in the Amana Society except in so far as it promotes the interests of the Community as a whole. This has been the *Weltanschauung* of the Community of True Inspiration for nearly two hundred years. In an old apothecary shop in one of the villages the chemist has worked with such zeal and to such purpose for half a century that his compounds are known throughout the Mississippi Valley as products of the Amana Society. But who knows the name of the skilful chemist? The patterns of the Amana calico are known from ocean to ocean. But who knows the name of the designer? Some of the machinery in the woolen mills has been copied (the members of the Society do not patent their inventions) in almost every woolen mill in the country. But who knows the name of the splendid young inventor? In every branch of industry men of marked ability patiently, and with apparent cheerfulness, are giving their best efforts for the common good with no thought of personal recognition.

The *me* spirit, as one of the members naively expressed it, is subordinated to the *we* spirit. Men of excellent attainments throughout the villages perform unhesitatingly the commonest kind of work. A folder of cloth in the woolen mills will long be remembered in the outside world as an artist who made many of the original drawings for *Gray's*

Botany. A musician of rare ability hoes thistles in the springtime and digs potatoes in the autumn. And a brilliant young fellow — a graduate of The State University of Iowa and a man of unusual ability in his profession — does not hesitate to work with his hands.

To be sure one can not truthfully say that there are no grumblers, no faultfinders, no wiseacres among the members of the Community of True Inspiration. Nor was there ever a congregation of eighteen hundred souls without its generous sprinkle of the dissatisfied — "and tatlers also and busybodies, speaking things which they ought not." Five generations of precept and practice in self-denial and brotherly love, in "genuine humility of heart and subjection of one to the other" have not completely annihilated suspicion, jealousy, and envy.

There are still "to the great grief of the Lord and of all faithful souls" the "self-willed and over smart" who do not "enter into the true harmony of soul and spirit" which is the ideal of the Community. There are those who "misjudge and oppose the well-meaning Brethren" and "hamper the important work instead of promoting it." But on the whole the members seem well satisfied and reasonably content with their plan of life and with the results they have attained under it. If this were not so, the Community could not be held together many years; for Amana is simply a voluntary association, depending for its perpetuity upon the good-will and the good faith of its members.

IV

CELIBACY AND MARRIAGE

In the Scriptures it is written: "He that is unmarried careth for the things that belong to the Lord, how he may please the Lord: But he that is married careth for the things that are of the world, how he may please his wife."[122] And so the problems of celibacy and marriage have at all times seriously confronted Christian communities. They are, indeed, the hobgoblins that have invariably tormented every community that has attempted to shape conditions so that its members might "without hindrance follow the lead of the Lord." In a powerful revival of earnestness the Harmonists, several years after their organization, adopted celibacy as one of their articles of agreement. It was, strangely enough, the younger members who took the lead in this movement; and their religious enthusiasm was communicated to the older members who, "convinced of the truth and holiness of their purpose", unanimously resolved "that they that have wives be as though they had none."[123] The Zoar Society began as a celibate community, but changed its policy regarding marriage some ten or twelve years after it had settled in America.[124]

The question of marriage does not appear to have been one of the fundamentals at the time of the founding of the Community of True Inspiration by Rock and Gruber; but with increasing religious fervor it arose to disturb the peace of mind of the Inspirationists. The *Jahrbuch* for 1727 contains this record:

> The marriage affair of Dr. ——— [a well educated and influential young physician] who had again resolved to unite in marriage with Fräulein ——— [a lady of noble birth] at the Court of ——— was also mentioned [in a testimony] concerning which the Lord prophesied thus: "Let the affair come to an end, that not a dangerous rent may result, for which the Enemy [Satan] lies in wait. I shall at my own time visit the couple, not as they think, but as I shall find it for good; and well shall I then strike hard with my rod, they will have to say, 'We have deserved and caused this'. Who is not satisfied with the pure embrace of my love [*Liebesumfassung*] must turn to the creature and finally feel the pangs which result therefrom." [125]

There seems to be some inconsistency on the part of Gruber in this testimony, since Gruber himself was married and had a son who accompanied him on some of his most important journeys and who was especially employed to detect false spirits whenever they made themselves conspicuous and to admonish them with earnestness to true repentance and change of heart. [126] But from the beginning there seems to have been a strong conviction in the Community that celibacy was more pleasing to God than the married state. Young people were constantly admonished to "resist the temptations of the Enemy", and to withdraw their "love entirely from the lusts of the flesh." But as far as can be learned marriage, while discouraged, was never absolutely prohibited.

During the Reawakening, a century after Gruber's death, the same doubts and perplexities regarding marriage reappeared, causing "dangerous rents" in the Community. At this time the marriage of the Elders is especially deplored as "setting a bad example to the young." Gottlieb Scheuner records that "in the month of October of this year [1828] it came about that Brother ————, of Ronneburg, who for a long time had been beset by manifold trials and temptations married contrary to the advice and will of the Lord and the Brethren, and thus for the time being made himself unfit for his calling in the Community and had to be separated from the latter until the Lord again raised him up and bestowed upon him his mercy." Two years later the "special act of grace" seems to have been granted by the Lord, for it is recorded that "Brother ————, who two years ago had been turned out, was again accepted by the Lord and He promised him a new grace, also for the benefit of the Community." [127]

As late as the year 1868 it is recorded that "on September first the great monthly Council of the Brethren was held in Homestead. Among other things they considered how to fill the place of *Kinderlehrer* in East Amana, since Brother ——— through his marriage had become disqualified for this calling." [128]

About the time of the removal of the Community to Iowa there was considerable agitation among the members over the question of marriage; and Christian Metz took the view that under right conditions and with proper restrictions marriage should receive the sanction of the Community. For this attitude he was sharply criticised by his "more unbending Brethren." Of this incident Christian Metz speaks in his *Tagebuch* thus:

> On November 28 [1846], the *Unterredung* at Nieder Ebenezer came to a close. I was under great trial and stress, and many testimonies occurred. There was also some disagreement with several of the Brethren concerning married life, which they wanted to denounce as wholly unchristian; and I was reproached because I had not been pure enough in the work of the grace of the Lord, which I, despite my many shortcomings and weaknesses, could not find to be the case. Oh would that the Lord may grant to me and to them clear insight in this so important matter, since it concerns the work of God. [129]

Long after the removal to Iowa, indeed so long as the Community had *Werkzeuge*, the strictly pious held (as a compromise) that marriage should be made only by and with the consent of God signified through his *Werkzeug*. Great emphasis was laid on the spiritual standing of the contracting parties. For marriage in any event is regarded as a spiritual fall; and the young couple, regardless of the high degree of spirituality they might have previously attained, are upon entering the marriage state reduced to the lowest *Versammlung* and are compelled to work up through deepening piety.[130] The utter hopelessness of the spiritual upbuilding of parties marrying "without grace" can well be imagined; and as the salvation of the soul is the supreme object of life in the Community, such marriages were sometimes interfered with by the *Werkzeug*. Barbara Heinemann was particularly free in denouncing such "godless marriages"; and on this very account she was the cause of a good many withdrawals from the Society during her later years.[131]

During the time of the removal from New York to Iowa it became customary to separate for one year the youth and maid who became betrothed. The one remained in Ebenezer; the other was sent to Amana. If at the end of the year they remained faithful to each other and steadfast in their purpose, and above all if their spiritual condition (ascertained in the yearly *Unterredung*) warranted, the marriage was allowed to take place. The wedding ceremony was treated with a degree of solemnity that was calculated to impress properly the young people with the importance of the step they were taking.

To-day the young people are still admonished that "a single life is ever a pleasure to the Lord", and that according to a revelation given through Christian Metz on October 23, 1850, "He has bestowed upon it a special promise and great mercy." The newly married couple are still reduced temporarily to the lowest spiritual *Versammlung*; and with the birth of each child in the family the parents suffer the same spiritual reduction and must win their way slowly back to grace by deepening piety.

At the same time it is true that the general attitude of the Community toward the institution of marriage has been greatly modified in recent years. This is clearly seen in one of their declarations which reads: "We believe that marriage was ordained by God, and it is therefore continued among us; but the first essential is that it be in the Lord, that God may bless it out of his mercy; and so it must be entered upon and continued according to the precepts of the Holy Scriptures, chaste and in the fear of God; but we do also regard as important the teachings of the holy Apostle Paul who repeatedly testifies that it is well to marry but better to remain single." [132]

A young man may not marry until he is twenty-four, and he must wait a year after he has received the sanction of the Elders before the wedding is permitted to take place. These are, however, merely prudential rules; for the head of the Amana household has none of the ordinary cares of his brother of the world. He has no rent, no grocer bills, no doctor bills — all these and more being secured to him and his family by the Society — hence certain restrictive rules have been found wise and necessary.

When a man and a maid wish to marry they present their case to the resident Trustee, who in turn lays the application before the Great Council for their sanction. If after careful consideration the Great Council finds no physical, mental, or spiritual obstacle to the marriage, the young people are "promised" and the wedding day is set for a year hence. On the wedding day the friends and relatives repair to the church. After a song, a prayer, and a scripture reading the young people stand before the presiding Elder while he expatiates "for a long time", with great earnestness and plainness of speech, on the sacred duties of husband and wife as set forth by the Apostle Paul in his epistle to the Ephesians (Ch. 5:22-23) and in the first epistle to the Corinthians (Ch. 7) as well as on their mutual duties and obligations to the Community. The marriage is then performed and the presiding Elder pronounces a benediction and a blessing. The newly married couple then take their places and each member present expresses a good wish for the future happiness and the religious peace of the bride and groom. The guests then repair to the kitchen-house where chocolate and coffee, and the marvelous variety of *Kuchen* that only a German housewife of the old school can make, await the company. After the modest wedding-feast the bride and groom go first to the home of the groom's parents and then to the home of the bride's parents where they receive the congratulations of the members of the Community in general.

In common with the Church of Rome — and be it remembered that Amana is primarily a church — the Community of True Inspiration does not recognize divorce. "As long as ye both do live" does not admit of the liberal interpretation given to it in the world at large. It is presumed that the married couple have thought long and seriously of the step they take, and they are expected to abide by it forevermore. Second marriage, even in the case of death of husband or wife, is not regarded with favor by the Community; it is especially reprehensible in an Elder who is expected in all of life's problems to set a good example to the youth.

The importance of the more friendly view of marriage as a factor in the growth and prosperity of the Community of True Inspiration can not be overestimated. Celibacy as a fundamental principle in such a Community carries with it the seeds of certain decline. One by one the celibate communities (many of them with greater material advantages than the Community of True Inspiration) have dwindled. Death has thinned their ranks and age enfeebled their members. And those that have not already died out are, like the Shaker communities, well on the road to dissolution.

It is the institution of the family that has been the salvation of the Community of True Inspiration. It is clear that the far-sighted Christian Metz perceived this long before his less "highly endowed and especially favored Brothers." Without it the growth of the Community would practically have stopped with the last accessions from Germany, and the splendid development that has taken place in the last quarter of a century would have been impossible.

V

THE INSPIRATIONIST AND HIS HOME

The newly married couple begin their housekeeping in two rooms which have been assigned to them by the Society. These rooms consist of a large airy sitting-room and a bedroom equipped in true German fashion with two single beds, each with its feather tick covered to match the comforter. If the house occupied by the parents of either bride or groom is large enough to admit of the setting aside of two rooms for the young people, such an assignment is often made by the Elders.

Formerly all of the house furniture was made in the Community; and there are still in the villages some fine old hand-made pieces which have done service for a century. Some of them bid fair to be used another century; for in the Community of True Inspiration the best a man can do has always been the standard from the making of a chest of drawers to the building of woolen mills. In recent years, however, machine-made furniture has been introduced, partly because of the growing worldliness of the younger people and partly because "it pays better to buy, than to take the time of a good workman."

With the growth of the family, larger quarters are provided by the Elders. Betimes a brand-new house is built; for there is no crowding in the Amanas. The same spirit which led the Community to adopt the village system has led it to provide plenty of room for its people.

While the Community of True Inspiration aims at the widest possible community of goods there is in the homes of its members a fine blending of individualism and communism which would hardly be possible in a community established with communism alone as its ideal. The Teutonic instinct of individual freedom, coupled with an intense love of home, led its members to preserve a wholesome sphere of domestic independence. Each family lives in a house which is the property of the Society. But the Amana "home" is nevertheless the sanctuary of its occupants. And to each member of the Community there is allowed, out of the common fund, enough personal property to assure personal comfort and to satisfy that desire of every human heart to have something of its very own. Indeed, the separatism of the Amana home, though not in accord with the principles of complete communism, has been an important factor in the perpetuity and prosperity of the Community of True Inspiration.

The cheerless cloisters of the Ephrata Community (notwithstanding the religious fervor of the early Brothers and Sisters, commonly regarded as the essential bond of successful communism) are empty to-day. One by one the Family Houses of the True Believers of the Shaker Communities have been closed. Even the great five-storied home of the Centre Family of Lebanon has been deserted; and the United Society of Believers is represented by only a small group of the old guard. The Oneida Community with its Mansion House "as a peculiar form of Society", to quote one of its own members, "is practically no more."[133] In truth the whole host of brotherhoods that have set sail on the communistic sea with the "Unitary Dwelling" and "Great House" ideal (despite the undeniable saving of labor and expense of such a plan) have miserably failed. The devoted men to whom the management of the Community of True Inspiration has been entrusted for the past century may not have been students of social science; but that they have been profound students of human nature is evidenced on every hand.

The Amana houses are substantially built, and quite unpretentious. It has been the purpose of the Community to construct the houses as nearly alike as possible. There is no hard and fast rule, but the aim is to make one as desirable as the other. There is in the private homes no kitchen, no dining-room, no parlor — just a series of sitting-rooms and bedrooms, which are, almost without exception, roomy and homelike. In addition to the general family sitting-room, each member of a household has as a rule his own individual sitting-room as well as his own individual bedroom. Here he is at liberty to indulge his own taste in decoration — provided that he does not go beyond his allowance or violate the rules of the Community. Here he may ride his hobbies or store his keepsakes without being disturbed — which accounts in part for the general content of the young people.

The average young girl is, with the suppression of everything pertaining to personal adornment, quite naturally given to bric-a-brac, painted celluloid boxes, Easter eggs, china doves, and similar souvenirs of the world brought from a rare visit to the city twenty miles away. And the "fancy work" instinct found in women of high and low degree finds vent in crocheted lamp mats for the center table and knitted laces for the pillow slips. The skill exhibited in "picking out" those wonderful "grape-vine" and "pineapple" patterns is a constant source of astonishment to her sister of the world. Such vanities are of course frowned upon by the more conservative members of the Community; but the ruling minds have found it best not to see too much.

Sometimes in the privacy of her own room the little Amana maid decorates herself with ribbons and cheap jewelry or dons a pair of red and gold slippers with high heels. "Well, maybe she does", says the Elder, "but it is not allowed." And if she really knew how much more attractive she is in her own simple little costume mere vanity itself would keep her from experimenting with "world clothes."

The Amana boy, likewise, has evidences of his handiwork in his room; for like his small brother in the world he likes to make things. He can whittle a chain out of a stick of pine; and make a top that is also a whistle and a box for marbles. There are many other wonders in his sitting-room that only a jack-knife in the hands of a growing boy can produce. The "collection" faculty, which makes its appearance at a certain age in every boy's evolution, is also present in the Amana lad, who sometimes far excels his American cousin in the thoroughness with which he pursues his "specialty." The Amana collections vary all the way from stamps and post-cards to botanical and archaeological collections of real merit. A few years ago an Amana lad was Secretary of the American Philatalist Society and discharged his duties in that office with great credit to himself.

In a community where religious meetings are the principal source of recreation a hobby is a splendid outlet for the penned up energies of the growing boy, and he pursues it with an enthusiasm that is refreshing. There is in a hobby a certain element of worldliness that is condemned, of course, by the more pious. But "young people will be some foolish", and so "there are some things the Elders must overlook."

Until comparatively recent years pictures were prohibited in the Community; for it is written: "Thou shalt not make unto thee any graven image, or any likeness of anything that is in heaven above or that is in the earth beneath, or that is in the water under the earth." [134]

Personal photographs were severely condemned and absolutely forbidden by the *Werkzeug*, Barbara Heinemann, as causing personal vanity and tending to idolatry. And her "ordinance" was apparently approved by the Great Council of the Brethren; for it is recorded that during the month of November, "after the work [the *Untersuchung*] had been again completed, a form of idolatry which had crept in and had become frequent was severely attacked, and the annihilation or surrender of the respective objects was demanded. This was, namely, the custom of having photographs or pictures of one's own self taken which is already prohibited in the Ten Commandments, and which the Lord, moreover, had expressly forbidden in his testimonies, but which of late had nevertheless become very popular, especially among our young people. Therefore a General Assembly for November 9, [1873,] was appointed through a resolution of the Great Council of the Brethren in order to read again a testimony in which the Lord condemned idolatry." [135]

To-day, however, the ordinance against photographs is not strictly observed. Indeed, there is scarcely a sitting-room in the seven villages without an album — which contains photographs not only of friends and relatives in the world, but many members of the Community who have had them taken (almost invariably in "world clothes" worn for the occasion) on some holiday to the city. These "worldly ways" are, of course, of the newer generation, who, loyal to the interests of the Community and to the faith of the forefathers, are nevertheless separated by two generations from Barbara Heinemann and her "ordinances" and are at times a little restive under some of the old regulations. "Well, young people will be some foolish" and so "some things the Elders must overlook."

Christmas presents are by the more pious regarded at best as "worldly" and "diverting" and were until recently condemned with the same severity as photographs. The *Jahrbuch* for 1849 records an "important revelation as a warning and rebuke because of the intruding abuse of Christmas presents and pictures." In 1873 the matter was seriously discussed by the Great Council of the Brethren, and "it was resolved to read once more an explanation and statement concerning these things in the Community," which on the following Sunday, December 14, 1873, was done in a general meeting in each village. At this meeting, in addition to the statement of the Great Council, the testimony of 1849 dealing with the "desecration of the Christmas feast through too many vain and sensual gifts" was read.[136] This ordinance also has undergone great modifications; so that to-day there is "allowed" among the members an exchange of simple Christmas gifts, and the little Inspirationist now has a reasonable variety of the enthralling collection of the toys that are displayed in the shop-window during the holidays.

To the lover of the antique the average Amana home has something of interest — as may well be imagined when one remembers that some of the forefathers of the present households were followers of Gruber and Rock and many, many more were witnesses of the "New Dawn" in 1817. As communism was not adopted until after the removal to America, each family brought to the new home its household goods. After the adoption of the "kitchen-house" system much superfluous material was disposed of; but a few families still have some pieces of old china and pewter, some brass candlesticks, or better still a pewter "tallow dip", or a "lard-oil lamp." There are still a few old clocks with wooden works and brass weights, and an occasional *Spinnrad von Deutschland.* There are a few rare old books of the fifteenth and sixteenth centuries, and some copper-plate prints of the same period. There are numerous Community books of the early eighteenth century, and manuscript letters not far from two hundred years old. There is a communion goblet used in the early *Liebesmahl,* and the compass carried by Johann Friedrich Rock on his missionary journeys. There are pictures older than the oldest living member of the Community, and old Bibles with wooden covers and huge brass clasps whose texts have been followed by the forefingers of six generations.

Whoever has seen an Amana *Grossvater* reading his old Bible by the light of a pewter lard-oil lamp has a memory picture that will live long after the old *Grossvater* has ended his earthly pilgrimage. Who can estimate the influence on the younger generation of the mere presence of this patriarch who embodies in his personality fourscore years and more of the romantic history of the Community; who was born, perchance, in the old feudal cloister of Marienborn; who still remembers the testimony of the Lord regarding the founding of a home "in the land of personal and religious liberty" and the farewell *Liebesmahl* at Armenburg; who shared in the hardships and privations of that first winter on the Seneca Indian Reservation at Ebenezer; and who helped to break the Iowa prairie for the new home which has seemed to be the fulfilment of the "gracious promise" of the early prophecies.

Shielded in a measure from the scientific doubt and social indifference of the surrounding world, and with the constant reminder in these "heroes of faith" of the noble self-sacrifice of the forefathers in a great cause, the present generation has much to challenge its loyalty "to cultivate humility, obedience to God's will, faithfulness, and love to Christ." Even the "outsider" and "unbeliever" feels sure that the "blessed continuation of the work of God's mercy" as the Inspirationist sees it and understands it is assured so long as the Community has with it these "still living witnesses of the great blessings of Inspiration."

With the exception of the Bible and a few volumes of testimonies and other religious texts published by the Society, books are conspicuously absent in the average Amana home. One gathers from the testimonies, particularly those of Barbara Heinemann, that general reading was not viewed with favor by the *Werkzeuge*. Reading for pastime was condemned as "soul dissipation" and as "diverting the mind from heaven and the things which are of the Lord." Reading for the acquisition of knowledge was denounced with equal severity, since it is written in the Bible that "knowledge puffeth up", and that "in much wisdom is much grief; and he that increaseth knowledge increaseth sorrow." [137]

There is still an aversion in the Community to mixing "philosophy and human science with divine wisdom" which bespeaks their Pietist ancestry. "It is surely known unto thee", declared Barbara Heinemann under Inspiration, "how it is written that much knowledge is not needed for salvation." Again in 1878 Barbara Heinemann under the influence of Inspiration said to an Elder who was of a scientific turn of mind: "It is not necessary that you should possess so great knowledge gained through pondering over the wonders and secrets of God." [138]

The reading of newspapers was to Barbara Heinemann's mind the chief cause of the "retrograding of the young people", and on numerous occasions she denounced the practice. In the *Jahrbuch* for 1863 there is a testimony, given during the *Unterredung* [139] of that year when the spiritual state of the young people was such that "the grace of God was withdrawn", in which "the Lord denounced especially the reading of so many newspapers and other worldly literature and commanded that this be entirely suspended for a while.''[140]

There is much of this old austere spirit still found at Amana among the older Brothers; but members are now ''allowed'' rather than encouraged to purchase books, newspapers, and magazines according to their own inclination. The Society subscribes for various technical and trade journals for the use of the different places of business in the Community.

There is a carefully selected library of ''good literature'' in connection with each village school, from which the children are at liberty to draw books at the end of the week. These are as a rule read by all the members of the family. In addition there is a township circulating library, and as the whole of Amana Township is owned by the Community this library, too, is selected and supervised by the proper authorities and is not destined to lead the young reader astray. Occasionally undesirable books and papers find their way into the hands of the young people; but if the Elders discover the fact, such books and papers are mentioned by name in open meeting and their further reading prohibited.[141]

General housekeeping in Amana is a comparatively simple matter. Here is at least one place in the United States where the old and ever present problem of the servant girl does not overshadow all other interests. At more or less regular intervals in each village there is a "kitchen-house"— a little larger than the ordinary dwelling — where the meals for the families in the immediate neighborhood are prepared and served. From sixteen to fifty persons eat at one kitchen, the number depending largely upon the location. The places are assigned by the resident Trustee, the chief consideration being the convenience of those concerned.

There are some three or four instances in the entire Community where for good and sufficient reasons an individual family kitchen is maintained — which illustrates the fact that when a rule is impracticable in its working (and there must of necessity be many such rules in a group of seven villages with a total population of eighteen hundred souls) the Elders do not hesitate to make exceptions to it. The important thing is to keep the machinery of the Community going with the least possible friction. To do this requires on occasion all the ingenuity and clear-headedness of the "captain of industry" of the world. And so in the Great Council of the Brethren there is required a genuine combination of spiritual and business leadership.

The kitchen-house system of Amana may lack the economy of the communistic ideal — the unitary dining-room — but there is much to be said in its favor. To the Great Council of the Brethren the purity and simplicity of the Community have ever been more important considerations than minimum expenditure. And they have felt that these could best be preserved by avoiding, what has proved to be the cause of the downfall of so many communities, frequent congregations of large numbers of individuals. Indeed, the mass-meeting is in no way a part of the working scheme of the Amana Society. Even in the church there are separate apartments or meeting-rooms for the young men, the young women, and the older members. Indeed, if Amana has made any distinctive contribution to practical, working communism it is in the combination, or rather the nice adjustment, between separatism and communism whereby mutual interest is maintained without inviting the pitfalls of "too much getting together." [142]

The Amana kitchen is large and airy, often extending through the full depth of the house. Each kitchen has its supply of hot and cold water and its sink and drain. Every pan and kettle has its shelf or hook; and there are more conveniences for paring and slicing, chopping and grinding, than the average housewife of the world ever dreamed of. But the really distinctive feature of the Amana kitchen is the long low brick stove with its iron plate top. This is built along one side of the room;

and back of it there is a sheet of tin several feet high which shines like a mirror. From its upper edge hangs a most surprising variety of strainers, spoons, dippers, and ladles. On top of the brick stove are the huge copper boilers and kettles which a community kitchen necessitates. In recent years there has been added to each kitchen a modern cook-stove, which is used during the winter for heating as well as for cooking purposes.

In the kitchen everything from the floor to ceiling is as clean and bright as can be made by soap and water, brooms and mops. The Amana woman knows none of the vexations of the village housewife of the world, in whose home as a rule proper conveniences for the kitchen are the last to be provided. Wood-sheds and store-houses are built in the most convenient places; there are covered passage-ways from the house to the "bake-oven" and outbuildings; and there is commonly a hired man at the kitchen-house for the carrying of water and hewing of wood. There is absolute system in every detail of the housework. Everything is thoroughly and effectively done; and the women do not appear to be overworked.

Each kitchen is superintended by a woman appointed by the Elders, who is assisted by three of the younger women, each taking her turn in attending to the dining-room, preparing vegetables, cooking, and washing dishes. The general rule as to service in the kitchen is two weeks on duty and one week off — which, it must be admitted, is a great improvement over the ceaseless routine of the life of the average housewife of the world. The older women do not work in the kitchen as a rule; hence it is sometimes necessary to hire help from the outside. It is the aim of the Community to have hired help in the hotel kitchens in order to shield its own young women from too close contact with the world. The fact that the average summer visitor too often leaves his manners in the city when he chances to take an outing makes the wisdom of such a rule evident.[143]

Wagons from the village bakery, butcher shop, and dairy make the daily rounds of the kitchens. Cheese and unsalted butter for table use are made in each kitchen; and any baking other than of bread is done in the big steel range found in connection with each kitchen-house. The brick oven has, in addition to the "bake-oven", compartments known as drying ovens where spinach, green beans, sweet corn, and a score of other things are dried for winter use. Ptomaine poisoning and adulterated foods have little chance to do their deadly work in Amana.

It is the aim of the Community to produce as far as practicable all the food consumed by the members. At the same time the Amana people do not deny themselves any comforts which are compatible with simplicity of life. The tables are bountifully laden with wholesome food; but the menu is practically the same from day to day, except as varied by the presence of fresh fruits and vegetables in their season. The Inspirationists are not faddists in their diet; they have no theories regarding the effect of a vegetable and fruit diet on "the health of the body, and the purity of the mind, and the happiness of society." They have no decided opinions regarding the relative merits of lard and tallow, and no rule against the "eating of dead creatures."[144] Tea and coffee are commonly used; and large quantities of home-made wine are consumed annually. In short the food throughout the Community is well cooked and substantial, but unmodified by any modern "dietetic philosophy."

Breakfast is served in the Amana kitchens at six o'clock in the summer-time and half an hour later in the winter-time. The dinner hour is 11:30 the year around. With the supper bell, which rings at half past six in the winter-time and at seven o'clock in the summer-time, the day's work closes. In addition to these three meals the Inspirationist takes a lunch in the middle of each half day. Those who work at considerable distance from the kitchen carry their lunches with them. When the men are working in the harvest field, home-made wine or cider is usually added to the afternoon lunch. When the supper things are cleared the members gather in small groups at different places in the villages for the evening prayer-meeting. Any announcements that are necessary for the proper organization of the morrow's work are made by the presiding Elders at the close of these meetings, and the members are then free for the evening.

The Amana dining-room is simply furnished with long narrow tables covered with oilcloth and surrounded with backless, unpainted but thoroughly scrubbed benches. While all the members of the family eat at the same kitchen, the men, women, and children sit at separate tables. This no doubt is designed to prevent "silly conversation and trifling conduct." There is some religious expression before and at the close of the meal, but very little general conversation. "Be quiet while at the table", admonishes the Catechism for the youth of the Community, "unless you are asked a question; the prattling of children while eating is a grave lack of manners."[145] The tongue has ever been held by the spiritual leaders of the Community to be an unruly member; and from Gruber's time to the present day the members have been admonished to "count every word", to "speak never without need", and to "avoid all unnecessary words".[146]

There was a time in the pioneer days of the Community (when all energies were bent to the building of a new home in the wilderness) when the women, in the manner of our Puritan grandmothers, shared almost equally the physical labors of the men. But as the Community prospered the lot of the women became easier; and to-day the woman of Amana knows nothing of the cares of the average housemother of the world who is expected to fulfil the combined duties of housemaid and nurse, hostess and church worker.

In every department of service in which woman participates the work is carefully apportioned to her strength. The woman with children under the age of two is not required to take part in the general village work, and her meals are brought to her home in a basket from the nearest kitchen-house. There is a nursery or kindergarten in each village well supplied with sand piles and the variety of playthings deemed necessary to keep children interested. Here the little folks between three years and school age are cared for when necessary to enable their mothers to take part in the village work.

In connection with every kitchen-house is a vegetable garden of from two to three acres. The heaviest of the garden work is always done by the hired man, but the superintendence and general care of the garden are entrusted to the women. This work is lighter than the kitchen work and the hours are shorter, hence the garden work is allotted to the middle-aged and older women.

Whoever has spent a summer in an Amana village and has fared on the produce of the kitchen-house garden can understand the feeling of the Amana prodigal who returned to the Community because there was "nothing fit to eat in the world." There is fresh lettuce from March to December, grown in hotbeds at one end of the season and kept in sand in the cellar at the other. There is ever-green spinach that is delicious the whole summer long; and the garden superintendent knows how to lengthen the green pea and wax bean season to the most surprising extent. There are great white cauliflowers averaging ten inches across; there is kale and salsify, red cabbage and yellow tomatoes, and much more that the visitor from the world does not even know by name. And such fruit as the garden superintendent brings to tempt the lagging appetite of the worn-out visitor who has sought refuge from the strenuous world for a brief respite in this peaceful village! Huge strawberries which before he has only seen pictured in the seed catalogues! Raspberries that even the gorgeously illustrated catalogue can not do justice! A score of varieties of apples, pears, and plums! And long after the visitor has returned to the city to take up once more his place in the noisy procession there comes a wonderful basket of grapes — big grapes and little grapes, white grapes, red grapes, and black grapes!

In their dress (like the Shakers, the Mennonites, and in truth all of the communities whose religion prohibits "a life of vanity") the members of the Amana Community are "plain." And like the Shakers, too, they do not profess to adhere to a uniform, but claim to have adopted and retained what they find to be a convenient style of dress. This is particularly true of the dress of the women.

There is nothing distinctive in the dress of the men of Amana to-day. While there is a great aversion among the pious to "looking proud", there is an equal dislike on the part of the younger members of being conspicuous on account of their clothes. And so the men, particularly those who come in contact with the world, dress in much the same fashion as do men of the world — a little more given to "plain goods", perhaps, and a little less responsive to the latest edicts of fashion.

Formerly the village tailor made all of the clothing for the men, but it was found to be cheaper to buy "ready-made" clothes for ordinary wear. The "best clothes" are still quite generally made by the Community tailor; for the young man gets his goods at cost from the woolen mills and, as the time of the tailor belongs to the Society, he is thus enabled to dress well on less than one-fourth of what it costs his brother in the world. The older Brothers are a little more orthodox and still wear trousers of the old-fashioned broad full front variety and a Sunday coat without lapels; but unlike the Amishman, with whom he is often confused, he does not regard the button as an "emblem of vanity", nor cut his hair in "pumpkin-shell" fashion. He does, however, resemble both the Amishman and the Shaker in the cut of his beard and in the absence of a moustache, which latter is regarded as a badge of worldliness.

The costume of the women might almost be called a uniform two hundred years old, the dress of to-day being practically the same as at the founding of the Community. Mothers and daughters, grandmothers and granddaughters dress alike — not in the silver gray of the Quakers, nor the more brilliant purples of the Amish, but in the black or blue or gray calico that is made by the Society and is known from Maine to California as "Amana calico." The waist and skirt of this costume are sewed together in a wide band: the former is short and very plain, the latter long and very full with the inevitable tuck for future reference. An apron of moderate length, a "shoulder-shawl" of calico which is long enough to reach the waist line both in front and behind so as to hide from view all lines of grace and beauty, and a small black cap designed likewise to suppress pride complete the summer costume. The only head-dress is a sunbonnet with a long cape. The winter dress differs from this only in being made of woolen goods; while a hood takes the place of the sunbonnet. "Do not adorn yourself in dress for luxury's sake", reads one of the precepts of the Community, "as a feast for the eyes or to please yourself and others, but only for necessity's sake. What you seek and use beyond necessity is sin."

Every woman makes her own clothes and every mother makes the clothing for her own small children. The most approved church costume is black throughout — apron, "shoulder-shawl", and all. There is a pathetic sweetness of expression and a serenity in the manner of the women that are seldom found in the world in this day of turmoil, haste, and discontent. And so the austere Amana costume seems a fitting frame for those kindly, placid faces.

Generations of right thinking and right living seem to have produced a distinct type in the Inspirationist. The older men and women are plain and direct of speech, self-possessed and sedate. They have strong faces and honest eyes — faces refined by much thought upon spiritual things and purified by sacrifice and high aims. There is a gentleness in their demeanor that reminds one of the Quakers, and a firmness and a seriousness in their manner that bespeak their Pietist ancestry. They live quiet and peaceful lives and do not like to admit strangers to their privacy. They have a reputation for honesty and fair dealing among their neighbors and wherever their products are bought and sold. "If you have made a promise so keep it, and beware of untruthfulness and lies",[147] is one of the fundamental precepts in the training of the Inspirationist. There is among the men an ample measure of the orthodox German sense of masculine superiority. The Inspirationist husband and father is the "true head and light of the household";[148] and the women are kept modestly in the background of life. The "housefather" has a heavy sense of responsibility. He aims to make his religion his life; and he unceasingly endeavors and earnestly hopes to conform to all the rules of Scripture and sundry of his own devising.

It is doubtful whether there are many places in the world outside of Amana where more tender care and respectful attention are given to the aged and infirm. Unproductive members of the Community enjoy all the privileges and comforts that the Community has to give. When the dissolution of the corporation was suggested in a recent lawsuit, it was the problem of the "old people" that caused the greatest concern in the Community. "It would be wrong to dissolve our brotherhood", said the Elders, "for if this should happen, what would become of our old people?"

There is no prettier picture anywhere than an Amana grandmother with her knitting (and what wonderful things she can do with those needles without seeming to look at them!) unless it is, perhaps, the homage she is paid by the younger members of the household. And what a wealth of stories the dear grandmother has to tell the eager little folks of "our forefathers in the old country", of the early days at Ebenezer and the trouble with the Seneca Indians, and of the long, long drive across the country to the Iowa prairie!

The Inspirationists do not approve of voting or of taking any part in "politics" — not because they consider it wicked to vote, but because they do not wish to create dissensions in their Community by the introduction of politics. "For the elections of the world are conducted amidst the feud and strife of the several parties struggling for diverse selfish ends." Christian Metz in particular was strongly opposed to the "spirit of partisanship", which he declared to be "an actual disobedience of the word of the Lord." During the residence of the Community at Ebenezer, Christian Metz records in his *Tagebuch* after a township election: "The Whig party elected our Brother ——— for supervisor and the Democrats elected him assessor which was preferable to us, but Brother ——— was too much inclined toward the Whig party and paid no heed; therefore the Lord had to testify concerning the intermingling with the world and the fact that the people desired to become mightier instead of humbler.''[149] Elsewhere he adds: ''Since party spirit fosters contention, and engenders hatred and strife, it is contrary to the principles of our faith and our rules for salvation.''

The young men have from time to time caused much anxiety by their manifest desire to take part in the political elections. But this ''intermingling with the world'' was some years ago pronounced through a ''severe testimony . . . . a contempt of the Lord's will and a grave transgression of His once-for-all established rules.''[150] ''We as believers'', reads a memorial written by the leading Brethren under the date of November 7, 1863, ''should pray for the best welfare of the land, and at the election of officials should implore, without regard for any party, that the Lord might direct the results according to his will and for the best of the country; but, according to the word and testimony of the Lord, we should not engage in party strife or participate in the fight of the election.''[151]

It appears, however, that in 1868 there were individuals who ''in spite of former warnings'' did vote at the election; but it is recorded that ''the offenders were excluded from divine service until the respective persons did report at the Council of the Brethren or to one of the First Brethren and confess and acknowledge their offence."

In recent years the Inspirationists have voted as a Society on questions that seemed to affect them in their industrial activities; but the "once-for-all established rules" are still in force for individual members and the transgressor is still "churched" by the First Brethren for his disregard and contempt of the will of the Lord.

While the Inspirationists do not approve of participation in elections they sincerely desire the peace and prosperity of the Nation. They give largely to charity. Be it a famine in Russia or in heathen China, an earthquake in California, or the failure of crops in the neighboring State of Kansas, Amana Society responds with equal generosity.[152]

Being non-resistants, the Inspirationists furnished no volunteers during the Civil War. They did, however, through the recruiting agent hire substitutes when recruits were called for in Iowa County. This was a little inconsistent; but as Christian Metz expresses it in a letter to the Brethren at Ebenezer, "Since war is contrary to our calling and faith we know no other way out than to pay the $300 prescribed by the law in order to show our patriotic attitude as citizens and supporters of the Union.''[153]

The suffering of the army presented a phase of the war with which the Community understood better how to deal. In a letter written at the time by Christian Metz to the Brethren of the Ebenezer Community, who were still in charge of the New York property, he gives an account of the collection among the Iowa villages of contributions for the army. ''We sent a circular letter'', he writes, ''to this and the other Communities that we considered it our duty that every member, household, or family should contribute a gift or offering each one according to his means, consisting of woolen blankets or stockings, socks, woolen shirts and jackets, underwear, etc. These were gathered in the evening before prayer-meeting . . . . Almost every one showed such willingness that it was real joy. We will now wait for the contributions from the other Communities and then send all of them to the place from which they are to be dispatched to the soldiers. The Brethren had indeed already sent $200 to the Governor; but I believe that this is or will be even more acceptable, for all these contributions consist of good warm clothing.'' These contributions, moreover, were repeated and amounted to thousands of dollars before the close of the war.

One would imagine that Amana's isolated and fraternal form of life would intensify sociability. Perhaps it does. Perhaps this very close relationship does away with the need of the so-called pastimes of modern society. Or perhaps owing to the freedom from care, worry, and hurry, and from the excessive physical labor and mental exertion of the world in this strenuous age, the members of the Community of True Inspiration do not require the relaxation deemed necessary by those who live in the world. However that may be, the life of the Inspirationist is almost devoid of amusements. There is no dancing — no cards, no games, no music, no parties, no sociables.[154] Such a thing as a lecture or concert or public entertainment of any kind seems to be entirely foreign to the Community.

Pleasures seem to have been discouraged in the Community simply because they were pleasures. "If we do what we wish", teaches the schoolmaster, "it takes our minds from heaven and increases our selfishness." It is the aim of the Elders to keep out everything that is calculated to lead to mere dissipation of time and energy and to lower the moral tone of those indulging. A group of young men may meet once a week during the winter-time as a study club (which is conducted very much in the manner of the college seminar, each member following a chosen line of work and reporting from time to time to the group); and this form of recreation seems to fall within the required bounds of sobriety. Very recently a little orchestra has been organized in one of the villages; but the "Older Elders do not like it", and so practice is for the most part *pianissimo*. The Zoar Society with all its religious fervor had its orchestra and an organ in the church; and the Rappites at Harmony, despite their austerity, had their village band. One deplores the fact that the First Brethren of the Amana Community still deny their young people so innocent a form of amusement.[155]

VI

INDUSTRIAL AMANA

Amana is far from being primarily an industrial organization. Nevertheless the system of community of goods which the Society has so successfully maintained for over half a century is one of the most interesting phases of its unique life. Amana has never boasted of "industrial enterprises established on correct fundamental principles." And yet its industrial history presents a strong argument in favor of communism as a practical economic principle.

The agricultural industries of the Community are carried on according to the most modern and scientific methods; and as the Society has more money than men to spare, every tested labor-saving device in farm machinery is gladly introduced. System prevails in everything; and in accord with German genius for organization, every branch of service is "functionated." Every department of labor has its superintendent or "boss", who in turn has his lieutenants; and so authority is transmitted from the head down.

The general plan of the field work is determined by the Board of Trustees or Great Council of the Brethren; but a field "boss" or superintendent is responsible to the Board for the proper execution of their orders. He sees that the farm machinery is kept in order; he appeals to the *Bruderrath* for more men to work in the field when necessary; and he obtains from the superintendent of the barns and stables the horses that are needed. Although the Society rents about one thousand acres to tenants at the present time, it is still necessary to hire from 175 to 200 "hands" from the world every year to carry on the field work — the members of the Society acting always as foremen and superintendents.

The members of the Community, particularly the spiritual leaders, deeply regret that it is necessary to introduce this "outside help"; for such a practice is not without its danger of leading the young members astray. At the same time there is not among the Inspirationists the strong aversion to the "hireling system" that is found in the Shaker Families. It is a question whether the Shakers were not more nearly right in this matter than the Amana Community; since the average "harvest hand" who floats into the Community for "work and wine" is mentally, morally, and spiritually a very different individual from the young Inspirationist with his heritage and training. "Good apples never yet made rotten apples sound", said an aged Amana field superintendent, "and we'd be better off without the hands."

The field hours of labor are from 6:30 to 11:00 in the morning and from 12:30 to 6:00 in the afternoon. The wages paid to the hired hands vary from $125 to $175 a year in addition to their "keep." This seems less than the neighboring farmers pay for the same kind of work. But in Amana there is always plenty of wholesome food to eat, plenty of home-made wine to drink, and the hired men are so sure of being made comfortable and of not being driven that the Society never has any trouble in getting the outside labor that it needs. It is a fact that the hired men in the Community are able to save more than help in the outside world can save.

Very often one department of industry is obliged, during its busy season, to call upon other departments for assistance. There is a meeting of the Elders and foremen once a day for the organization of the morrow's work; and at the close of every prayer-meeting the presiding Elder appoints the helpers required. The great advantage of being able to command at any moment a large laboring force for an emergency is evident. The quickness and thoroughness with which a hay-field is cleared, the harvest gathered, or the potatoes stored for the winter, and the apparent pleasure the workers find in the doing clearly illustrates the efficiency of combined industry.

The care and the thoroughness with which the Amana Society has cultivated its fields and selected its seeds have done much to raise the standard of farming in the immediate neighborhood. No farmer cares to plant inferior grain when for the asking he can get better seed from his neighbor. Furthermore, the Society furnishes a market for the surrounding country and is in position to dictate as to the quality of the produce.

The products of agriculture are for the most part rye, barley, oats, corn, potatoes, and onions. The average annual yield for three years as taken from the records of the Secretary of the Society was 1,269 bushels of rye; 8,934 bushels of barley; 42,464 bushels of oats; 55,208 bushels of corn; 31,622 bushels of potatoes; and 9,779 bushels of onions.

The Society makes no attempt to raise live stock for the market. It buys and sells stock when the market is favorable, but aims to have in the long run only enough for home consumption. During three years the live stock of the Society averaged annually 930 steers and heifers; 607 cows; 273 horses; 2,817 sheep and 2,580 swine.

It is, indeed, the aim of the Amana Society to raise only enough agricultural and dairy products for home consumption. In a recent civil action in which the Community was alleged to be conducted for pecuniary profit it was shown that while the

Society for convenience may sometimes sell a small surplus of one kind of grain that invariably other grain has to be purchased, so that upon the average all the product of all the land under cultivation does not supply the needs of the people of the Society and the animals owned by the Society. It was also shown that as a rule money derived from other enterprises must be expended in order to buy the necessaries in agricultural products.

In contrast with the modernity of all that pertains to the Amana fields and more in keeping with the foreign aspect of the village and its people are the ox-teams that ever and anon one sees meandering down the flower-bordered village street. There are from fifteen to eighteen ox-teams used in the Community for heavy hauling, it being the experience of the Society that oxen are more profitably used than horses for work which requires heavy and steady pulling. With the visitor's first glimpse of an Amana ox-team in its picturesque setting he feels that he has suddenly stepped into a strange land; and as he listens dreamily to the "gee" and "haw" of the driver and the laborious creaking of the heavy two-wheeled cart, he quite resents the shrill whistle of the incoming passenger train which reminds him that only twenty miles away street cars are clanging and delivery carts rattling over the hot pavements while street venders are screaming the merits of their wares.

There is probably no place in the United States where work is more thoroughly or effectively done than in the Community of True Inspiration; and while money-making is as pleasant an occupation for communities as it is for individuals, it is not the end and purpose of living at Amana. The members have learned that in order to have a moderate surplus for "hard times" it is not necessary to labor exhaustively. Steady but comfortable industry, regularity of living in general, and the sensible pursuit of wealth and happiness make for the prevailing good health and longevity in the Community. At the age of eighty-four, the watchmaker at Old Amana was still at his post as regularly as the sun rose; while another still more remarkable Brother is active in the fields at the age of eighty-seven. Indeed, there are several less active members in full possession of their faculties who are over ninety years of age.[156]

In *Inspirations-Historie* we learn that as early as 1740 the Community of True Inspiration had to care for certain of its mechanics who "came into difficulties and perplexities." "At this time", reads the record for 1740, "the Brethren, especially those at Himbach and Bergheim had come into difficulties and perplexities, on account of a new trade guild which had been established and which the Herrnhuter and the hostile Brethren had joined. But since the members of the Community could not and must not meddle with this affair for conscience sake they lost their jobs and means of support, since no mechanic who was not a member of this guild was permitted to ply his craft in these places. This caused trouble and anxiety to the Brethren and there was no other remedy than to leave the towns in which these guilds existed."[157] It is interesting to observe that while the Community still persists in its attitude of not "meddling with such affairs", there is scant sympathy for labor unions in Amana. It was the custom of the Community in those "troublesome days" to find for the unfortunate Brethren, who for conscience sake had lost their jobs, employment in the more tolerant towns and provinces.

A hundred years later at the time of the renting of the first estate near Ronneburg it was found necessary to rent mills and factories for those who knew not how to till the soil but were skilled in the trades. The *Jahrbuch* for 1829 records that at the time of the arrival of a large number of souls at the Haag whom the Lord had called to the Community from the surrounding country "it was approved and confirmed by the Lord that Br. ——— should move from Marienborn to the Haag and set up at the latter place a spinning-machine in order to provide for the poor members a means of earning their livelihood."

The building of their own mills and factories in the new world followed quite naturally. Article III of the Constitution adopted in 1859 reads: "Agriculture and the raising of cattle and other domestic animals in connection with some manufactures and trades shall under the blessing of God form the means of sustenance for the Society." In these later years the Community has decided that a simple branch of manufacturing employing only a few hands yields a more satisfactory income than a large acreage cultivated with hired labor — which accounts in part for the present tendency of the Society to rent more of its own land and enlarge its manufacturing plants.

The Shakers believed that every commune must, in order to prosper, be founded on agriculture. Elder Frederick Evans even declared that "whenever we have separated from this rule to go into manufacturing we have blundered." And proceeding on this policy they bought farm upon farm until they became land-poor. On the other hand, the advice of the Oneida Community to all "associations" owning a "domain" was to "sell two-thirds of that domain and put the proceeds into a machine-shop. Agriculture, after all, is not a primary business. Machinery goes before it, always did and always will more and more.''[158] The Shaker Families with their enormous farms have dwindled sadly and the Oneida Community with ''the whole range of modern enterprise open to its people'' is no longer a commune. How nearly the Amana Society has hit upon the ideal adjustment of the two industries, time alone will tell.

Amana's mills and factories were among the first erected in the State of Iowa. The two flouring and grist mills, one at Old Amana and the other at West Amana, were important centers half a century ago for the pioneer farmers for fifty miles around.

But it is through its woolen mills that the Society is best known in the business world. These mills, moreover, have been in active operation for fifty years. In them over half a million pounds of raw wool are used annually. As this is considerably more than the Society's three thousand sheep can furnish, a great deal of raw material is purchased in the outside market. Formerly this raw material was obtained through jobbers who imported it from Texas, Colorado, and other western States, and from Australia. But since the imposition of a high tariff on wool no foreign wool has been used, and at present most of the wool is bought in the Chicago market.

The latest and most improved machinery for woolen manufacture is found in the Amana mills.

Some of it has been imported directly from Germany. Numerous very clever devices have been invented by the workers in the woolen mills to add to the efficiency of the best models which the Society has been able to obtain in the world. The Society does not patent its inventions, as they are made to facilitate its own work and not for pecuniary gain. The shrewd and not over scrupulous Yankee has discovered this fact; and so most of the Amana inventions have been copied and patented in the world.

While water was originally the motive power used in the mills and factories, it has gradually been supplanted by steam, so that during low water, or when for any other reason the water power furnished by the canal is insufficient, all of the mills and factories can be run by steam.

There are about one hundred twenty-five persons employed in the woolen mills. Of this number only from sixteen to eighteen outsiders are hired by the Society — and to these is given almost without exception the heavy and more unskilled labor. The woolen mill workers are carefully selected for their places, and are still more carefully trained. The outsider with the same skill and efficiency demands and gets in the world a very high wage — and so it is deemed best by the Great Council not to disturb the peace of mind of the members of the Community by a too intimate knowledge of the value of skilled labor.

The capacity of the mills is at present taxed to the utmost, and the demand for their product far exceeds the supply; but the Society has not members enough to warrant immediate extension. Nor is there the slightest desire to get rich at the expense of the "solidarity" of the Community, which would necessarily result from the employment of much skilled labor from the world.

The only place in industrial Amana, outside of the kitchen and the garden, in which women are employed is in the woolen mills; and even here there are only six or eight to be found and these are women who are not strong enough or are too old to work in the kitchen. Their work in the woolen mills is largely simple hand-work, such as tying threads as they are wound on the large reels, or spinning together broken threads on genuine old spinning-wheels stationed in out-of-the-way corners.

The placid matron of the Amana mills in her austere costume sets one to dreaming of the patient industry of our pilgrim foremothers of New England. Indeed, it is such touches as these, such unexpected linking of the old and primitive with the latest and best methods of the new century, that gives to Amana its inimitable charm.

One half a million yards of flannel and ladies' cloth are manufactured in the mills annually, ranging in price from twenty to eighty-five cents per yard. Certain times of the year are devoted to the weaving of blankets, of which 10,000 pairs are made annually, selling at from $2.75 to $9.00 per pair.

It has always been the aim of the Society to manufacture "good goods", and their rigid honesty has secured them a market Nation wide. Ten men, seven of whom are members of the Society, are on the road for a part of the year in the interests of the woolen mills. The extreme East and the extreme West are as a rule worked by outsiders. Some of Amana's best customers have handled their woolen goods every year since the establishment of the woolen mills at Ebenezer; for wherever their products are bought and sold "Amana Society" is a guarantee of rigid honesty and fair dealing.

The hours of labor in the woolen mills for the greater part of the year are the usual Amana hours of from 7:00 to 11:00 A. M. and from 12:30 to 6:00 P. M. But during the summer months when the orders for the fall trade are being filled, the mills run from 4:30 in the morning to 6:00 in the afternoon; or from 7:00 in the morning to 11:00 at night. When the men work more than the required number of hours they receive extra compensation — sometimes in credits, sometimes in cash, and sometimes in preferment of position or other special perquisites.[159]

In spite of the long hours and the noisy machinery there is a very unusual factory air about the Amana mills. The rooms are light and airy. There is a cushioned chair or stool for every worker "between times." An occasional spray of blossoms on a loom frame and the humming of a psalm tune by an Elder whose calling as a shepherd of souls does not interfere with the labor of his hands reflect the spirit of the workers. The product of the Amana mills comes as near being what William Morris called "the expression of a man's joy in his work" as can be found anywhere. Here and there in different parts of the factory is a well equipped cupboard and a lunch table where the different groups of workers eat their simple luncheon of bread and coffee in the middle of each half day.

In the villages where the factories are located the boys of thirteen or fourteen years of age who are about to leave school are employed for a few hours each afternoon "to learn." If they show special aptitude and the work is congenial they are carefully trained and are given every opportunity to "work up"; but if this employment is not agreeable they are at liberty to choose some other line of work. "Each according to his calling or inclination" is the ruling principle of industrial Amana.

The natural result of such a system is intelligent and efficient workmanship.

In Old Amana there is a calico-printing establishment where 4,500 yards of calico are dyed and printed every day. The heavy cotton goods used here are manufactured for the Society in the Southern States. The printing patterns for the calico are not only designed but made by a member of the Society. The colors used in the dyeing are chiefly blue, brown, or black. Only the severest of these patterns are considered sufficiently "plain" for the dress of the Amana women and children.

In this connection it is interesting to note that during the prosperous days of the Icarians in Iowa the women dressed for the most part in Amana goods. There is a remnant of an Amish Mennonite settlement in the vicinity; but the Amish women, whose idea of "plain" clothes runs to brilliant purples and greens, find the modest Amana calicoes a trifle worldly. When the Amishman with his broad hat and buttonless coat and his gentle little wife with her purple gown come to Amana, as they frequently do, the inspection is quite mutual; for the Community regard the Amish as rather a queer people. Yea, verily, "all the world is queer except thee and me; and I sometimes think thee a little queer."

The Amana calico, particularly the "Colony Blue", is quite as favorably known as the woolen goods, and is sold at ten cents a yard throughout the United States and Canada.

There are from twenty-five to thirty-five men employed in the calico-printing establishment, ten or twelve of whom are outsiders. The working hours are the same as in the woolen mills.

The flouring and grist mills employ about sixteen men, five or six of whom are outsiders. The working hours are from 7:00 to 12:00 A. M. and from 1:00 to 6:00 P. M. Recently a large addition to the flouring-mill at Amana has been erected. Most of the grain used in the mills (about 5,000 bushels of rye, 16,000 of barley, 10,000 of wheat, and 90,000 of corn) is purchased in the outside market; and a large part of the products is sold to jobbers in this and neighboring States. A few years ago the Society paid a premium on white corn, and in two years time almost the entire yellow corn crop of the vicinity had been replaced by white corn. The Amana Society is such a convenient market for the agricultural products of the surrounding country that the neighboring farmers find it profitable to respond to the wishes of the Community.

The industrial efficiency of the operatives in all of the Amana mills and factories is noticeably great even to the casual observer. Each worker labors with the air of a man in physical comfort and peace of mind, and with the energy of a man who is working in a partnership in which he expects to enjoy all the fruits of his labor.

There is a printing-office and bookbindery at Middle Amana. The job work for the stores and mills, the text-books used in the schools, the hymn-books used in the churches, and all other religious books commonly read in the Community are printed at this Middle Amana printing-office. But the Society publishes no newspaper or magazine, official or otherwise.

Nearly all of the communes in the United States have published an "organ" in which were freely discussed their fundamental principles with a view to uniting "all friends of humanity in one world-wide socialistic fraternal brotherhood."[160] The Amana Society, on the contrary, has never had any desire to recruit its membership from the world, and has never cared to take the public into its confidence. The members live quiet, peaceful, honorable lives. They attend strictly to their own affairs; and the curious public is given to understand that it would be much pleasanter for all parties if it in turn would do likewise.

Nor is there any need of newspaper communication within the seven villages. All necessary information can be transmitted daily through the

Elders to the people at the evening prayer-meeting; and the "personals" and "local news" travel, in spite of the admonition to "avoid all unnecessary words", quite fast enough without a daily paper. With the absence of nearly all forms of social intercourse other than religious meetings, it is but natural that in so human a community as Amana the affairs of one's neighbors should be of absorbing interest.

In three of the villages — Amana, Homestead, and Middle Amana — there are licensed pharmacies. The quantity of drugs prepared for the outside market is not large, as no effort has ever been made to build up a drug trade. As a rule only special orders are filled. Some physicians of the State prefer to get their supplies here rather than to send farther east for them. Moreover it is interesting to note that the Inspirationists were the first people west of Chicago to begin the manufacture of pepsin, and their manufacture is still considered one of the best in the market. The old apothecary, a typical gentleman of the old school to whom is due in a large measure the excellent reputation of the Amana pharmacies, still works assiduously in his laboratory, where all unconsciously amid his quaint surroundings he presents a picture which one longs to be able to transfer to canvas.[161]

It is the aim of the Community to produce and make as far as practicable everything that is needed by its members, not alone for the better grade of goods thus obtained but for the independence from the outside world thus secured. And so, in addition to the industries mentioned above, each village has its shoemaker, tailor, tinner, harness-maker, and even its watchmaker—for one finds that watches and clocks are classed as necessities in Amana. These tradesmen as a rule do not devote their entire time to their occupations, but only make and repair what is needed in their line by the people of the village. During the busy season they are called to the factory or the field as circumstances demand.

There is in each village a slaughter-house, a piggery, and a huge power saw for the cutting of fire-wood; while beneath the meeting-house there is a great wine-cellar in which the village supply of wine is stored. In one of the villages there is a soap-boiling factory. These with the dairy, the bakery, and the extensive Amana gardens suggest how completely the Community is supplied with all the wants of daily life.

In the early days the Amana Society operated its own breweries for the manufacture of beer for home consumption. But believing thoroughly in the reign of law the Community promptly shut down its breweries with the passage of the prohibitory law in 1884. Since the enactment of the mulct law this industry has not been revived; but wine in generous quantities for home consumption is still made. The output when ready for use is measured with German accuracy and precision and apportioned with that same "justice and equity" which pervade the Amana system in all its ramifications.

Owing to the recent winter-killing of some of the vineyards the output of wine is at present smaller than usual, but still averages some twelve gallons annually for each adult male and half that quantity for each adult female. Boys over fourteen years of age who are taking part in the village work, particularly in the fields, likewise receive their proportionate share. A "wine-keeper" (often an Elder) has charge of the village supply; and each member is furnished with a wine ticket, the punching of which, together with the keeper's record, precludes the possibility of an overdraft.

The Community raises its own tobacco and makes its own cigars. There seems never to have been in the Amana Community the prejudice against the "vile weed" that is found in some other German communistic settlements — particularly among the members of the Zoar Society and the Rappites at Harmony. There is, however, a strong sentiment against the abuse of the wine privilege. [162]

It is not the Inspirationist's way to take his allotted labor as an affliction. He labors cheerfully and industriously but not exhaustively; for of this there is no need. He works less rapidly than his brother in the world; but he lives longer. Some years ago the grain elevator in one of the villages was destroyed by fire; and owing to the season enough members of the Community could not be spared from their routine work to rebuild it. Accordingly a contractor from a neighboring city was engaged for the work, with the understanding that the available Amana masons should be employed by him and paid on the same terms as his own men. In the course of a few days it was very evident that the Amana masons could not keep up with the masons of the world; and so the fair-minded superintending Elder agreed that the Community workmen should be paid only in proportion to the work actually done. With this stimulus the Inspirationists set to work with a will; but while their work was unquestionably well done, the average amount accomplished and paid for was only two-thirds that of the masons from the city who had learned to labor under the influence of competition.

An unmistakable atmosphere of industry pervades the Community; but the elements of hurry and worry have largely been eliminated. To the outsider, escaping for a few days from the high pressure of the business world, Amana's "ways are ways of pleasantness, and all her paths are peace."

The personal or proprietary interest of each man in his work is apparent everywhere. There is nothing mechanical in the work of the factory operative. He handles his machine as if it were a thing alive and quite capable of responding to his loving ministrations. Indeed, the amount of ingenuity, inventive skill, and general business talent developed by the Amana industrial system is a telling argument in its favor. The industrial training of the young Inspirationist, covering as it does a variety of trades, increases his dexterity and broadens his faculties to a degree not found in his fellow tradesmen of the world.

With all of its conservatism in manners, customs, and religious observances, the Community of True Inspiration keeps pace with the times in the matter of business methods. The latest inventions, the newest improvements in machinery, in truth anything that is designed in any way to facilitate work, are promptly tested. And all changes in modes of conducting commercial affairs are eagerly watched and gladly adopted.[163] Economically considered there seems to be no immediate danger that the Community of True Inspiration will decline.

VII

SCHOOLS AND EDUCATION

If it is true that a man's education and training should begin some two hundred years before he is born, and that, as the founder of the Oneida Society declared, "men and women need to be trained to live contentedly in a community", then surely the younger members of the Community of True Inspiration are well fitted for the great responsibilities which will come to them when the men of strong hands and strong minds who have so successfully guided the affairs of the Community have passed away. For the special education and training of the Inspirationists began, in truth, in Württemberg at the beginning of the eighteenth century, under the guidance of those "heroes of faith", Eberhard Ludwig Gruber and Johann Friedrich Rock; and the chief aim has always been the preparation of the youth for membership in the Community.

The First Brethren, those who have formulated and determined the *Weltanschauung* of the Community through the many years of its inspiring history, have been men of intellectual capacity who have fully understood the importance of bending the young twig in a manner that would insure the proper inclination of the full grown tree. And so they have made the preservation of the pristine earnestness and religious zeal of the *Urgrosseltern* the mission of the Community school. Naturally the text-book has been of minor consideration, where learning has always been of less account than piety. "What our youth need more than study", says the *Kinderlehrer*, "is to learn to live holy lives, to learn God's commandments out of the Bible, to learn submission to His will, and to love Him."

The philosophy of the Community school and the fundamental principles in the ethical training of the children of Amana are set forth most clearly in the *Kinder-Stimme*, which is a "brief guidance for children and those of child-like heart to the most commendable practice of virtue, and to their duties toward God, their superiors, their fellow members and towards themselves." This little volume was published originally in 1717 under the inspiring influence of Rock and Gruber.

To inculcate the precious doctrines of the *Kinder-Stimme* in the minds and hearts of their children, separate schools were established by the *Urgrosseltern* against the protest of the Lutheran clergy. And gladly did the *Urgrosseltern* suffer the fines and imprisonment that followed, feeling that they had "through God's grace recognized and found something better" and had planted the spirit-

[Facsimile of the title-page of the first edition of the *Kinder-Stimme*]

Kinder-Stimme

Oder

Anleitung zum kindli-
chen Lob und Jugend-Ue-
bungen der Kinder;
Durch Trieb des Geistes verfasset
Von einem/
Der nach dem kindlichen Geist
Christi in Auffrichtigkeit des
Hertzens sich sehnet.

ANNO 1717.

ual seed that would in time bring forth a harvest acceptable to the heavenly gardener. Five times since that "dark and gloomy period" the little *Kinder-Stimme* has been reprinted; and it is still used to guide the budding Inspirationist into "the ways of humility and simplicity" and to inspire him with that profound respect for authority and unquestioning obedience to superiors which have always been taught as fundamental principles in the Community of True Inspiration. Some of the "orders and regulations" of the *Kinder-Stimme* read as follows:

Ever pray for a truly repentant, submissive, and humble heart.

Implore God in all earnestness to shatter in you stubbornness, self-will, and self-love.

Let not Satan undermine your earnestness through indolence, laziness, and drowsiness.

Do not seek your desires and ambitions in great knowledge and understanding, but rather in self-negation and self-denial.

Let the fear of God fill your tender hearts, and do not offend him through your sinful self-willed deeds, nor offend him in your superiors.

Do not elevate yourself because of a few good deeds, for thereby you rob God of the honor.

If you feel a divine impulse in your soul to seek quiet seclusion and meditation for intercourse with God in prayer, by all means do not disregard it. For the gate of Love then stands open for you.

When you have sinned or misused the grace of God, behave not like wicked children who avoid the punishment, flee continually from the presence of their father, and so make the approach in the end only the more difficult; but come voluntarily and submit to the correction of your heavenly Father. Confess to Him your evil deed and excuse it in no wise. Ascribe to yourself the greatest blame, nay all the blame, and pray for mercy and patience. And thus do also with your earthly parents and persevere in watchfulness over yourself.

Direct your eyes ever and only upon Jesus, your beginning, aim, and goal.

Guard yourself against the misuse of the name of God or of Jesus. Do not use either in vain or from habit.

Accustom yourself to be silent and let your heart speak more than your tongue, that is to say, with God.

If you feel dislike for prayer, watching, and beseeching, make simple plaint to your heavenly Father. And speak of it indeed also with others, particularly with your superiors, that they may help you with their good advice.

Choose with purpose whatever serves to break your will, or for your humiliation. What serves for the mortification and annihilation of your old self choose. For whatsoever inflicts pain upon self-love brings true well-being to the spirit. The cross brings salvation. Remember!

Pray that God may teach you the true art of dying. Without daily dying, self-negation, renunciation, and the mortification of your old being you can never obtain the true life.

See to it that you practice an entirely voluntary obedience and submission to the superiors set over you by God in all things, if their commands are not plainly contrary to God and your conscience.

Let no grumbling, disrespect, or opposition towards the orders and regulations of your superiors arise in you or, worse still, become permanent or break forth in words or deeds.

Do not regard the shortcomings of your superiors, if they have any; nor seek to shield yourself through them and do not allow any disrespect toward them to arise in you, look rather upon yourself and into your own heart, there you will find enough to condemn. Tear out the knavish eye that seeks to see evil in others.

Think always better of others than of yourself.

When you are punished or reprimanded because of your faults, do not excuse your wrong-doing since this makes the matter only worse before God and your superiors. Come forth, confess your sin openly, accuse yourself, and ask sincerely for forgiveness but not for exemption from punishment; receive the latter readily and willingly and let it serve for your humiliation and betterment. Thus you gain the love of your superiors.

Do not esteem yourself wise. Suppress your supposed wit and cleverness, and obey the counsel of your superiors without reasoning.

Gladly give up your plans, and submit to the advice of others. That will not be harmful, but on the contrary beneficial for you.

If you, without the knowledge of your superiors, have committed offence against them or otherwise, be not ashamed to accuse yourself of it. It will be of great benefit to you and will despoil the Enemy.

Conceal and cloak nothing of your faults. The revealing of the Enemy indeed weakens his strength.

If you or your works are treated with disregard or contempt, though they be blameless in your own eye, let it produce no bitterness in you. It is but a test of your humility and patience.

Learn to take willingly from one another admonition and punishment, and let no one think himself better than the others, for you all are dust and shall again become dust and the food for worms.

Avoid useless words for they deprive you of the strength of the soul.

Flee from wicked, talkative, boastful and vain company, for you are infected and spoiled by it.

Seek and love seclusion, concealment, and separation.

Let no one envy the other because of superior talents or because he seems to be more pleasing to the superiors.

Let every one seek to be most humble. Flee ambition and exaltation of one over another.

The smaller you are in your own eyes the better can the grace of God reveal itself in you.

Let the thought of how you may die in Christ be often the subject of your meditation. Remember that your time is short and that you do not know when your time to die is going to come. Therefore make the best use of the time in season.

Guard against mental and physical idleness as a state in which the Enemy is able and likely to overpower you most easily.

Do not love the world and do not follow the customs of the world. Do not love beauty nor daintiness of dress, much less boast in them. For what are you? A vile maggot.

Do not adorn yourself in dress for luxury's sake as a feast for the eyes or to please yourself and others, but only for necessity's sake. What you seek and use beyond necessity is sin.

Take care however that you wash and cleanse your spiritual dress in the blood of the Lamb.

Let your words be few and, together with your manners, not overbearing and impertinent but chaste and modest.

Do not accustom yourself to a proud bearing. Keep your eyes under control. Perform your physical work actively, quickly, industriously, and carefully.

Be not concerned with what is neither commanded to you nor your duty, and be not forward. Whatever you do perform it with sincere prayer.

Be moderate in food and drink. Remember that nature is satisfied with small and plain fare. Give to the body what it requires, but see to it that under the form of necessity no superfluity be concealed. Therefore bridle your uncontrolled appetite.

Seek all your joy and desire in God, and not in the objects of His creation. Ever bear in mind the purpose for which they are given to you, namely, to use them for your wants and to the praise of God.

Mortify the body that it may be subject to the spirit. Care for the needs of your souls.

Keep your body in proper manner and cleanliness.

Shun much sleep. Do not sleep readily when in good health in the day time. Battle against indolence of body and soul. Love watchfulness.

Let not the sun set upon your anger and enmity. Strive that you may have a conciliatory heart for those who offend you.

Learn to do what you practice in the performance of your virtuous duties as easily and freely as you eat and drink and breathe.

Before you go to bed at night go over the account of the day between yourself and God and diligently scrutinize your heart. See whether you have lived as you are commanded to live or as you pledged yourself to live in the morning. If you find your conduct unfaithful, repent of it sincerely and pray for mercy.

When you have made to the Lord your simple evening sacrifice, let nothing further enter your thought and mind. Go to bed and submerge yourself in the peace of God and the wounds of Jesus, and thus go to sleep. Then the Enemy will have no power to torment you with dreams and pictures of fancy. And whenever you awake at night, lift your heart at once to God.

Finally in all that you do let your heart be lifted up to the Lord and refer everything to your heart or pious meditation.

a. When you undress, pray to the Lord that he may free you from the tatters of sin.

b. When you dress, pray for the garb of salvation and the purple garment of Christ.

c. When you wash yourself, pray for the true cleansing from sin and for sanctification in the blood of the Lamb.

d. When you use fire, pray for the kindling and augmentation of the fire of divine love in your souls.

e. When you behold the rays of the sun penetrate the air, pray that the eternal sun may tinge and adorn your heart, and that it may free you from all self-pride and superficiality.

f. When you till the ground, pray to the heavenly gardener that He may prepare your spiritual garden for the right harvest, that He may turn your mind heavenward and away from all earthly thoughts.

And so do with all objects of creation and you will thus find God in all things. Everything will then be a ladder and a guide to God for you. And finally take care lest your prayer and sacrifice become a mere habit.

There is in the Community of True Inspiration to-day a school in each village which is conducted in the main like any other village school under the laws of the State; for the Amana schools are public, not parochial, sharing in the school-fund of the State. Strictly speaking the Amana schools belong to the regular school system of the county in which the Community is located. But it happens that the whole of Amana Township is owned by the Society. Like other townships this particular township is divided into independent school districts with a schoolhouse in each of the seven villages. Thus the Amana Society in fact levies its own school tax, builds its own schoolhouses, chooses its own directors, and employs its own teachers. The teachers are of course members of the Community; but they attend the county institute along with their fellow teachers of the county.

To guide and train the Amana youth in the "so important ways of God" requires unflagging energy; and so the Amana school has no vacation. Between the ages of five and fourteen the Amana boy and girl attend school six days in the week and fifty-two weeks in the year.[164] The sessions of the school open early and close late; for when mothers, grandmothers, and grown sisters are busy in the kitchen or in the garden during the greater part of the day, some provision must be made for the proper training of the children in their absence. To those accustomed to the short hours and long vacations of the modern public school, the young Inspirationist's hours, his rigorous religious training, and his long school year seem rather strenuous. We are, therefore, somewhat surprised to find in the Amana school the merriest, most contented group of little folks that ever spelled in concert or did sums in duet.

The school yard is a veritable German *Kindergarten* with plenty of green grass, big shade-trees, enticing grape-arbors, and a profusion of flower-beds. With modifications less individualistic and more in harmony with the communism of the Community, Froebel's idea that every child should learn to cultivate a plot of ground is a principle of the Amana school; for all of the school gardens are planted and cared for by the children under proper guidance. Here each little Inspirationist takes his turn at sowing seed and hoeing weeds, in watering the flowers and cutting the grass.

The pleasure that these school children take in their surroundings fills the visitor with wonder. The little Inspirationist with scarcely English enough to make himself understood will timidly call the attention of the visitor to the catbirds in the lilac bush, to the apple orchard in full bloom, or to the beautiful view from the schoolroom window. A love of Nature in all of her varying moods is a marked characteristic of the Inspirationist. Indeed, this is the one aesthetic side of his nature that seems not to have been repressed as "a vanity" in the past six generations.

The first floor of the schoolhouse is devoted to school purposes. The second floor is the home of the schoolmaster and his family, if he is married; or it may be the dwelling-place of the spinster knitting teachers. For it is the aim of the Community "to have things handy." And so the pharmacist and the doctor live above or near the drug store; and the kitchen superintendent lives in the upper story of the kitchen-house. The women who care for the church and its surroundings live in the building. The members take their meals at the nearest kitchen and attend prayer-meeting at the nearest meeting-house.

The school opens with the singing of a psalm followed by prayer offered in the manner of the Community — the teacher and the children falling on their knees and each in turn repeating a supplicatory verse. Then one of the older pupils repeats the *Glauben* slowly, distinctly, and impressively, to which the teacher responds with the Lord's Prayer.

What would otherwise seem like a long tiresome daily session in the Amana school is broken up into three parts: (1) the *Lehrschule,* when all the common branches are taught; (2) the *Spielstunde,* or hour of play, when the children play their quaint little German games; and (3) the *Arbeitsschule,* when manual training and the trades are taught. It is in the *Arbeitsschule* that, during the winter-time, the younger boys and girls are taught to knit and crochet. Here the stranger is amazed to learn that five year old Minchen is knitting her second pair of stockings, and that little Wilhelm, brim full of mischief, is knitting his father's hose.

Each child has for his yarns and needles a stout round basket which is stored away "between times" in enclosed shelves in the *Arbeitsschule.* These baskets of domestic manufacture are as near alike as the hats of Amishmen; and with the same inexplainable accuracy with which the Amishman picks out his head-gear the little Inspirationist finds his basket.

Just before the knitting lesson is given a lunch of bread and butter is served by the older girls to the children in the knitting-room. During the knitting lesson the older boys, who have in their turn helped to knit the family stockings, usually go to the different shops and factories for instruction in the trades; while the older girls clean up the schoolhouse and help in the knitting department.

While the "big" boys are learning a trade and the "little" boys are learning to knit, the "middle-sized" boys under the superintendence of the schoolteacher hoe thistles in the spring-time and work in the orchards during the summer. Sometimes in the late fall, when the apples and grapes are to be gathered and "many hands are needed", school work is suspended for a week or ten days and all the children who are large enough help to garner the harvest. Thus the Inspirationist learns, along with his catechism and his *ah, bay, tsay,* the habit of regular and patient industry, of occupying himself "with serious work." While the Community values education, it lays special stress on that which makes most strongly for good character and fits for the useful activities of life.

The atmosphere about the Amana school is more like that of a large household than of the ordinary school. The perfect equality maintained has eliminated that shrinking timidity so common among small children. It is seldom that one sees a group of children so uniformly well-mannered, pleasant-spoken, and courteous. Each child has the air of being a member of a great family; and a visitor at the school is the guest of every boy and girl present, as well as of the teacher. If he chances to arrive for the first time during the *Spielstunde,* he may be somewhat bewildered by the array of little hands extended in welcome; but he soon learns that the parting guest is speeded in the same cordial manner — the little ones reaching under and the big ones reaching over the middle-sized ones in an effort to shake hands. If recitations are in progress, the friendly chorus of goodbyes follows the departing visitor, making him decide at once to come again.

School discipline as a burden is reduced to a minimum. When it is remembered that this Community of men and women have for generations maintained the same high standards of living and of thinking it is easy to understand why the school children of to-day are so well-mannered and obedient. There are to be sure some mischievous boys and giggling girls; but such types as make our city teachers grow old before their time are wholly wanting. No Amana boy or girl has ever been sent to the State Industrial Schools.

Absolute faith in the wisdom and integrity of their leaders and an almost military obedience to their commands are and always have been taught as fundamental in the Community of True Inspiration; and so the schoolmaster is a man of great authority in his little world — and this is as it should be, for his responsibility is a grave one. With him rests not only the elementary education of the child in obedience and good habits, but to a large degree the spiritual guidance of the youth is in his hands.

Formerly the schoolmasters were appointed by Inspiration for their "gracious calling." In the *Jahrbuch* for 1878 there is recorded a testimony, given for the benefit of a Brother whom the Great Council of the Brethren and Sister Barbara Heinemann had chosen for schoolmaster, but who pleaded his inexperience. "Thou shalt", reads the testimony, "receive this grave and gracious calling with reverence though thou dost deem thyself unworthy and unable. This is as it should be; for then the Lord can be teacher and reformer within thee, and thou canst therefore render Him good service."

Where the villages are large enough to admit of such an arrangement, the work in the *Lehrschule* is divided into three grades, each of which is presided over by its own schoolmaster. The teachers in the *Lehrschule* are all men; but there are women among the "working teachers" in the *Arbeitsschule*. In the smaller villages there is but one schoolmaster who is usually assisted in the primary work by one of the older girls who is about to graduate.

Most of the teachers in the Community are old men — men who have devoted a lifetime to the training of Amana's youth. Some of them have taught so long that their pupils to-day are for the most part the children and even the grandchildren of their former pupils. There is thus established a relationship between teacher and pupil of which the world with its rapid changes and eager desire for "new blood" knows nothing. The white-haired schoolmaster of the Community remembers that Hans' father was a little rascal in school, but he turned out all right; and so mischievous Hans in consequence often escapes a "ruling." Minchen is like her mother, very conscientious, but a little slow; so Minchen is helped over the hard places. If ever there was a school where the "do-learns" had a proud and appreciative teacher, the "can't-learns" a kind and sympathetic helper, and the "won't-learns" a firm and upright judge who never runs the risk of spoiling the child by sparing the rod, it is in the Community of True Inspiration.

Much of the reciting in school is done in concert. In the "primer class" the pupils spell and pronounce long columns of words. They accent with some vigor the first letter, and take just enough time between words to catch breath while the schoolmaster beats time on his desk with a ruler. The result is a pretty little chant in perfect time and tune.

The "Johnny-book" method of spelling may be more modern, but it lacks aesthetically the charm of the *tay-hah-ee-ay-air — thier; tay-ee-ess-tsay-hah-ay — tische* of the Amana "primer class." To one who has listened in passing to that chant as it floats out of the vine-covered school window, reciting in concert will always recall the Amana primary room with its sanded floor and its long well-scrubbed benches, a row of tiny lassies in severe black caps on one side, and a row of embryo Inspirationists in blue over-alls on the other, each with a huge flannel-bound slate with a sponge suspended by a string — for which latter in true child fashion the sleeve or apron is substituted in an emergency.

Since "it is in the play-day of childhood that social sympathy, a social sense, and a social habit are evolved", one is impressed with the fact that the *Spielstunde* is as essential a part of the training of the future Inspirationists as the *Arbeitsschule*. As a rule the boys have their own games and the girls theirs. They are constantly admonished to "take no pleasure in boisterousness and immodest plays"; and the exclusive games — those enjoyed only by a few — make way for those in which every one can take part. Most of the games are of the "all-hands-round" type, accompanied by rhymes of ten, twelve, and fifteen complicated verses which the children in the inexplicable manner of childhood repeat without a slip. Their favorite rhymes are (as they probably have ever been with the children of all tongues) those that require acting out.

With the sustained enthusiasm of childhood they chant for the hundredth time:

Armes Häslein, bist du krank
Dass du nicht mehr hüpfen kannst?

Then there are of course the games in which are acted out the daily vocations, as in the following:

Maulbeerbaum, Maulbeerbaum
Wir tanzen um den Maulbeerbaum
  Des Morgens in der Frühe
Dann ziehen wir die Strümpfe an
  Des Morgens in der Frühe.

And when the stranger has listened to verses enough to don each bit of wearing apparel separately, to wash faces and comb hair, to laugh and to weep, to go to school and home again, he feels that the day of perpetual motion is near at hand.

Some of the Amana games are adaptations from the English; but the majority of them were brought from the Fatherland, and with their picturesque setting still retain the inimitable charm of the old German folk songs. Some of them, as *Sieben Jahr,* sound the same mystic note of the seventeenth century that is found in the *Jahrbücher*.

The Great Council of the Brethren has general supervision over the Community schools; but each schoolmaster, as a rule, is free to follow his own particular methods. The instruction for beginners is very naturally wholly in German, and is confined rather closely to the orthodox "Readin, Ritin, and Rithmetic", with a seasoning of prayer and catechism. In the more advanced classes instruction in English and German go hand in hand. The English texts of the United States History, Physiology, and Geography are translated into the German; and the German texts of other branches are translated into the English paragraph by paragraph.

There is the same variety of branches taught that we find in the Grammar School of the world, with daily Bible readings and catechism. At definite times during the week the schoolmaster devotes an hour to the history of the Community, to reviewing the lives of their spiritual leaders, to recounting the suffering and devotion of the *Urgrosseltern*, and to impressing upon the youth the solemn obligation of fitting themselves to take their places in the Community and to carry on the work "according to the holy command of the Most High."

The methods of the Amana schools may not be modern. But let us not forget that it is "by their fruits ye shall know them."

At the end of the school catechism there are "Sixty-Six Rules for the Conduct of Children" covering all the relations of life; and in the knowledge of these it is the aim of the schoolmaster to have his pupils well grounded. Herein are set forth in considerable detail and with great plainness of speech piety, orderly habits, obedience, truthfulness, cheerfulness, discretion, industry, politeness, cleanliness, and in general all "that is pleasing to the Lord." To live up to these rules of conduct are the first steps towards salvation. The following are some of the more essential:

Let your first thoughts be directed to God after the example of David who said: "How precious also are thy thoughts unto me, O God! how great is the sum of them! If I should count them, they are more in number than the sand: when I awake, I am still with thee"; and "Because thou hast been my help therefore in the shadow of thy wings will I rejoice." (*Psalms*, 139:17, 18; and *Psalms*, 63:7)

Instead of useless chatting with others endeavor to have good thoughts while you dress yourself. Remember the garment of justice of Jesus Christ and its innocence, and make the resolution not to stain it that day through any intentional sin.

Be quiet while at the table, unless you are asked a question; the prattling of children while eating is a grave lack of manners.

Pray before you fall asleep once more to your Father in heaven and direct your heart to Him without distracting thoughts, then remain quiet until you go to sleep.

If you awake during the night do not pursue idle thoughts but think of the Lord and His omnipresence.

When you come to school sit down quietly at your place and be mindful of the presence of God.

When the prayer is said, pray aloud and devoutly; when singing do not seek to drown the others. When studying the word of God be quiet and reverential and do not forget that it is God who speaks with you.

If you are punished for your misbehavior, do not show yourself resistant or impatient either through words or gestures, but let it be for your betterment.

If you have not been asked, remain quiet and do not help others because this works only harm to them.

Show yourself kind and peaceable towards your fellow pupils, do not kick them, or make them dirty with your shoes or in some other manner; call them no bad names, and behave yourself always towards them as you wish that they should behave towards you.

When going home avoid all noise and jumping, and walk quietly and mannerly.

Go quietly and with collected mind to the meeting, sit down at your place, and let the fear of the presence of the Lord fill your heart.

Let your eyes not wander about, but turn your heart and your mind to the Lord. If you are overcome with sleep struggle against it and arise.

On your way home avoid everything unmannerly, all prattling and standing about.

Think wherever you are that the Lord your God is present and resolve that you will strive against all sin and misbehavior.

In the winter-time do not go on the ice, do not throw snow balls at others, and do not go sliding with wicked boys.

Take no pleasure in boisterousness and immodest plays; do not stand at the road when people quarrel or fight or do other knavery; never associate at all with licentious boys, for there you learn only wickedness; refrain also from playing with children of the opposite sex.

Be polite and friendly towards everybody, and let this be from genuine love of God and your fellow men, not from mere habit.

Be never idle, but seek to occupy yourself more and more with serious work, in order that rambling and playing may cease at last entirely.

If you come to someone who has money or the like lying on the table, do not approach closely and do not remain alone in the room.

Do not listen at the doors, and close them gently when entering or leaving the room.

Be polite also towards strangers who come into the house.

Avoid boisterous laughing and resentful weeping on all possible occasions, because both these are foolish. Rejoice never over the misfortune of others, for this greatly displeases the Lord and is always punished.

If you have made a promise so keep it, and beware of untruthfulness and lies.

Let whatever good or mannerly you see in other Christian persons be an example to you.

Twice each year there are "solemn religious meetings" intended to ascertain and promote the spiritual condition of the children. These meetings are conducted by one or two of the First Brethren "who are endowed with much grace, insight, and discrimination." The first meeting is the *Kinderlehre*, and consists in the main of an impressive review of the fundamental doctrines of the Community and of the supreme importance of keeping the faith. The second meeting is the *Kinder-Unterredung*, which is the children's part of the yearly rigorous spiritual examination of the entire Community. "It is my profound belief", said one of the Community schoolmasters recently (one who has himself grown gray in his lifelong effort to bring it to pass) "that no other children on the whole earth are more richly instructed in religion than ours."

There are special songs for the children in the *Kinder-Stimme* for each church festival of the year — songs for Ascension Day, Christmas, and New Years, for the Resurrection, Renewing the Covenant, and for Harvest Time — each with its admonition or appeal to "learn early to pay heed to the inner voice", to "pray for true childlike obedience", "to love the ways of humility" and "drink the bitter cup of dying", and "to make use fully of your time." Every anniversary, every important happening, is one more precious opportunity of pointing a moral.

Graduation from the Community schools takes place twice a year. Formerly both of these ceremonies were rather elaborate. All of the graduates, all of the teachers, and the entire Great Council of the Brethren congregated in one village for the impressive exercises. But the First Brethren are growing too old to go about in wind and weather; and so in the graduation exercises, as in all other activities, the Community has adjusted itself to the advancing age of its "experienceful" leaders. In the autumn when the weather permits, there is a general ceremony in Amana; but in the spring when the weather is more uncertain more simple exercises are held in each settlement, presided over by those members of the Great Council who can attend with the least inconvenience to themselves.

The graduation exercises take place in the school-room, and are opened by a song from the *Kinder-Stimme.* All the children then kneel while a member of the Great Council pronounces a prayer. The First Brethren then proceed with the examination, beginning with the Catechism and then reviewing the history, significance, purposes, and solemn obligations of the members of the Community. The spiritual examination is followed by an examination in all branches, the questioning in this case being led by the teacher in charge.

At the close of the examination some one asks a blessing, the children sing a psalm, and all noiselessly file out of the room except the candidates for graduation, who come forward and occupy a row of chairs in front of the Elders. After a moment of silent meditation one of the Brothers offers up a petition for the proper guidance of these children to whom so soon is to be entrusted the deep responsibility of guiding the affairs of the Community. Another Brother follows with a brief address to the graduates, chiding each (in all kindness) for his shortcomings and impressing upon all the importance of the step they are taking and the solemn obligations it involves. Each of the young people in turn then arises and reads his graduation essay which is a simple child-like review of his school life, of his faults, of his aspirations, and of his future intentions as a member of the Community.

The whole exercise is, in the words of the schoolmaster, "a ceremonious solemnity", so awe-inspiring that the graduates are sometimes seized with stage fright and are obliged to stand while the kind old schoolmaster reads the essay. After all of the essays have been read, the presiding Brother pronounces a benediction and a blessing, and the school days of the little group are over — except of course for the occasional lad who for "character and capacity" is chosen by the Great Council to be a pharmacist or a doctor in the Community. These receive their professional training in due time at The State University of Iowa.

The following is a translation of one of the more recent graduation essays:

As the time has arrived that I am to leave school, I write in looking back upon my life in school the following:

I was born at Homestead on February 25, in the year 1891. At the age of five I began to attend the school in which Brother A——— B——— is the teacher. I received instruction in reading, arithmetic, writing, drawing, grammar, geography, physiology and history of the United States. I also was instructed in the word of God, in catechism, biblical history, and also in singing and reading of the songs in the children's hymn book.

Our teacher took great pains with us, and besides the work of instruction he always found time to read to us a beautiful story or to tell us something interesting and instructive. After the hours of instruction we went to the knitting school which was conducted by Sister C——— D———. In the knitting school we were taught besides knitting, also sewing and embroidery. I owe great thanks to my teachers for the many good and useful things they have taught me and for the patience they have had with me. The recollection of my school years will ever be a pleasant memory to me, marred only by the knowledge that my conduct has not always been as faultless as it should have been and that I often caused my teachers grief through my disobedience and lack of attention. I deeply regret it and ask their forgiveness from the bottom of my heart. I am now leaving school with the sincere desire to become a faithful member of the Community and to do what I am bidden.

Your grateful pupil,

E——— F———.

"I have chosen the trade of locksmith for my calling", writes a boy graduate of the same year. "It is furthermore my desire, and may God help me to this end, that I may become a faithful and obedient member of the Community and that I may ever remain such."

The solemn and impressive graduation exercises are a sort of preparation for the *Bundesschliessung* (Renewing of the Covenant) in which they are allowed to take part for the first time between the ages of fifteen and sixteen. Indeed, their nine long years of school life may be regarded as a special preparation for and as culminating in this event, when for the first time the children openly consecrate themselves to the work of the Lord.

The *Bundesschliessung* is, to quote again the naive Amana phrase, the most important "ceremonious solemnity" of the year. In it every member of the Community and every boy and girl fifteen years of age or more takes part. The time and place of holding this meeting was formerly divinely appointed through the *Werkzeug*; but it is recorded that in 1863 "when the annual common Thanksgiving-day of the land came around the Lord gave direction through His word that henceforth this day should be annually observed solemnly in the Communities as a day of Covenant" which has been and is still observed.

At this meeting, after the usual song and silent prayer, two chapters of the books of Moses are read — particularly the words of the Covenant which the Lord commanded Moses to make with the children of Israel. There is an exhortation by the Head Elder on the majesty of the Lord, the great mercies promised unto the repentant, and the curses which shall come upon those who disobey His commandments. This exhortation is concluded by the most earnest appeal to every member of the Community (particularly the young people who find so much in the present day to draw their thoughts away from the things that are of the Lord) to hearken unto the voice of the Lord, to walk in His ways, and to keep His commandments and His statutes and His judgments.

At the close of this address, the Elders pass in turn to the Head Elder who gives them a solemn shake of the hand, signifying thereby their renewed allegiance to the work of the Lord. Formerly the *Werkzeug* while under the influence of Inspiration administered the hand-shake and pronounced upon each member a blessing. After all of the Elders have passed in solemn procession, the Brothers one by one according to age and spiritual rank come forward and similarly pledge their fidelity by a silent solemn hand-shake with the Head Elder and three or four of his most highly endowed assistants. When all of the Brothers, old and young, have taken part in this ceremony, the Sisters in the manner of the Brothers come forward according to their spiritual standing and pledge themselves to "cleave unto the ways of the Lord that they may dwell in the land which the Lord sware unto their fathers." At present in order that all may participate in this most important ceremony the Brothers take the pledge in the forenoon and the Sisters in the afternoon.

PART III

THE RELIGION OF THE INSPIRATIONISTS

'hurch benches and baskets

[Facsimile of the title-page of an early pamphlet dealing with the faith of True Inspiration]

J. J. J.

Kurtze und deutliche

Grund = Sätze

Von der

Wahren allgemeinen

Liebe;

Zur Unterscheidung deren

Von der

Eingebildeten und Falschen.

Um der

Unberichteten willen

Entworffen/

Und nebst einem Anhang

Etlicher Lieder

Mitgetheilet

1719.

I

THE FUNDAMENTAL DOCTRINE OF TRUE INSPIRATION

Although the Community of True Inspiration is unique in its successful practice of communism, the interesting and picturesque Amana of to-day is not primarily the outgrowth of a philosophy of economic life but essentially an expression of the religious enthusiasm of the *Urgrosseltern.* Indeed, the history, the life, and the institutions of the Community clearly reveal the fact that the *real* Amana is Amana the Church — Amana the Community of True Inspiration.

The fundamental doctrine upon which the Community is founded is that divine inspiration and revelation are just as real and potent to-day as in the time of Moses. The prophets that have arisen in their midst are to the Community but the fulfilment of the promise of the Old Testament to the children of Zion: "And it shall come to pass afterward that I will pour out my spirit upon all flesh; and your sons and your daughters shall prophesy, your old men shall dream dreams, your young men shall see visions."[165] And so the Inspirationists feel and believe that every step in their own eventful history is evidence of the fact that "God is ever present in the world and will lead His people to-day as in olden times by the words of His Inspiration if they but listen to His voice."

Sincerely and most devoutly do these people believe that from the beginning of the "New Spiritual Economy" they have received in all spiritual matters, and in those temporal affairs which concerned their spiritual welfare, divine guidance through specially endowed individuals — *Inspirations-Werkzeuge.* They believe that the beautiful Amana of to-day is simply the expression of the Lord's will as revealed directly to them from time to time through the *Werkzeuge.* They believe they were commanded by "a decisive word of the Lord" to dwell together in the Fatherland, to come to America where they might "live in peace and religious liberty;" to adopt communism in the "new home in the wilderness"; to leave Ebenezer and move to Iowa; and there to buy land and establish factories in order that the brotherhood might be maintained in "the faith which has love and the bond of peace for its essence."

"In all these important undertakings and changes, nay in the whole external and internal leadership of the Community, the *Werkzeug* had to bear the bulk of the burden and care, since the Lord ordained and directed everything through him." [166]

During the lifetime of the *Werkzeuge,* wrongs and evils in the Community were revealed by Inspiration, new-comers were admitted to full membership, unworthy members expelled, spiritual leaders chosen, hymns dictated, and love-feasts commanded. Even the *Werkzeuge* were appointed and removed by "a decision through the word." For in the words of Christian Metz, "the strong God can do and bring about whatsoever He will; what is required in all weighty matters is complete submission to and faith in God."[167]

II

THE DIVINE ORIGIN OF TRUE INSPIRATION

When Eberhard Ludwig Gruber had identified himself with the Inspirationists early in the eighteenth century and claimed that he was compelled by the Spirit of God to give utterance to His direct word, he was denounced by the Lutheran clergy as an "instrument of the Devil." To this accusation Gruber replied after the manner of the German Reformation with a pamphlet in which he gives the reasons whence he personally gets the assurance or conviction *(Ueberzeugung)* of the divine nature of Inspiration. This pamphlet is of special interest since Gruber himself had "struggled against the Spirit of Inspiration" and had previously written much opposing it. Gruber's assurances or convictions as given in his *Bericht von der Inspirations-Sache* are as follows:

Because I have not light-headedly and without test and experience come to the approval of these things.

Because the testimonies of the inspired persons, although being at first adverse to me, have not in the least troubled me, nor aroused and stirred my emotions, as certainly would have happened to some extent if they had originated from a wicked and dark spirit.

Because I have thereby not been hindered in the usual quiet introspective prayer granted to me by the mercy of God.

Because during such a deep and earnest self-examination all scruples and objections to this matter were without effort on my part so completely removed and dispersed that not one remained which irritated me or which I could not comprehend.

Because such prayer, which was absolutely without prejudice in the matter, has again won for me the precious gift of tears, which had become almost unknown to me.

Because the Spirit of Inspiration penetrated into and laid bare those things which occurred in the most hidden corners of my heart, so that no creature could know them; and because it [the Spirit of Inspiration] also approved and commended those ways of mercy and sanctification in which the Lord had hitherto led me in affairs external and internal.

Because the promises pronounced in regard to myself have not dazzled me or made me vain.

Because at the same time the extinguished love was again renewed in the hearts of many.

Because the assemblies of prayer recommended by the Spirit, and up to that time vainly striven for, were at once established to our joy and bliss and without opposition of the then well-disposed individuals.

Because I was led into the severest struggle for purification instead of expecting at once the fulfilment of the great promises given me.

Because this struggle searched my innermost self and has deeply impressed upon me the most vivid lessons of complete denial and negation of myself.

Because in this matter also all external hindrances were removed and I indeed was made willing and confident to throw them behind me and to take upon me all the disgrace and suffering of this service, often confirming my faith under tests and with proofs not mentioned here but known to God and also to others.

Because the inner word was laid open and led forth from the depths of my heart, whither no divine creature much less a satanic spirit could reach, deeper and more abundantly than I ever possessed it before.

Because those inner emotions known to me from my youth, but having now become stronger and more numerous, have ever either held me back from some evil deed or encouraged and urged me to some good act

Because they [inner emotions] often must with certainty reveal to me the presence of hidden false spirits rising against me or others.

Because in all this I do not found my conclusions on Inspiration alone, as may be the case with others, but moreover upon the undeniable work of God in my soul which has gone on there for long years out of sheer mercy and which under this new economy and revival is becoming ever more powerful.

Because my son, together with many others, has been brought into a state of deepest repentance and wholesome anxiety of the mind through the powerful testimony of the Spirit in the inspired persons.

Because the word of the Lord was unsealed to him [the son] by the very first *Bewegungen.*

Because the Spirit of Inspiration promptly appeared as when it had been foretold that a certain married woman [Johanna Melchior] [168] would testify on the day mentioned in Bergheim.

Because my son came to testify with great fear and trembling, nay even through the severest struggle and surely not through his wish and vain desire.

Because he was enabled and compelled in his first testimony, as a foreshadowing of the future, to denounce with great certainty an impure spirit, to the sincere humiliation of the latter.

Because he was led in these ways of Inspiration contrary to the inclination and habit of his youth, to deep introspection and seclusion, and was also endowed with many extraordinary gifts of mercy.

Because he made far beyond his natural abilities such pure, clear, and penetrating statements [utterances] that many well-learned in divine and natural things were led to wonder about them.[169]

III

THE CHARACTERISTICS OF TRUE INSPIRATION

In another pamphlet, entitled *Kennzeichen der Göttlichkeit der Wahren Inspiration,* Eberhard Ludwig Gruber attempts to answer "certain professors, extra-ordinaries, priests, first and second assistants, and students" who "in their inquiries and disputes concerning the work of Inspiration all concurred in this cardinal question: How can the inspired individual, and all those who are joined and participate in this work, be assured and feel certain that the Spirit of Inspiration is truly the Spirit of God, who testifies and speaks through the *Werkzeug?*" Gruber's reply was as follows:

The certainty which a person truly inspired from the Spirit of True Inspiration possesses, and which from firm conviction he can give to those who demand proof, may be obtained from the following, in part external, in part internal, infallible characteristics:

INTERNAL CERTAINTY

First. The Spirit of True Inspiration cleanses and purifies the *Werkzeug* in all his inner and outer faculties through daily training in repentance, faith, and obedience, that not self-will and foolish reason, not ill guided affections may intermingle with the divine working or hinder or destroy the same.

Second. He anoints his [the *Werkzeug*] spirit and his faculties with the true fear of God and humility, with childlike willingness, forbearance, and simplicity, so that one only seeks and thinks of what is of God and of Christ.

Thirdly. He pours into such receptacle divine revelation and teaching accompanied by violent trembling and commotions *(Bewegungen und Erschütterung)* of the body through the service of His good angels, who make themselves master of the inner and outer senses and through the external voice and sound of the mouth announce the inner word so that one may understand and record it, even as Baruch has recorded all the words and speeches out of the mouth of Jeremiah. [Then took Jeremiah another roll, and gave it to Baruch the scribe, the son of Neriah; who wrote therein from the mouth of Jeremiah all the words of the book which Jehoiakim king of Judah had burned in the fire: and there were added besides unto them many like words.]

Fourth. The *Werkzeug* does not control this inward spiritual gift and agency *(Geistes- Gabe und Wirkung)* through its own might or will, but it possesses the same only as a precious deposit, which it may preserve through careful watching and praying, obedience and suffering, but which it also may hamper and lose, nay even become subject to false powers and forces, if it mingles its own perversions, affections, desires, and insincere purposes with the effort and desire to be itself the mover and doer in this work, wherefrom result confused, incorrect, false utterances, which only those can test who possess the eye of simplicity and the spirit of discrimination, that they may know if the spirits are of God, but not those who regard this work with the knavish eye of the Pharisee, and when their faults and follies are made manifest through Inspiration either defend or deny them or attack the Spirit of Inspiration and mock it and blaspheme against it, where they should confess and abandon their sins and humble themselves before God and men.

EXTERNAL CERTAINTY

First. The word and the testimony of the Spirit of True Inspiration proves upon investigation in each and every fundamental truth to be concordant with and conforming to the scriptures of the prophets and the apostles, and that it has these truths in common with the scriptures.

Second. It aspires for no preference; on the contrary it gives the preference to the word of the witnesses first chosen [prophets and apostles] just after the likeness of two sons or brothers, in which case the oldest son as the first born has the preference before the younger son who was born after him, though they are both equal and children begotten of one and the same father. Thus it is also with the word of Inspiration and the word of the prophets and apostles. The latter has the preference before the former, especially and above all, first in point of time of revelation, and second in the degree of spirituality, that is to say, with regard to the unfathomable depth of the manifold wisdoms, ways, wonders, and secrets of God, which are contained in the writings of the prophets and apostles, but so that minors and babes in wisdom may draw from them their nourishment. But both the old and the new revelation, of which we here speak, are of divine origin and the testimony of one and the same Spirit of God and of Jesus Christ, just as the sons mentioned above are equally children of one and the same father though there exists through the natural birth a slight difference between them.

Third. It [the word of Inspiration] has in, with, and by itself divine powers and effects, namely:

It terrifies the wicked and godless sinners and puts them in fear and awe before its divine power while the motion [*Bewegung*] of the Spirit lasts. (Character.) [170]

It arouses to godly repentance and atonement, of which we have numerous examples near and far which have remained in this state to their blessed end.

It lays bare the hidden and innermost bottom of the heart of the good and wicked as all those have confessed and still must confess to whom such word and testimony has been addressed and who accord the honor to God.

It rebukes and punishes without difference all hidden and all known sins, all sins committed knowingly and unknowingly, of the old and the young, of the great and the lowly, without respect of person, rank, sex, or age, of which enough testimonies are on record and have become known through publication in print.

It purifies, as it is a divine fire, the senses, thoughts, desires, affections, impulses, passions, and the life and conduct of those who give room and place to the word and testimony, and become submissive and obedient to it; but those who despise and reject it, for those it becomes the breath of death and a testimony against them on the day of judgment.

It implants in souls and hearts thus purified a new creature, which is Christ in us, the hope of glory. To this end tends the whole economy of Inspiration (this spiritual husbandry) with all its testimonies and spiritual effects, namely; that the image of God, Christ, the new creature, be restored in man through the obedience of faith, which acts through love. Therefore it is no wonder that Satan and the old evil serpent of reason unceasingly rage and foam against this work.

It keeps the wicked in check and control, so that often they are not permitted to work harm although they would like to do so, of which many instances are known. Yes, it even often compels such persons from a hidden fear and emotion of their conscience to do good instead of evil so that not infrequently blasphemers of the truth come to glorify God.

It punishes and often brings death of body and soul to those who with heart, mouth, or hand have offended and persecuted the work of the Lord, His Spirit, and His messengers, of which many instances are known.[171]

On the other hand it often anoints, refreshes, consoles, and strengthens those, who in struggle and strife and in many trials loyally endure and are of a faithful and upright heart.

It promises and threatens from near by and from afar, but always under certain conditions, as is also the case in the Old and New Covenant, namely; if the ungodly repent, the curse is changed into a blessing, and if the just man becomes godless, then the promised blessing is changed into curse and wrath, (*Jeremiah* 18:7-10, and 9 *Sammlung,* p. 47-48.) as a warning for us since God punishes both opposition and backsliding with death.[172] (I Moses, 2:17. Romans 5:21. Proverbs 1:11. 1 *Sammlung* chapter 15, 23. Chapter 16, 14. Chapter 31, 6.)

These have ever and ever been the infallible characteristics of the words and testimonies of the prophets and the apostles that their word was a divine word and testimony, for the sake of which they had to endure, to suffer, and to die; but in spite of all this they enjoyed the calm, and the consolation of eternal bliss through the Spirit of God who was their hidden *Urim und Thumim (Licht und Recht)* whereby He anointed and sealed them for the divine

Solte es Gott leiden, so wäre [illegible] mit einem wort nicht, [illegible]
hertzen liebe, dazu aber [illegible] im stande nicht zu reden, so [illegible]
zu können einem andern schriftlich [illegible] das nicht [illegible] [illegible]
[illegible] wird. ich tröste mich das ich [illegible] gehorsam an [illegible]
halten [illegible] mir [illegible] Mündlich wäre wol viel zu reden.
Gott wolle sich nach allen Nöthen und Zuständen [illegible] erbarmen.
und liebe [illegible] wird von mir [illegible] hertz [illegible] Gr[illegible]
gegrüßet [illegible] Schwester [illegible] und alle alte Nachbarn
das ich nicht [illegible] mir sonst wolte sie alle mit Namen nennen
Gottes [illegible] hertzlich [illegible] befehlen, und
uns [illegible] Gott [illegible] mit demselben
Meines [illegible] Herrn [illegible] verbleibe [illegible] langjährig
[illegible] Caspar [illegible]

FAC SIMILE (WITHOUT REDUCTION) OF THE HANDWRITING AND AUTOGRAPH OF CASPAR LOW, A PROMINENT WRITER AND SPIRITUAL LEADER IN THE EARLY YEARS OF THE COMMUNITY OF TRUE INSPIRATION

certainty that indeed the Spirit of God dwelled, acted, spoke, and testified within them; and thus the Spirit of God still acts in his witnesses and gives to-day as he did yesterday the same assurance through which the prophets and apostles were certain that the Spirit of God and not a false spirit spoke through them and urged them on. . . . "Believe in the Lord your God, so shall ye be established; believe His prophets, so shall ye prosper."—[II *Chronicles* 20:20.] [173]

The writings of the early Inspirationists—especially those of Johann Adam Gruber, Gottfried Neumann, Blasius Daniel Mackinet, Georg Melber, Caspar Löw, and Johann Nicolaus Duill—contain many additional arguments in support of the divine origin of Inspiration. [174] Nor is it possible to discern wherein the testimonies of the *Werkzeuge* are regarded as of any less authority than the words of the Bible. Indeed they seem to be regarded as of equal rank, unless it be with the exception of the preference that Gruber speaks of as naturally given to the eldest brother (See above p. 230). "There are diversities of gifts," said Paul in his *Epistle to the Corinthians,* "but the same Spirit. And there are differences of administrations, but the same Lord. And there are diversities of operations, but it is the same God which worketh all in all."

In the religious services as conducted in the Community to-day the readings consist almost wholly of testimonies. It has become customary to read from the testimonies which were given subsequent to the Reawakening in the morning service on Sunday; while in the afternoon selections are usually made from the older testimonies.

IV

THE WERKZEUGE AND THEIR TESTIMONIES

In the New Spiritual Economy it was not enough that an individual should feel called upon to announce the word of the Lord in order to be recognized as a *Werkzeug* of Inspiration. For there were "false" as well as "true spirits" in the early congregations. Nor was it alone sufficient to receive appointment through a testifying *Werkzeug*. It appears from the records that as a safeguard against "false spirits" a committee of the congregation was usually delegated to ascertain the genuineness of the *Bewegungen* (violent shaking of the body accompanying the state of Inspiration) and *Bezeugungen* (testimonies).

While in the earlier days of the Community the *Werkzeug* Johann Adam Gruber was "especially employed by the Lord to detect false spirits", subsequent to the Reawakening an "Overseer of the *Werkzeuge*" was appointed by the Brethren to have special supervision of the work of the *Werkzeuge* even after they had been fully recognized and declared instruments of True Inspiration.

In his *Historische Beschreibung der Wahren Inspirations-Gemeinschaft* Christian Metz records:

"I was rebuked for my humiliation by Brother ————, who was then Overseer of the *Werkzeuge,* and for more than half a year I had no Inspiration." Likewise Barbara Heinemann was for a brief period in her early career "declared false and banished to her native place."[175] "It is no easy thing", wrote Christian Metz in his *Tagebuch,* "to be a *Werkzeug* of the Lord in which the Spirit of Inspiration is to labor and rule. I have often found how the grace of God is hindered through subtle self-love and one's own wisdom, but how on the other hand through self-denial and an absolute surrender and abandon to the fathomless abyss the divine grace can create something new after the will of God."

The testimonies (variously called *Zeugnisse, Bezeugnisse,* or *Bezeugungen*) given under the influence of Inspiration seem always to have been accompanied by a violent shaking of the body *(Bewegung).* An interesting account of the *Wewegungen* is given by the Scribe, Blasius Daniel Mackinet in his *Schreiben von der Göttlichkeit der Wahren Inspiration* in which he says:

> With regard to the *Bewegungen* the *Werkzeuge* were not alike, although they were all moved by one Spirit; there was considerable difference in regard to their gifts and convulsions. When they had to announce punishments and judgments of God, they all did it with great force, majestic gestures, strong *Bewegungen,* and with a

true voice of thunder, especially if this occurred on the public streets or in churches. But when they had to speak of the love of God and the glory of the children of God, then their motions were gentle and the gestures pleasing; but all, and in all attitudes assumed by them, spoke they with closed eyes. Often they had, previous to the *Bewegungen*, a feeling of its approach. Again they were seized suddenly, often at their meals, by day and by night. At times they were aroused from their slumber and had to testify, frequently on the public highways, in fields and forests. In short they were instruments in the hands of the Lord and had no control over themselves.

As violent as the commotions of the body [*Leibes-Bewegungen*] often were, still they did no harm to the body; on the contrary they served often as remedies if the *Werkzeuge* were ill, as in the case of the *Werkzeug* who, on a journey, lay seriously ill at Halle in Saxony and was very weak in body, when he suddenly to the terror of those present was seized with violent convulsions and had to testify. In the utterance he received orders to start on the journey, at which all were surprised. After the testimony the *Werkzeug* arose and was well at the very moment, and on the following day they departed.

Elsewhere in the same essay this Scribe describes his own sensation in the presence of a testifying *Werkzeug* in these words:

It has also often happened to me, although I was only a Scribe, that when the *Werkzeug* fell into *Bewegungen* previous to an utterance I was able to write before the very words had been spoken; nay, even the whole meaning and the content of the prophecy was clear to my mind. [176]

V

THE OLD AND THE NEW REVELATION

Under the date of January 30, 1716, there is an account of an interview between the younger Gruber and his Scribe and two old Jewish Rabbis in a synagogue at Prague in which are compared the manner of prophesying of the old Hebrew prophets and the *Werkzeuge* of the Inspirationists. This account is regarded very highly by the Community as it proves conclusively to the mind of the Inspirationist the divine nature of the *Bewegungen*. The account of the interview reads in part as follows:

Hereupon came two old gray-haired Rabbis and questioned us. (This is the reason why I have recorded the happenings.) They asked in the first place, where we had our home. Answer: Near Frankfort. Question: Of what religion? Answer: We call ourselves Christians. They said, they believed that and knew full well that not all are Christians who call themselves Christians, just like among themselves not all were Jews who called themselves Jews; and that they asked only for the sake of the outer distinction. Thereupon I [the Scribe] replied that one of us had been reared in the reformed church, the other among the Lutherans. They asked: Which of you is then the Prophet of the Lord? I pointed to Gruber. Now they questioned further. How does the word of the Lord come to this Prophet, does it come through an external voice into the ears or from within? Answer: Not from without, but from within, and to be explicit, in the following manner:—The *Werkzeug* or the Prophet feels at first in his innermost being a gentle and pleasant glow which gradually becomes more intense and also fills the external body. Thereupon results an inflation of the nose, trembling of the whole body and at last violent motions of the whole body, often attended by kicking with hands and feet and shaking of the head. And in the centre of this internal fire the word of the Lord is born; and the Prophet is enabled through the *Bewegungen* to pronounce the word of the Lord without fear or awe, as it was born in him, at times syllable by syllable, at times word by word, now slowly now rapidly, so that the *Werkzeug* had no choice of its own, but was used solely as a passive instrument in the hands of the Lord. Now you will be able to inform us (we said to them) since you are better acquainted with the Hebrew language than we, whether the old Prophets among the people of Israel have also announced the word of the Lord through such strange gestures of the body and through *Bewegungen?* They replied in kindness and humility: The word of the Lord had not been made known to them otherwise than from within, and if you should have said that the word of the Lord came to the Prophets of the present day from without, we should have rejected it; nor do the commotions of the body [*Leibes-Bewegungen*] surprise us at all, since this was a positive characteristic of the old Prophets; for he who spoke without these commotions of the body, was not considered a true Prophet, wherefore we in imitation of the Prophets of old unceasingly move when we sing our psalms. [176]

Rock relates in his autobiography a number of instances where ''out of respect of person'' he ''resisted the promptings of the Spirit'' and thereupon underwent sincere humiliation. ''On one occasion'', he writes, ''I was to testify against the selfishness of a Brother who did much good to us, but his presence made me womanish (*weibisch*) and I resisted. Soon after I learned that he had fallen into false *Bewegung* and had made false *Bezeugungen*, for which may the Lord pardon me and him.'' [177]

VI

THE GIFT OF PROPHECY : EINSPRACHE AND AUSSPRACHE

From the very beginning of the New Spiritual Economy there was a difference between the *Werkzeuge* as to their gift of prophecy. Some, though recognized as "true receptacles of God's mercy", were unable to give voice to their "strange and mysterious impulses" and therefore were obliged to resort to written expressions of the "inner promptings." And so a distinction was made between the written word (*Einsprache*) and oral prophecy (*Aussprache*), the latter being regarded as the higher gift. It appears that Barbara Heinemann, being at first endowed simply with the gift of *Einsprache,* was sorely hampered because of her inability to read or write; and she seems to have devised a cipher of her own "in order to obey the inward impulse and the demand of God", until on Christmas Day of the year 1818 she was granted by the Lord "the miraculous gift of *Aussprache.*"

The spiritual Christian Metz entered the "service of the Lord" with the humbler power of *Einsprache.* This "first period of the Lord's mercy", we are told, lasted nine years. *Inspirations-His-*

torie records in full his last *Einsprache* in which the Lord admonishes the Community "to render thanks to My great name in deepest humility (*Demuth*) and reverence (*Ehrerbietigkeit*) and worship and honor it"; for "it is pleasing to the Divine Love to announce to them soon its word from without" to be "written down by Scribes." [178] The second period seems also to have lasted nine years; when the *Werkzeug* passed through a third period. [179] "Of this the Lord made announcement to all the Communities in a most important word and testimony on October 15, [1841], at the Haag."

> I announce to you that the number nine conditions a change in the manner of the communication of My testimony and that the third period begins. Therefore My *Werkzeug* shall be subjected to Me to announce My word in a twofold manner, both in writing and through speaking as it pleases Me. [180]

At least twice during his lifetime the peace-loving Christian Metz was "deprived of his gift by the Lord." But each time, after a period of deepest humility, "it was pleasing to the Divine Love" again to bestow this grace upon him. [181]

VII

THE NATURE AND SCOPE OF THE BEZEUGUNGEN

The *Bezeugungen* or *Zeugnisse* vary in length from a few sentences to several hours in duration. In his *Historische Beschreibung der Wahren Inspirations-Gemeinschaft* Christian Metz records that at Bischweiler there occurred through him on a Sunday in the presence of two Brothers, who acted as Scribes, "a testimony which lasted from nine in the morning until ten at night. Everything uttered was in rhyme. Whoever came and gave me his hand received a message and a blessing."

In the days when the Community was fortunate enough to have two *Werkzeuge*, it sometimes happened that both "were befallen by a powerful spiritual emotion" at the same time, and then occurred a *Bezeugung* through both *Werkzeuge* in which they spoke alternately. Under the date of January 12, 1819, a testimony of this nature is recorded as having been given through Michael Krausert and Barbara Heinemann at the home of one of the Brethren. It reads in part as follows:

Barbara Heinemann: Well then oh souls! Michael Krausert: Arm yourself for the battle and be faithful unto death; follow Jesus Christ in truth and make a path in your hearts. Barbara Heinemann: And take no offence at the raging and raving of Satan, but wander on without delay and hesitancy or considering this or that; nay, follow unwaveringly the narrow path after your Savior, then He will be in and with you and His strength shall invigorate you, that no enemy can harm your soul, but that everything shall increase your strength and perseverance, if you receive it in the right spirit. Michael Krausert: Yes, the mighty prince of victory, Jesus Christ, has everything in His power, how soon may He not come forth as a strong support and destroy all ungodliness. Barbara Heinemann: Yes, yes, I will come forth, says the Eternal Son, Jesus Christ, from within and without, and I will assail the wicked men who want to hinder the progress of the divine work of mercy. [182]

The contents of the *Bezeugungen* vary from admonitions to live a holier life to explicit directions for the buying of machinery; but by far the larger number are of the former order. There are numerous promises of the "love of the great Father-heart" for "the truly pious and faithful souls." There are numerous appeals to the "God of Salvation" to "remove everything which has brought offence" and "to seek to till a new spiritual field, break the sod of the hard and thick self-will and self-righteousness and drive away the great wild monster called dissension." [183] There are warnings, often in the severest language, against *Leichtsinn,* lukewarmness, and ungodly pride, and threats of the wrath of God for those who persist in acting *selbstständig* and *eigenmächtig* in His presence. There are appeals to the Elders "to work upon a deeper foundation, to learn better to understand the Lord from within, and to give more heed to His immediate advice and guidance." There are vigorous denunciations of "those who do not enter upon repentance concerning the state of their souls."

The later testimonies of Barbara Heinemann are full of threats of "the hellish torture" and of "Satan's open door to the gloomy abyss." There is much "grieving of the Spirit of the King of all below and above" over the "wavering" of the young people, those whom "the *Schlange* and *Schlangenbrut* have assailed with the spirit of doubt and unbelief," and those who "through lack of watchfulness have allowed the tempter to sneak in." And many accounts are given of "how dearly lost grace has to be paid for."[184]

Humility, obedience, and self-negation are continually emphasized in the *Bezeugungen* old and new; and many assurances are made of the "glory and adornment, the blessed peace and rest of the Spirit" for those who "act not according to their own inclinations" but "as the Lord directs."[185]

Eternal vigilance that the enemy may not enter seeking whom he may devour"; a firm battle against "selfish and private purposes"; against "the flesh and its lusts"; against the world and the devil''—these have been the key-notes of the *Bezeugungen* from the beginning. ''Be earnest and brave and be ever on your guard'', said Christian Metz at the very beginning of his service as *Werkzeug.* ''Drive the enemy on all sides off the field and keep close watch that Satan be deprived of all advantage. Battle and fight firmly and see how the eternal friend of souls can pardon sinners and fit them for His service, how He can arm them with strength and power, yes even impart to them His spirit which can teach and refresh them with the dew of heaven.''[186]

The *Bezeugungen* were not always addressed to the general congregation but often to individual members after the manner of the personal criticisms of the Oneida Society and the Perfectionists. They were often cruelly severe, from the standpoint of the worldly; but were given in all love to bring the erring Brother or Sister to a proper state of humiliation and repentance.

The manner of accepting ''the judgment of the Lord'' thus delivered indicated the amount of grace possessed by the one reproached and punished. If ''he found sufficient grace to acknowledge the judgment of God concerning him as just, to submit to it and humble himself, and to confess his fault and guilt openly before the Community'' he was joyfully ''granted pardon and peace''; but if he had "seated himseif so high in his conceit that he neither could nor would find the grace for submission and humiliation" then "the Lord against whom he wished to contend proved to be too powerful for him."

A typical instance of "open humiliation before God and the Community" is the case of a leading Brother who was severely reproached and punished by the Lord for treating unkindly His handmaid, Barbara Heinemann (who seems to have had as much difficulty in getting along with the Elders after the return of her gift as before). It illustrates beautifully the spirit of humiliation before the will of God and the heed of brotherly admonition and punishment which have ever been the guiding forces in the Community of True Inspiration.

My sin is great and I have fully deserved the severe but just judgment of God which has come upon me; nay, I even thank God from the bottom of my heart that I was cast down from the height of self-will, whither I had gotten unconsciously, and that I have again been admonished to humility and lowliness of heart. My grief is great, may the honest tears of remorse which I have shed reconcile the Lord that before and with Him I may again find pardon and peace, as also in your sight, beloved Brother [Christian Metz], for I have caused you to suffer much, and also the beloved Sister [Barbara Heinemann] who may forgive me all offences and insults which I have inflicted upon her in the pride of my heart; and may the dear Brethren also pardon and forgive me, and retain no rancor against me.

There is much of the philosophy of Job running through the *Bezeugungen,* and ever an absolute faith in the Lord's "saving and protecting hand of grace." Death, misfortune, sorrow, and suffering are permitted by the Lord "as a severe warning" to the Community; "to humble and lower the *selbstständige und eigenmächtige*"; to arouse the religious fervor of the lukewarm; and in general to maintain the high standards that have from time to time been set for the Congregations of the Lord. "The Spirit of God", said Barbara Heinemann under Inspiration, "has a sharp knife; nay, a two-edged sword, wherewith He cuts off all that is ungodly."

On the occasion of the sudden death of a young girl, the Community was told through "the Spirit of Grace" that "it grieves Me to have permitted it; but I can not find entrance in any other manner except by sending the angel of death here and there. Would that thou wouldst heed it and mightest divine what is threatening that still in timely season thou mightest begin to fear and repent before the second beat of the knocker sounds." [187]

When in 1871 an unprincipled individual made an attempt to extort a certain sum of money from the Community by means of blackmail, it is recorded that "aside from all other considerations, the fact that the Lord had permitted such a wicked man to go thus far was a most serious warning to the Community that it might come to consider what would result if the Lord should permit hostile people to gain power and control over the Community." It was plainly the "intention of God that the Community was to be aroused and to search and acknowledge its faithlessness to God and humble and lower itself before Him, as it behooves the faithful and as they have ever done . . . . At the same time the Lord directed that the religious instruction of the children *(Kinderlehre)* be again held to earnestly warn the *freche* youth lest the Lord would stretch out his hand over them and send the destroyer." [188]

When Barbara Heinemann "suffered severe condemnation and banishment together with inward trouble and desolation" in 1819 through the instrumentality of the "overbearing" First Elder and "the other Brothers who had also incurred guilt through their dumb submission to his despotic decree", it is recorded that "all this did not befall her without the wise consent of God for a deeper knowledge of her own self, and for a more thorough grounding and founding in her divine calling." [189]

Under the date of November 21, 1853, there is recorded the death of a young man which seems to have been regarded in an exceptional light. The young man was crushed while alone in the mill at

Nieder Ebenezer; and the historian Gottlieb Scheuner records that "it caused great terror and fear that the Lord had permitted this. He was a loyal, young single Brother, who had come to the Community in 1846 and was not quite thirty-two years old at the time of his death." The Lord expressed His sorrow in these words: "The bloody avenger had seized his victim while not watching."[190]

The one supreme object of "the pilgrimage on earth" in the Amana theology is the salvation of the soul. The Community is but a school of preparation for the next world, and the awful fate, after death, of the soul that has not been thoroughly purified and sanctified during its earthly sojourn is best described in an old *Bezeugung* as follows:

> Such souls will wander in pathless desolation; they shall seek and not find; they will have to endure much torment and grief and be wretchedly plagued, tortured, and tormented by misleading stars.[191]

VIII

THE TESTIMONIES OF BARBARA HEINEMANN AND CHRISTIAN METZ

Barbara Heinemann was quick to condemn an erring Brother and to announce rules and regulations "through which arose many temptations, offences, and provocations." Christian Metz, on the other hand, was always the great pacificator in the Community, and felt obliged ever and anon to rebuke gently "the elder Sister" for her "human severity and arbitrariness" [192] which grew upon her with advancing years. "According to my feeling and opinion", said Christian Metz in his *Tagebuch* after the return of Barbara Heinemann's gift, "she shall have still to undergo a deep and more complete spiritual rebirth . . . . For it is indeed true that we achieve nothing through our own will, effort, endeavor, and toil; nay, it is born amidst anxiety and the complete annihilation of self."

Barbara Heinemann's earlier *Bezeugungen,* uttered before the time of her marriage and subsequent fall from grace, breathe a somewhat deeper spirituality. When she was scarcely nineteen years of age the "Lord urgently admonished her and all allied, especially the called workers, to preserve to themselves the deepest humility and self-negation in spite of what the Lord had hitherto accomplished in and through them, and not to become weakened through human considerations."[193] "Give heed and test yourself", said Barbara Heinemann in an early testimony, "that you fall not into ways of your own, for even the greatest and wisest one must often let himself be taught by the most lowly."

The phraseology of the early *Bezeugungen* of Barbara Heinemann is largely that of the Old Testament, which is but natural as it was the instrument through which she learned to read and write. The following *Bezeugung*, given as an important instruction to a group of the First Brethren, is typical:

Go confidently with great repose and in whole-hearted trust, for the almighty protector is everywhere, and will and shall everywhere be with you. For I will close the jaws of the lions, though they show their teeth. I shall satiate them with sheer miracles, that they shall astonish and everyone must say: Now we see that it is the living One and the all powerful who is with you. But see to it that ye do not become of little faith when the tempests and the billows of trial and temptation surge around your craft. Only believe firmly, though the storms press your ship ever so hard, that the help of the Lord is ever with and amongst you. Only hold the mouth of your faith to the hidden force, thence you will draw sufficient strength to endure to the end; for the enduring ones, though they shall pass through many sufferings and trials shall in the end inherit the kingdom of heaven; but a lasting and enduring faith is required. This shall be given you as a staff on your journey on which you ever can repose and rely.[194]

The testimonies of Christian Metz were throughout much freer from personalities than were those of "the elder Sister"; and even where he was obliged "by the promptings of the Spirit of Mercy" to give a testimony as a personal admonition to a member there was in it all a beauty and a dignity that even the offender must have recognized. When Michael Krausert "became timid and undecided and ran, so to speak, before he was chased", Christian Metz was obliged "by a special inner prompting" to give a testimony as a warning to him. This testimony, which is here quoted in part, illustrates the style of the greater part of his *Bezeugungen* which are recorded in the *Jahrbücher*.

Thus speaks the eternal God: I will give a word of testimony to my servant Krausert, who knows not now what to begin, so bewildered is he. But listen, then, what has prompted you to act and deal thus according to your own inclinations? You run before you were sent away, says the almighty God of Love. Alas, how troubled is my spirit, that you have failed thus, and do not want to be found again! Oh come back again and resign yourself in and to the faithful tie of Brotherhood which I have established, and which I have again strengthened through you. You run about thus and are like a hireling who has seen the wolf and has abandoned to him his flock and deserted. Is this the true faithfulness of the shepherd? Do faithful servants act thus, when the wolf comes that they run away and do not step into the gap to ward off harm? . . . . Can you then say that I have deserted you a single time when you were persecuted for holy causes alone? Have I not ever helped you again and satisfied you? . . . . Listen then what the God of Eternal Love furthermore testifies in regard to you: You were then not as faithful in your office and service as you were, and you do not sufficiently submit yourself in and to My will. You have become too self-willed, and you do not want to heed the others, whom, too, I have summoned and through whom I instruct you. Alas I do not wish to make known and have recorded all that I have to record against you, says the mighty God. But, nevertheless, you shall never succeed in this manner if you do not soon and quickly return again in and to the training of My love and more carefully tend to My flock than at present. Oh, I still love you and see you in your erring state. Return, then, and care more diligently for the souls whom I have called.

Indeed I shall help and always have helped you! Why then do you lose courage now and desert ere you were sent away? Has it ever been heard that My witnesses whom I have called from time to time have not also thus believed that they know no fear? And though the whole world should rise and appear in the field against them, and they themselves should be so weak that they could hardly stand on their feet, I will still be their God and their mighty protector, if they trust me in all things. Thus you may see that I take no pleasure at all in your present course of action.

Alas, My soul is troubled, that the wild beasts have broken in, in such number. Will you then, too, turn a hireling and scatter the sheep, which I so miraculously have led together? says the mighty God. Alas, return then again and lead them on as a faithful servant and shepherd; with the staff of the true love of the shepherd seize firmly upon faith, then I will assist you again and give back again the inward peace, love, and simplicity. Submit cheerfully to this punishment, for it is My will that it may become known thus that no mortal may boast of his importance. [195]

IX

THE PRESERVATION AND PUBLICATION OF THE TESTIMONIES AND RECORDS OF THE COMMUNITY

The testimonies, or *Bezeugungen des Geistes des Herrn,* with their exhortations, warnings, reproofs, admonitions, and prophecies, were from the time of Rock and Gruber "correctly written down from day to day in weal or woe", usually by specially appointed Scribes (See above Part I, p. 23).

From the rise of the New Spiritual Economy to the death of Johann Friedrich Rock in 1749 the many *Zeugnisse* which were uttered through the *Werkzeuge* were not only recorded in manuscripts and preserved in such collections as the *Diarium* and the *Tagebücher* of the Congregations of True Inspiration, but a large number of these important revelations were published in *Sammlungen,* of which there are forty-two printed volumes. However, not all of the *Zeugnisse* of this period have been printed; for an examination of the manuscripts in the *Archiv* at Middle Amana reveals the fact that many of the older testimonies, especially those of Johann Friedrich Rock, remain to this day unpublished.

[Facsimile of the title-page of a volume containing extracts from a *Diarium*]

J. J. J.

Fortgesetzte aufrichtige

EXTRACTA,

Aus dem allgemeinen Diario

Der wahren

INSPIRATIONS-

Gemeinden,

Im

Ysenburgischen/

De Anno 1734, 5, 6, 7, und 1738.

dem geneigten und abgeneigten/ glaubigen

und unglaubigen

Leser/

Zum Spiegel und Stachel, ans Licht gestellt,

Mit GOTT.

Hiob XII, 4. 5.

Der Gerechte und Fromme muß verlachet seyn. Und ist ein verachtetes Lichtlein vor den Gedancken der Stoltzen; Stehet aber/ daß sie sich daran argern.

ANNO 1738.

During the Decline (1749-1817) no testimonies were recorded since there were no *Inspirations-Werkzeuge.* The Congregations were content with the reading and rereading of the old *Zeugnisse* — especially those of Rock and Gruber. But with the Reawakening in 1817 and the appearance of *neue Propheten* in the New Community the Spirit of the Lord was again revealed through testimonies which have been reverently recorded and published in *Jahrbücher* of which there are fifty-eight *Sammlungen* covering the period from 1823 to 1883.

In the Yearbooks, which are uniformly entitled *Jahrbücher der wahren Inspirations-Gemeinden oder Bezeugungen des Geistes des Herrn,* each testimony or *Bezeugung* is not only numbered but is usually introduced by a paragraph setting forth the circumstances under which it was given. The following are typical introductions:

[From the twentieth *Sammlung*]

No. 54. Nieder Ebenezer, October 12, 1845. Sunday afternoon in the meeting of the Sisters, Brother Christian Metz fell into Inspiration while an old testimony was being read, and he had to utter the following testimony from the Lord to the members of this meeting.

[From the thirtieth *Sammlung*]

No. 5. Mittel Eben-Ezer. February 4, 1855. Sunday afternoon in the *Brüderversammlung* at the close of the first hymn (*Erneure mich, o ewigs Licht*) Br. Christian Metz fell into Inspiration and there occurred this important testimony of the Spirit of the Lord: first concerning directions of a *Liebesmahl*, then concerning the Elders and Community at Nieder Ebenezer, the whole Community, and also concerning those present and a few in particular.

[From the fifty-fourth *Sammlung*]

No. 27. West Amana, October 12, 1879. In the afternoon after the general meeting Sister Barbara Landmann fell into Inspiration, and thereby occurred the following severe rebuke and punishment owing to the manner in which the opening hymn was sung, in which notes and voices stood out above the rest, which caused a withdrawal of the divine grace and despoiled us (the Community) of the intended blessing. [196]

It would be strange, indeed, if in the Community of True Inspiration "demons of doubt and unbelief" had not at times caused the Elders of the Community to "suffer grief and oppression." Indeed, we are told that sometimes an individual would "rise up high in the air and investigate everything", in spite of the fact "that it is written that much knowledge is not needed for salvation." And once, it is recorded, "there arose worldly-wise and self-willed people who interfered with the divine guidance and criticised the word and the work of the Lord, whereby the Lord was greatly offended, so that he testified sternly against it and also prohibited the reading of the recent testimonies for the time being." [197]

At the time of Krausert's desertion there occurred at Ronneburg, through the "presumptuousness'' of the Head Elder, an examination of books and manuscripts with a view to the condemnation and destruction of the *Bezeugungen* of Krausert ''since he had gone astray and did not endure.'' Indeed, this ''*selbstständige und eigenmächtige*'' Elder, who had from the first opposed the leadership of Barbara Heinemann, took this occasion also to condemn her early utterances, since they were given largely under the influence of Krausert.

In her *Kurze Erzählung von den Erweckungs-Umständen* Barbara Heinemann relates that ''because Krausert had not persisted in the good and because his later utterances were not purely divine but intermingled with his own spirit . . . . [the Head Elder] found it well to give to the flames all testimonies which had hitherto occurred through him and me. With this I could not agree, and asked that a distinction should be made. But he replied, that the One who had given these testimonies could also again inspire others, and it could do no harm to burn up all. Thus those testimonies were burned. In how far this was wrong I dare not judge, but leave the decision to the Lord.'' [198] The Community historian, Gottlieb Scheuner, regrets that since the Head Elder ''went so far in this examination and scrutiny it is difficult to establish the exact succession of the events of that period.'' [199]

The lovable Christian Metz, who in his spirituality had risen far above the pettiness of personal likes and dislikes, ever encouraged the recording, collecting, and preserving of all of the testimonies "since they all contained some truth." Furthermore, he encouraged the reading of these and all other records of the Community. As late as November 1, 1846, the Lord gave directions through Christian Metz "not to allow the destruction of the writings of the old, that is, of the founders and faithful followers of the first Community of True Inspiration."

"Behold the work of the old, who no longer are", reads this testimony, "they have bequeathed unto you a treasure, which is still a blessing: but it is being forgotten and lies for the most part in the nooks and corners; much is being lost, is already lost, and you no longer have it. Listen to the counsel and will of Divine Love: Let nothing be lost, but induce your youth that they renew and rewrite it, especially what is not printed, for a profitable pastime. Bring the blessed past into good order and safe keeping."

At the same time (1846) "this word went forth to Brother Christian Metz: Thou, child of man, let not be lost along with other things that which the Lord has done in your days, but bequeath it likewise, as a memory, treasure, and blessing."

Whereupon Brother Christian Metz wrote his *Historische Beschreibung der Wahren Inspirations-Gemeinschaft* which was published as a supplement to the twentieth *Sammlung*. This *Beschreibung* is a brief account (189 pages) of the Community "as it has existed and continued from the year 1714 to the year 1845." After the establishment of the new home at Ebenezer, Christian Metz kept a diary with great faithfulness and precision. This practice he continued until the year before his death, when he made this last entry:

Ich kann nun nichts mehr schreiben
Mein Reimenspiel ist aus —[200]

The *Tagebücher* of Christian Metz are more than a chronological account of the Community's happenings. They are full of his own philosophy of life, of hopes and plans for the future of the Community, and of deeply devotional exhortations. Here too are found many of his more beautiful poems and songs written (often under the Spirit of Inspiration) on the occasion of some important happening to "point a moral or adorn a tale." From these *Tagebücher* Christian Metz made extracts "containing the most important things which have happened to the *Werkzeug* himself, as also in and to the Community." These were "arranged and collected", edited, and supplemented by his loving Scribe and co-worker, Gottlieb Scheuner, as

rape trellis and swing— 1890s

Arnsburg den 6ten Juli 1841 –
von C Metz

Wenn Gottes Gnaden Quell das Herz aufschliesst
so fleusst es aus von seiner reinen Liebe
die andern Seelen [illegible]
dass sie auch suchen solche Triebe
o finstres Herz schau diesen Adel an
den nur dein Jesu dir allein geben kann

2

was hindert aber Gottes reines Licht
dass es das finstre Herz nicht kann erleuchten
der Glaube ist o Seele daran liegt
der muss in Liebes Kraft das Herz befeuchten
o finstres Herz ergieb dich deshalben
die Gottes Lieb lass deinen Adel sein

a "continuation of the *Historische Beschreibung* contained in the twentieth *Sammlung*."

To the faithful Scribe, Gottlieb Scheuner, quite as much as to the *Werkzeug*, Christian Metz, the Community is indebted for the bringing together of the "work of the old, who no longer are." He was only thirty years of age at the time of Christian Metz's death; and was spared to the Community for thirty years more. During that time he devoted his energy and his talents to carrying out, in so far as he was able, the plans formulated by Christian Metz. He searched the Community for manuscripts and documents; he recorded accounts "orally related" by the still living witnesses; he wrote many poems and hymns; and he bequeathed all, including *Inspirations-Historie,* to the Community as a "treasure and a blessing" in the spirit of the *Werkzeug* who was "recalled from the field of his endeavor" before the fulfilment of his plans could be accomplished.[201]

FAC SIMILE OF TWO VERSES OF AN ORIGINAL MANUSCRIPT POEM IN THE HANDWRITING OF THE *Werkzeug*, CHRISTIAN METZ

X

THE BASIS OF FAITH

The Community of True Inspiration has never regarded itself as a distinct religious sect in any partisan sense; nor has it ever acknowledged any basis of faith other than the literal word of God as contained in the Scriptures and in *Bezeugungen.* In truth at the very beginning of "this spiritual husbandry" one of the arguments set forth for the divine origin of Inspiration was the fact that the "inspired ones reject all sects and point to Jesus Christ alone as the living foundation."

Since the Inspirationists believe that the Lord has ever revealed his will directly to them and "gives to-day as he did yesterday the same assurance through which the prophets and apostles were certain that the Spirit of God spoke through them and urged them on", a rigid orthodox creed would be contrary to the theory and spirit of True Inspiration. "I will reveal myself ever more powerfully, holier, and more glorious . . . . in and among you", reads the early promise of the Lord, "as long as you will bring forth to meet me the honest and sincere powers of your will." To keep this covenant "faithfully and sacredly" has been of more consequence to the Community than the formulation of a church creed.

Although the Community of True Inspiration can not, therefore, be said to profess a creed in the orthodox sense of the word there are three documents which may properly be regarded as statements or bases of Community faith. These are: (1) *Der Glauben;* (2) The Twenty-four Rules of True Godliness; and (3) The Twenty-one Rules for the Examination of our Daily Lives. The Ten Commandments and the Lord's Prayer are also taught in the schools and repeated at the religious services of the Community.

Der Glauben, which is prayed in the religious services and in the schools, is substantially the Apostles' Creed as used in the orthodox evangelical churches of the world. It is given in the Community Catechism under the title of *Die Artikel des christlichen Glaubens.*

Ich glaube an Gott Vater, den allmächtigen Schöpfer Himmels und der Erden.

Und an Jesum Christum, Seinen eingebornen Sohn, unsern Herrn, der empfangen ist von dem heiligen Geist, geboren von der Jungfrau Maria, gelitten unter Pontio Pilato, gekreuziget, gestorben und begraben, abgestiegen zur Hölle, am dritten Tage wieder auferstanden von den Toten, aufgefahren gen Himmel, da sitzet Er zur Rechten Gottes, des allmächtigen Vaters, von dannen Er kommen wird, zu richten die Lebendigen und die Toten.

Ich glaube an den heiligen Geist, eine allgemeine christliche Kirche und Gemeinschaft der Heiligen, Vergebung der Sünden, Auferstehung des Leibes, und ein ewiges Leben. Amen.

XI

TWENTY-FOUR RULES FOR TRUE GODLINESS

The "living foundations" of the Community are the "Twenty-four Rules for True Godliness and Holy Conduct", which were received by the Community as a "most important revelation of the Spirit of the Lord through Johann Adam Gruber" at Büdingen on July 4, 1716, and in accordance with which the New Communities were established and received into "the gracious covenant of the Lord." Nor have these rules with their directions, warnings, and admonitions lost any of their force or authority in the nearly two hundred years that have elapsed since they were regarded as such a menace to the established church that copies of them were gathered by the civil authorities and ordered "publicly burned by the executioner." [202] They remain the basis of the faith of the Community, and are, indeed, the foundation on which the whole religious edifice of the Community is erected.

The Twenty-four Rules for True Godliness are part of a lengthy *Bezeugung* in which the Community is commanded by the Lord to renew the covenant "before My holy face and in the presence of My holy angels and of the members of your Community'' and ''once more avow openly with hand and mouth to My servant, the Elder, given unto you, what I shall speak unto you and also what you have promised with words and in your heart.'' These holy commands were given ''for careful regard and sincere observation'', with threats of ''a fiery and heavy burden . . . . as a quick witness . . . . if you break this vow.''

The concluding paragraph of the admonitory introduction and the Twenty-four Rules for True Godliness and Holy Conduct are as follows:[203]

Hear then what I say unto you. I, the Lord your God am holy! And therefore you, too, shall be and become a holy Community, if I am to abide in your midst as you desire. And therefore you shall henceforth resolve:

I. To tear all crude and all subtle idols out of your hearts, that they may no longer befool you and mislead you further to idolatry against your God, so that His name be not defamed and He not suddenly go forth and avenge and save the glory of His name.

II. I desire that you shall have naught in common with the fruitless works of darkness; neither with grave sins and sinners, nor with the subtle within and without you. For what relationship and likeness has My holy temple with the temples of pride, unchasteness, ambition, seeking for power; and of the useless, superfluous, condemning prattling, which steals the time away from Me. How could the light unite with the darkness? How can you as children of the light unite with the ungodly, the liars and their works, the scoffers and blasphemers, who are nothing but darkness?

FAC SIMILE (WITHOUT REDUCTION) OF THE HANDWRITING AND AUTOGRAPH OF THE *Werkzeug*, JOHANN ADAM GRUBER. TAKEN FROM A LETTER ADDRESSED TO BROTHER NAGEL

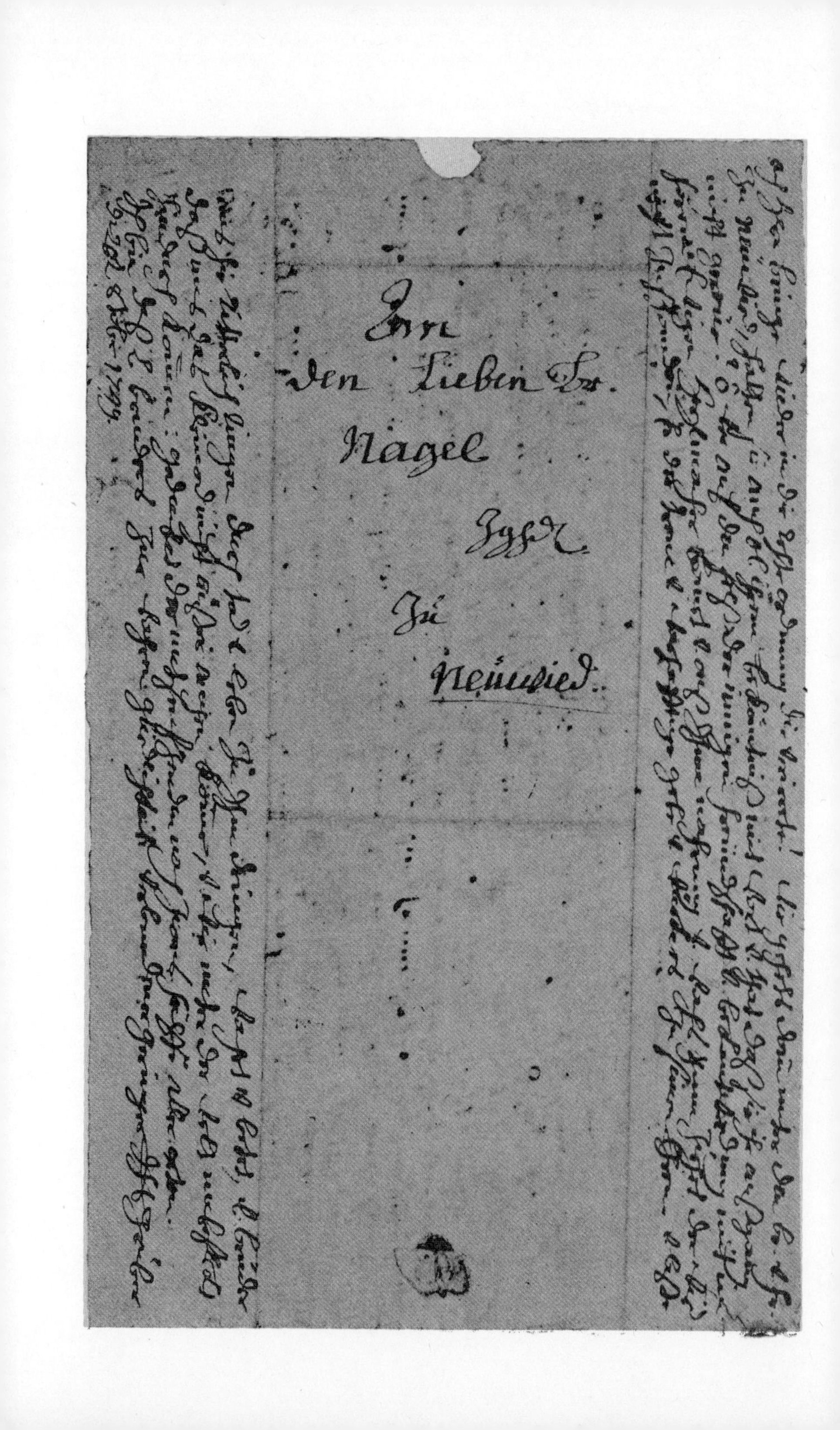

Ahn

den Lieben Br.

Nagel

Eyßer

zu

Neuwied.

III. You shall henceforth in your external life conduct yourself so that those standing without find no longer cause for ill reports and for defaming My name. Suffer rather the wrong if you are abused. But above all flee from associations which hinder you from growing in godliness. All mockers and scoffers and those who recommend you unto vanity, you shall shun and have no dealings with them.

IV. You shall also perform your earthly task the longer the more according to the dictates of your conscience; and gladly desist from that which My spirit shows you to be sinful — not heeding your own loss, for I am the Lord, who can and will care and provide for the needs of your body — that through this you may not give cause for censure to the scoffer. The time which I still grant you here is very short; therefore, see to it well that My hand may bring forth and create within you a real harvest.

V. Let, I warn you, be far from you all falseness, lying, and hypocrisy. For I say unto you that I will give the spirit of discernment and will lay open unto you through the Spirit of Prophecy such vices. For to what end shall clay and metal be together? Would it not make for Me a useless vessel, which I could not use and should have to cast away with the rest. Behold, My children, I have chosen before many, many, many, and have promised to be unto you a fiery entrenchment against the defiance of your inner and outer enemies. Verily! Verily! I shall keep my promises, if only you endeavor to fulfil what you have promised and are promising.

VI. You shall therefore, none of you, strive for particular gifts and envy the one or the other to whom I give perchance the gift of prayer or maybe of wisdom. For such the enemy of My glory seeks ever to instill into you, especially into the passionate and fickle souls, to impart to you thereby a poison destructive to the soul. You shall, all, all, all of you be filled with My pure and holy spirit when the time will come to pass, if you will let yourself be prepared in humility and patience according to My will. Then you too shall speak with tongues different from the tongues you now speak with. Then I shall be able to communicate with you most intimately.

VII. Put aside henceforth all backbiting, and all malice of the heart toward each other, which you have harbored hitherto! None of you are free from it!

Behold I shall command the Spirit of my Love that He as often as you assemble in true simplicity of heart and in humility for prayer be in your very midst with His influence and may flow through the channels of His Love into the hearts He finds empty.

VIII. You must make yourself willing for all outer and inner suffering. For Belial will not cease to show unto you his rancor through his servants and through his invisible power. It is also pleasing to Me and absolutely necessary for you that you be tried through continuous sorrow, suffering, and cross, and be made firm and precious in My crucible. And he who does not dare (but none must be indolent himself in this) to exert all his physical and spiritual powers through My strength, let him depart that he may not be later a blemishing spot upon My glory.

IX. Do not lend in future your ears to suspicion and prejudice and take, because of your lack of self-knowledge, offence at each other where there is none. But each one among you shall become the mirror for the other. You shall, moreover, also endeavor to stand every day and hour before the Lord as a oneness, as a city or a light on a high mountain, which near and far shines bright and pure.

X. At the same time practice the longer the more outer and inner quiet. Seek ever, though it will be for the natural man which is inexperienced in this a hard death, to hide yourself in humility in the inner and undermost chamber of your nothingness, that I may bring in this soil to a befitting growth My seed which I have concealed therein.

XI. Behold, My people! I make with you this day a covenant which I bid you to keep faithfully and sacredly. I will daily wander amongst you and visit your place of rest, that I may see how you are disposed toward Me.

XII. Guard yourself. I, the Lord, warn you against indifference towards this covenant of grace and against negligence, indolence, and laziness which thus far have been for the most part your ruler and have controlled your heart. I shall not depart from your side nor from your midst, but shall Myself on the contrary reveal Myself ever more powerfully, holier, and more glorious through the light of My face in and among you, as long as you will bring forth to meet Me the honest and sincere powers of your will. This shall be the tie with which you can bind and hold Me. Behold I accept you this day as slaves of My will, as free-borns of My kingdom, as possessors of My heart! Therefore let yourself gladly and willingly be bound with the ties of My love, and the power of love shall never be wanting unto you.

XIII. And you who are the heads and fathers of households hear what I say unto you: The Lord has now chosen you as members of His Community with whom He desires to associate and dwell day by day. See, therefore, to this that you prove truly heads and lights of your households, which, however, always stand under their faithful head, your King; see that you may bring your helpmates to true conduct and fear of God through your own way of living, which you shall strive to make ever more faultless, more earnest and manly.

XIV. Your children, you who have any, you shall endeavor with all your power to sacrifice to Me and to lead to Me. I shall give you in abundance, if you only inwardly keep close to Me, wisdom, courage, understanding, bravery, and earnestness mingled with love, that you yourself may be able to live before them in the fear of God and that your training may be blessed — that is, in those who want to submit to My hand in and through Me. But those who scorn you and do not heed my voice in and through you and otherwise, shall have their blood come upon their own heads. But you shall never abandon hope but wrestle for them with earnest prayer, struggle, and toil, which are the pangs of spiritual birth. But if you neglect them through indifference, negligence, half-heartedness, and laziness, then every such soul shall verily be demanded of such a father.

XV. Do now your part as I command you from without and frequently inwardly through My Spirit; do not desist, just as I never cease to work on you my disobedient children; then you will abide in my grace and save your souls. And such women and children shall bear the fruits of their sins as do not want to bow themselves under you and Me. I will henceforth no longer tolerate those grave offences among you and in your houses about which the world and the children of wrath and disbelief have so much to say; but I have commanded the Spirit of My living breath, that He pass through all your houses and breathe upon every soul which does not wantonly close itself to Him. The dew of blessing shall flow from the blessed head of your high priest and prince of peace upon every male head among you, and through them it shall flow upon and into your help-mates, and through both man and wife into the offspring and children, so that all your seed shall be acceptable, pure, and holy before the Lord, since He has nourished and will nourish the same among you.

XVI. And none of your grown up children shall be permitted to attend your meetings, who have not previously received from their parents a good testimony according to the truth, not appearance, and without self-deception, as also from the Elders and leaders especially from the one who with his fellow workers has to watch over the training of the children, which is to be carried on with earnestness and love, but without all severity and harshness. This training is to be watched over with all earnestness; and should the parents be negligent and the case require it, so shall the latter be temporarily excluded [from the prayer-meetings] for their humiliation.

XVII. Prove yourselves as the people whom I have established for an eternal monument to Me, and whom I shall impress upon My heart as an eternal seal, so that the Spirit of My love may dwell upon you and within you, and work according to His desire.

XVIII. And this is the word which the Lord speaks of these strangers who so often visit you and cause so much disturbance: None, whom you find to be a scoffer, hypocrite, mocker, sneerer, derider, and unrepenting sinner, shall you admit to your Community and prayer-meetings. Once for all they are to be excluded that my refreshing dew and the shadow of My Love be never prevented from manifesting themselves among you. But if some should come to you with honest intentions who are not knowingly scoffers, hypocrites, and deriders, though it be one of those whom you call of the world, if he to your knowledge does not come with deceitful intentions, then you may well admit him. I shall give you My faithful servants and witnesses especially the spirit of discrimination and give you an exact feeling, whether they are sincere and come with honest intentions or otherwise.

XIX. If they then desire to visit you more frequently, you shall first acquaint them with your rules and ask them whether they will submit to these rules and to the test of the Elders. And then you shall read to them My laws and commands, which I give unto you; and if you see that they are earnestly concerned about their souls, then you shall gladly receive the weak, and become weak with them for a while, that is, you shall with them and for them repent and make their repentance your own. But if a scoffer or mocker declares that he repents, him you should only admit after considerable time and close scrutiny and examination of his conduct, if you find the latter to be righteous. For Satan will not cease to try to launch at you his fatal arrows through such people. Be therefore on your guard and watch that not the wolf come among you and scatter or even devour the sheep.

XX. And those who pledge themselves with hand and mouth after the aforesaid manner to you shall make public profession before the Community and also make an open confession of their resolve, and I shall indeed show you if this latter comes from their hearts; the conduct of those you shall watch closely, whether they live according to their profession and promise or not, lest the dragon defile your garments with his drivel.

XXI. (To the Elders.) Thus My Elder and his fellow-workers shall frequently visit the members of the Community and see how things are in their homes and how it stands about their hearts. I shall give to you my servant (E. L. Gruber) and to your Brothers keen eyes, if you only pray for it. And if you find that one is in uncalled sadness, or lives in negligence, impudence, boisterousness, or the like, then you shall admonish him in love. If he repents you shall rejoice. But if after repeated admonition he does not mend his ways, then you shall put him to shame openly before the Community; and if even this does not help then you shall exclude him for a while. Yet I shall ever seek my sheep, those who are already excluded and those who in the future because of their own guilt must be excluded, and I shall ever try to lead them in their nothingness into my pasture.

XXII. And to all of you I still give this warning: Let none of you reject brotherly admonition and punishment, so that secret pride grows not like a poisonous thorn in such a member and torment and poison his whole heart.

XXIII. You shall not form a habit of anything of the external exercises [forms of worship] and the duties committed to you, or I shall be compelled to forbid them again; on the contrary, you shall make your meetings ever more fervent, more earnest, more zealous, in the true simple love towards each other, fervent and united in Me, the true Prince of Peace.

XXIV. This the members and brethren of the Community shall sincerely and honestly pledge with hand and mouth to my Elders, openly in the assembly, after they have carefully considered it, and it shall be kept sacred ever after.[204]

XII

TWENTY-ONE RULES FOR THE EXAMINATION OF OUR DAILY LIVES

In the year 1715 Eberhard Ludwig Gruber published the "Twenty-One Rules for the Examination of Our Daily Lives" for the benefit of his little band of followers. They constitute a fundamental ethical code rather than a basis of faith. At the same time they are an expression of the religious ideas of Pietism and True Inspiration. Having been handed down from generation to generation they still endure in the Community as an ideal standard of conduct for all those who in their daily lives strive to keep the faith of the *Urgrosseltern.*

I. Obey, without reasoning, God, and through God your superiors.

II. Study quiet, or serenity, within and without.

III. Within, to rule and master your thoughts.

IV. Without, to avoid all unnecessary words, and still to study silence and quiet.

V. Abandon self, with all its desires, knowledge and power.

VI. Do not criticise others, either for good or evil, neither to judge nor to imitate them; therefore contain yourself, remain at home, in the house and in your heart.

VII. Do not disturb your serenity or peace of mind — hence neither desire nor grieve.

VIII. Live in love and pity toward your neighbor, and indulge neither anger nor impatience in your spirit.

IX. Be honest, sincere, and avoid all deceit and even secretiveness.

X. Count every word, thought, and work as done in the immediate presence of God, in sleeping and waking, eating, drinking, etc., and give Him at once an account of it, to see if all is done in His fear and love.

XI. Be in all things sober, without levity or laughter; and without vain and idle words, works, or thoughts; much less heedless or idle.

XII. Never think or speak of God without the deepest reverence, fear, and love, and therefore deal reverently with all spiritual things.

XIII. Bear all inner and outward sufferings in silence, complaining only to God; and accept all from Him in deepest reverence and obedience.

XIV. Notice carefully all that God permits to happen to you in your inner and outward life, in order that you may not fail to comprehend His will and to be led by it.

XV. Have nothing to do with unholy and particularly with needless business affairs.

XVI. Have no intercourse with wordly-minded men; never seek their society; speak little with them, and never without need; and then not without fear and trembling.

XVII. Therefore, what you have to do with such men do in haste; do not waste time in public places and worldly society, that you be not tempted and led away.

XVIII. Fly from the society of women-kind as much as possible, as a very highly dangerous magnet and magical fire.

XIX. Avoid obeisance and the fear of men; these are dangerous ways.

XX. Dinners, weddings, feasts, avoid entirely; at the best there is sin.

XXI. Constantly practice abstinence and temperance, so that you may be as wakeful after eating as before.

XIII

THE SPIRITUAL ORDERS OR VERSAMMLUNGEN

Spiritually the members of the Community of True Inspiration (with the exception of the Elders who very naturally are in a class by themselves) are divided into three grades or orders (*Versammlungen*) which are in the main based upon age, the presumption being that the degree of piety increases with years of "sincere repentance and striving for salvation and deep humility of spirit." But unfortunately years do not always bring the requisite amount of "heart resurrection and grace", and therefore it remains for the Great Council of the Brethren at the time of the yearly spiritual examination (*Unterredung*) to "take out of the middle order here and there some who belong in the first, and out of the third order some who belong in the second, not according to favor and prejudice, but according to their grace and conduct."[205]

"My Elder and his fellow-workers", reads the divine law and command, "shall frequently visit the members of the Community and see how things are in their homes and how it stands about their hearts." To the "shepherds of souls" the same divine law promised at the very beginning of the

New Community "keen eyes, ... the spirit of discrimination, and an exact feeling" to ascertain the spiritual state of the members of the Community.

The *Versammlungen* were originally established through Inspiration; and during the lifetime of the *Werkzeuge* the placing of the members was made with "great accuracy"; for then indeed "the Spirit of Inspiration penetrated into and laid bare those things which occurred in the most hidden corners of the heart" and all grading was accomplished without "human consideration."

The *Versammlungen* are referred to as the First *Versammlung*, the Second or Middle *Versammlung*, and the Third or *Kinder Versammlung*. For convenience in conducting the *Unterredung* the *Versammlungen* are subdivided into *Abtheilungen,* the number of which varies according to the inhabitants of the village. Reduction from a higher to a lower *Versammlung* is one of the Community's methods of discipline. It is comparable to and quite as effective as the "setting back in meeting" of the Amish Mennonites. Indeed, every religious community has devised some similar "regulator"; and such punishment seems always to have been sorrow enough for all but the most hardened sinner. Marriage in the Community being still deemed a fall in spirituality, the newly married pair, though belonging to the highest order, are reduced to the lowest order and compelled to work up through deepening piety — the length of time required depending of course on the "amount of grace" of the parties.

XIV

THE SPIRITUAL EXAMINATION OR UNTERREDUNG

The practice of ascertaining the spiritual condition of the members of the Community by a yearly examination *(Unterredung* or *Untersuchung)* is an ancient ceremony which is still observed. "Confess your faults one to another", reads the *Epistle of James,* "and pray one for another that you may be healed. The effectual fervent prayer of a righteous man availeth much." It is upon this scriptural injunction that the spiritual examination of the Community of True Inspiration is based.

The *Unterredung* is searching and thorough, including every man, woman, and child in the entire settlement of seven villages. It is conducted by the First Brethren, who examine the members by orders, that is, by *Versammlungen.* The Elders of one village are examined in the presence of Elders from other villages. Each member when examined is expected to make "a public confession of his spiritual state"; and the Elders are admonished by divine command to watch closely their conduct to learn "whether they live according to their confession and promise." [206]

The burden of the *Unterredung* formerly fell largely upon the *Werkzeug.* For naturally none of his fellow-workers, however spiritual, were so well fitted to ascertain whether each and every member of the Community spoke the whole truth in his confession. Under the date of April 28, 1833, it is recorded that at a personal examination that was ordered (by the Lord) at the Haag "every member was examined by Brother Christian Metz."

All of the details regarding assistance for the *Werkzeug,* the manner of holding the *Unterredung,* and the character of the examination were formerly arranged through Inspiration. In the *Jahrbuch* for 1851, in one of the *Bezeugungen* of Barbara Heinemann, there are directions upon which were formulated the principle questions to be asked of each person at the time of the *Unterredung.* They follow closely the spirit of Gruber's questions of nearly a century and a half before and read:

I. Soul what is thy purpose? Why hast thou joined this Community? For what art thou longing and seeking?

II. How and in what manner hast thou recognized and found the work of mercy or of True Inspiration? In how far dost thou agree with the ways of sanctification and the testimonies through which I [the Lord] have hitherto led my servants and my Community?

III. Art thou agreed in matters internal and external with the grace of common possession and the ways and precepts thereof, not after the faults and disorders which creep in and intermingle through the weakness and disobedience of men, but after the sacred ordinances? And how art thou disposed to submit thy natural will and the inclination of thy heart henceforth to the workings of grace and spiritual training for the purification and sanctification of thy soul? [207]

The results of this personal examination were not always pleasing to the *Werkzeug;* and repeatedly "there occurred a most earnest and urgent word in which the Lord expressed His sorrow and grief over the retrogression and decay after the period of grace, and especially over the carelessness and the unconcerned mode of living of the young people and also of many older ones." [208]

Sometimes the "sorrow and grief of the Lord" was occasioned by the ungodliness of a particular individual who was admonished with great freedom for the good of his soul. "Self-will", said Barbara Heinemann under Inspiration to an *eigenmächtig* Brother, "is called one of the devils — and it will lead thee into hell . . . . it would have been better if thou hadst not deceived and hadst confessed and acknowledged that thou hadst acted foolishly, then the reproach against thee would have been removed." [209]

There is less in condemnation of particular sins and more in exhortation to holier living and to a more thorough consecration to God in the personal criticisms given through Christian Metz, as seen in this admonition to an erring Sister: "Oh, weep over your ill-spent squandered time! Esteem the grace of your God more highly and go out of yourself . . . . Strive for your salvation. Oh, make better use of your time; go forward with careful step and seek with tears for thy lost grace." To another Sister he says: "Oh that you were not given to the external and that your eyes were directed inward. Pray the Lord, the God of your salvation, pray with your whole heart and spirit, pray with fervent desire, pray with the whole power of your soul that He the mighty Creator may arouse you and create in you a new being." [210]

Sometimes the examination of a certain division was adjourned from day to day, owing to the fact that the *Werkzeug* was "oppressed and anxious" because the members "did not really possess the deep foundations and experience in divine things." [211]

"Oh ye souls", lamented Christian Metz in a *Bezeugung* on one occasion, "the salvation of God does not come unto you unless you hasten to meet it, that you may storm the kingdom of heaven, and that you may take the key of true knowledge, of pure grace, and unlock the door of the heart through prayer and beseeching, through sincere anxiety for your own and others' sake in order that the good may be accomplished and that the house of God may be built and that there be no scoffing of the enemy . . . Therefore give heed how you serve the Lord for his eyes look upon you."

There is in addition to the *Unterredung* (although in no way connected with it) a Conference of Elders, which is in a way a special examination of the spiritual condition of the Community and of the Elders themselves. This Conference is held every two years at Amana, and alternates with the *Liebesmahl.* It is regarded as one of the most important spiritual meetings in the Community; for at this time not only is the spiritual welfare of the Community most seriously considered, but the spiritual state of the Elders themselves is freely discussed and all their differences, disagreements, and misunderstandings frankly expressed and adjusted.

XV

THE LOVEFEAST OR LIEBESMAHL

The *Unterredung* with its attendant sanctification and purification is a preparation for the *Liebesmahl* (Lovefeast) or celebration of the Lord's Supper, which dates back as a Community observance to the beginning of the eighteenth century and which has always been the most solemn religious ceremony observed by the Community. At the present time it is held once in every two years; but during the ministration of the *Werkzeuge* it took place "not after human customs or decrees at stated times, but only after the will of the Lord has been revealed." [212]

When important testimonies occurred during the progress of the *Liebesmahl* a full account of them, including "how they are announced, ordered, and held by His word and witness", was printed in a separate volume and distributed in the manner of the *Bezeugungen*. The account of the *Liebesmahl* for 1855, appointed by the "gracious word and determination of the Lord through Brother Christian Metz", is prefaced in part with these words:

> The beginning and progress of it [the *Liebesmahl*] shall be like the previous one . . . . There will be

on this occasion humiliations and revelations . . . . You shall choose and appoint the day of Ascension as the opening of the first *Liebesmahl* [that is, of the first order], make ready then and cleanse all your hearts . . . . of all sin and everything idle and useless, and cherish pious thoughts, so that you shall put down the flesh as you are commanded.[213]

The *Liebesmahl* is observed by each *Versammlung* separately, beginning with the first and ending with the children. Moreover, the ceremony of foot-washing is observed at the *Liebesmahl,* but only by the highest spiritual orders. In this connection the thirteenth chapter of the Gospel according to St. John is read, and the Elder dwells at great length and with great impressiveness upon the lesson of humility taught by Jesus in the lowly service of foot-washing.

"After the necessary preparations had been made", runs an account of a *Liebesmahl* held at Ebenezer in 1844, "and the membership of the three Communities — Mittel, Nieder, and Ober Ebenezer — had been, according to the grades of the *Versammlungen,* divided into three *Abtheilungen* exclusive of the children, the first of these came, 158 souls in number, on Christmas Day at eight o'clock in the morning together in the hall at Mittel Ebenezer." Then follows a very complete account of the Lovefeast which lasted two days and ended with the ceremony of foot-washing. "On Sunday, December 29th, the second *Liebesmahl*, at Mittel Ebenezer, was celebrated to which the members of the second or middle *Versammlung*, 148 in number, gathered themselves.'' This Lovefeast, being of a lower spiritual grade, was a less elaborate affair than the first, lasted but one day, and was held without foot-washing. ''The third Lovefeast was held a week later, on Sunday, January 5, 1845, at Mittel Ebenezer, and some 130 souls came together . . . . Thus, this Lovefeast likewise became in its further progress a day of blessed grace, although it had been gloomy and oppressive at first . . . . On the following day a feast was spread to some fifty children.'' [214]

Every phase of the *Liebesmahl* is functionated with the same thoroughness which is exhibited by the Community in every detail of its organization. This is manifest in Gottlieb Scheuner's account of the appointments made for the *Liebesmahl* of 1868.

The entire membership, excluding the young people under fifteen, was divided into three classes according to the conviction and insight of the Brethren and the *Werkzeug* [Barbara Heinemann] [215] as to the spiritual state of the respective persons. Also the servants for the foot-washing, for the breaking of the bread and for the distribution of bread and wine, also those who were to wait at the supper as well as the singers and scribes had to be chosen and arranged . . . . The number of those who were to serve had to be determined in proportion to the great membership. Thus there were appointed for the foot-washing at the first Lovefeast 13 Brothers and 12 Sisters . . . . For the second Lovefeast likewise 13 Brothers and 14 Sisters from the first class . . . . For the breaking of the bread and the passing of the wine two times twelve Brethren were selected . . . . For the leading and the support of the singing 8 Brethren and 4 Sisters were chosen. Besides those many of the best singers among the Brethren and Sisters of their respective class were selected and joined to the leaders so that the whole choir consisted of 20, sometimes 22 persons, who in the afternoon during the meal had their place at a separate table in the middle of the hall. To write down the testimonies of the Lord those then being teachers at the different Communities were appointed.[216]

The period of the *Liebesmahl* is still a very solemn and important occasion; but in the days of the *Werkzeuge* it was preëminently a time of great religious fervor, since the Lord was sure on such holy occasions to reveal Himself to the Community; and so it behooved every individual to be spiritually prepared to receive "the divine message."

One of the most interesting accounts is that of the last *Liebesmahl* held in Armenburg just before the departure of the divinely appointed committee for the divinely directed journey to America "to prepare a new home in the wilderness and establish a dwelling where there was none." This account is given in full since it is typical and includes the ceremony of Renewing the Covenant:

The Elders of the Communities assembled for the announced discussion and for the Lovefeast and the farewell supper following it at Armenburg on August 27 . . . . It was an important day and one on which the Lord revealed himself to the Community as a whole as well as to all the individuals who were present singly. In the afternoon when the work was completed the Lord gave orders to hold the next morning, since it was on a Sunday, a general meeting for the whole community and to celebrate then in the afternoon the *Liebesmahl.* So all the Elders assembled again on Sunday afternoon when the Lord at once again sent His divine message while the hymn, *O heil'ger Geist, kehr bei uns ein,* was being sung. Among other things the message declared: "You shall again unite for life and death in the spirit of divine childhood according to the will of the three times holy God." And they [the Elders] were further admonished thus: "You shall now, one after the other, give Me your hand as a pledge of faith, quietly for an outward sign." They now passed the *Werkzeug* [Christian Metz] one by one and shook hands with him while he continued to speak: "Holy is My name and you shall be sanctified through it. Yes Amen! Thus you are baptized to be of one spirit through the one Spirit who is three-fold, that of the Father, the Son, and the Holy Ghost; and you are sprinkled with the blood of the new covenant. Oh, Jehovah is the God of your covenant, your Alpha and Omega, beginning, middle and end! . . . ." After this holy outpouring of mercy *(Gnadenausfluss)*, the hymn which had been begun was finished, while the *Werkzeug* and all present were lying prostrate with their faces to the ground. Then they prayed and after a short silence the foot-washing was held while they sang the hymn, *O Haupt voll Blut und Wunden.*

After this ceremony they sang the hymn *Die Seele Christi heil'ge mich* during which the *Werkzeug* was again inspired, when bread and wine were brought and blessed by the Lord. While these were passed and partaken of they sang again *Wohlauf, zum rechten Weinstock her* and the chapter on the foot-washing was read. Thereupon they partook, after a silent pause, of their supper and then sang *Wie wohl hast du gelabet,* and the *Werkzeug* was once more inspired and pronounced at the close of this holy and important act the song of praise which ended "Now I have anew joined this holy tie of love with you, receive it and preserve it each of you in your heart as a holy pledge. Let this be the conclusion: I give to each soul which clings to Me as a bridegroom a kiss of love. This pertains to the soul which possesses My grace and strives for it early and late. To all of the members I shall be a confidential lover, to each one individually and again to all as a whole in the true enjoyment of love." Then they closed this day of mercy and blessing with the hymn *Nichts soll mich von Jesu trennen.* [217]

XVI
THE COMMUNITY CATECHISM

The catechism published by the Community of True Inspiration is in two separate parts or volumes — one for the instruction of the younger children (*Jugend*), the other for the more mature youth (*für die Glieder*).[218] The former is similar to the catechisms of the orthodox Protestant churches of the world and contains, in addition to the usual questions and answers regarding the Father, the Son, the Holy Ghost, and the Ten Commandments, several chapters under the general title of *Denksprüche, zur Beherzigung für fromme Kinder,* the *Sittenregeln,* and *Das goldene A. B. C. eines frommen Kindes.* Much time and attention are given in the schools to this little volume, and most of its ninety-six pages are committed to memory.

The second volume of the catechism is also written in the form of questions and answers, but deals more with a discussion of the fundamental principles of the religion of the Community. It is divided in the main into three parts: *Die erste Oekonomie* deals with the time of the Prophets; *Die zweite Oekonomie* with the time of the Apostles; and *Die dritte Oekonomie* is entitled *Das Gnadenwerk der*

Inspiration and deals particularly with the unique doctrines of the Community with numerous references to the Old and New Testament by way of corroboration.

The imprint of the latest edition of the catechism is 1905; but the spirit of this *Catechetischer Unterricht von der Lehre des Heils* is the spirit of the "heroes of faith" who founded the New Spiritual Economy in the early part of the eighteenth century.

The following scattered quotations from *Das Gnadenwerk der Inspiration* set forth some of the fundamentals of the belief which has so long held the pious Inspirationists together in the fellowship of mutual service:

When did the work of Inspiration begin in the later times?

About the end of the seventeenth and beginning of the eighteenth century. About this time the Lord began the gracious work of Inspiration in several countries through these new messengers of peace, and declared a divine sentence of punishment against the fallen Christian world.

What were these Instruments or Messengers called?

Inspired or new prophets. They were the living trumpets of God, which shook the whole of Christendom, and awakened many out of their sleep of security.

What is the word of Inspiration?

It is the prophetic word of the New Testament, or the Spirit of Prophecy in the new dispensation.

What properties and characteristics of divine origin has this Inspiration?

It is accomplished by a divine power, and reveals the secrets of the heart and conscience in a way which only the all-knowing and soul-penetrating Spirit of Jesus has power to do; it opens the ways of love and grace, of the holiness and justice of God; and these revelations and declarations are in their proper time accurately fulfilled.

Through whom is the Spirit thus poured out?

Through the vessels of grace, or *Werkzeuge,* chosen and fitted by the Lord.

How must these *Werkzeuge* be qualified?

They must conform themselves in humility and child-like obedience to all the motions and directions of God within them; without care for self or fear of men, they must walk in the fear of God and with attentive watchfulness for the inner signs of his leading; and they must subject themselves in every way to the discipline of the Spirit.

Upon what is the Constitution of the Communities of True Inspiration founded?

Upon the divine revelations of the Old and New Testaments together with divine directions, precepts, and revelations in general and in particular given through the word of True Inspiration.

Through whom are the divine laws and ordinances administered in the Communities?

Through the Elders and Wardens appointed by the Lord.

In what do the duties of these consist?

Every Warden or Elder of the Community is, in consequence of his calling bestowed upon him by God, in duty bound to promote the temporal as well as the spiritual welfare of the Community after the measure of grace given to him, in which, however, the spirit of Prophecy renders the true and valid decision in difficult and important cases.

Is it therefore of great importance to fulfill the calling of a shepherd of souls?

It is indeed a precious duty that he with the keys entrusted to him unlock the kingdom of heaven, not close it, and that he be a guide for his flock and a true follower of his Lord and Master. He furthermore must use the word of admonition, rebuke, and instruction with divine love and earnestness, so that he may justly and wisely censure and punish the fallen ones, cast out the wicked and impure from the Community, and also receive those who repented again at the proper time. I Timothy, 4: 12, 16. II Timothy 2: 15, 24-26, I Peter 5: 1-4.

What is necessary for this?

An ample measure of divine enlightenment and discrimination.

Is this constitution supported by the Scriptures?

Yes. The first Christian Communities at the time of the Apostles had the same arrangement and constitution. Paul addressed to the Elders of the Community of Ephesus these earnest and important words:

"Wherefore I take you to record this day that I am pure from the blood of all men.

"For I have not shunned to declare unto you all the counsel of God.

"Take heed therefore unto yourselves, and to all the flock over which the Holy Ghost hath made you overseers, to feed the church of God, which he hath purchased with his own blood." Acts 20:26-28.

Is the divine power to bind and to loosen which according to Matthew 16:19 was entrusted to the apostle Peter valid for the Elders of the Communities of True Inspiration?

It is given to all Teachers and Wardens of the Community of the faithful called by our Lord Jesus Christ through his Holy Spirit, who exercise the power of their divine calling and divine power given to them without abuse of the Flock and Community entrusted to them.

What are the duties of the members of the Community of True Inspiration?

A pure and upright life in the fear of God, sincere love and affection for their fellow members, and childlike obedience towards God and their superiors. Psl. 15:2-18, 24. Phil. 1:27. Col. 1:10. I Thes. 2:12. I Timothy 5:17. I Peter 1:15, 17. Hebr. 13:17, 18. Jak. 3:13, etc.

Will there be any distinction between the pious in the life to come?

Yes; for the Apostle says: "There is one glory of the sun, and another glory of the moon, and another glory of the stars; for one star differeth from another star in glory." I Cor. 15:41. But blessed are the dead who die in the Lord, though they will differ in the degree of their sanctification as our Lord Jesus spoke: "In my Father's house are many mansions." Joh. 14:2.

Is there accordingly for the damned, who go to the fire of God's wrath, also still a redemption to be hoped for?

Yes; for the word "eternal" or "eternity" has still its limitation. Since according to the wise will of God the fallen man Adam and with him the whole race of his descendants, groaning under the curse of sin, was to be brought back to God, the saving and redeeming power of the blood and death of Jesus Christ extends over all fallen spirits of the visible and invisible world and brings them after the lapse of many eternities again back to their origin, that is, to God. (Joh. 12:32.) Sin was not from everlasting, therefore it does not remain unto everlasting; it had a beginning, and therefore will have an end.

What does the Lord demand of each soul that desires admission to the Community of True Inspiration and wishes to continue and endure in the same?

Thorough repentance and change of heart; the belief in Jesus Christ; a sincere striving for purification and sanctification; pure love of God and the brethren. Joh. 13:34-35.

But if hidden sins and abominations occur in the Community whereby a curse comes over it, can these be cast out?

As long as they are hidden the matter lies between God and the soul; if the correcting grace of God can punish the soul therein, so that it repents and casts out the evil, so does the Lord not lay open its transgressions; then the soul says: "Whither shall I go from thy spirit? or whither shall I flee from thy presence? If I take the wings of the morning and dwell in the uttermost parts of the sea; even there shall thy hand lead me," etc. Ps. 139:

7-12. If, however, in this manner the soul cannot be brought to repent and mend its ways, then it is dealt with, after its sins have been revealed according to the direction of the Lord. Matthew 18:15-17. And if this too should be of no avail, it is expelled from the Community.

Is such a person, that must be expelled because of sin and disobedience and does not later repent, also excluded from the heavenly kingdom?

If all has occurred after the ordinance and will of God, this exclusion remains in force, and its effect extends into eternity, according to the words of our Savior: "Whosoever sins ye remit, they are remitted unto them; and whosesoever sins ye retain, they are retained." Joh. 20:23.

Are those who have repented of their sins again admitted?

Yes; in order that the wealth of Jesus Christ and his compassion for that which was lost and has been found again, may become known. . . .

But there are also hypocrites, who preserve the appearance of godliness and whose heart and conscience nevertheless are full of filth and abomination; what becomes of those?

Such cannot carry on their deception forever, for God is the judge of the Community, who also brings to light what is hidden, but everything at his own time. Judas also, who betrayed the Lord, was among the small number of the disciples; however, he could not remain and came to a terrible end.

How is the Supper and Lovefeast of our Lord and Savior celebrated in the Communities of True Inspiration?

Not after human customs or decrees at stated times, but only after the will of the Lord has been revealed is it celebrated such as Jesus Christ established it, and with the necessary tests and preparations whereby the grace of God flows in abundant measure intc the hearts of those assembled.

What is and ever remains thereby the chief essential in this respect for the Communities of True Inspiration?

The partaking of the inner (spiritual) Lovefeast. Joh. 6:54.

Is there any religious faith which alone of all leads to salvation, or has the Community of True Inspiration represented itself as such or claimed to be such?

No. The invisible or spiritual body of Jesus Christ consists of all the true followers and worshippers of God in spirit and in truth, and those may be found among all Christian people and denominations although hidden and unknown to the natural eye. Acts 10:35. ["But in every nation he that feareth him, and worketh righteousness, is accepted with him."]

What does it mean to worship the flesh and to bear its mark?

It is the earthly and false teaching of reason among the Christians which in its falsely famous art has risen above all which is divine, for it seats itself in the temple of God and says, I am God. "Little children, it is the last time; and as ye have heard that anti-christ shall come, even now are there many anti-christs; whereby we know that it is the last time." I John 2:18. Revelations 14: 11-12.

What furthermore are characteristics of the flesh?

Many other things. Behold! test and examine yourself, whether you do not even now bear them in and on you in subtle form. The great security of the flesh, pride and vain dress, the empty honor of the flesh and self-will, the earthly unjust gain, not to mention the great vices and terrible wickedness, at which heaven and earth shudders and prepares itself for a great judgment.

Whither go the souls of the ungodly, of the unconverted and persistently unrepenting after their death?

To hell, to the place of unspeakable torment, of eternal darkness and imprisonment, to the devil and prince of darkness, where there will be howling and gnashing of teeth. And the smoke of their torment will rise from eternity to eternity. Revelations 14:11.

Why is baptism through water not observed among us?

Since baptism by water is only external and hence not essential for salvation, so has God exempted us from its observance and directed us to the baptism by fire and by the spirit, through which alone we can become children of God.

Has our Lord Jesus Christ commanded the baptism of children?

No. We find nothing concerning it in the Scriptures.

XVII

THE PSALMS AND HYMNS OF THE COMMUNITY

An old collection of psalms of more than nine hundred pages written by Dr. Johann W. Peterson in the seventeenth century is sometimes read by individuals in the Community of True Inspiration. But the hymn book (*Psalter-Spiel*) in regular use in the Community to-day is a volume of twelve hundred and eighty-five pages with the unique title: "Psalms after the Manner of David, for the Children of Zion: or a Collection of Old and Newly Selected Spiritual Songs, Brought Together with Zeal for the Blessed Use of All Souls Desirous of Salvation, and Sucklings of Wisdom; but Particularly for the Congregation of the Lord."

In the table of contents the hymns are grouped under fifty-seven subject headings, of which the following are characteristic:

Of Longing after God and Christ	76 hymns
Of Spiritual Battle and Victory	61 hymns
Of Denial of Self and the World	51 hymns
Of Suffering and Temptation	41 hymns
Of Christian Living and Conduct	42 hymns
Of True Repentance, Conversion, and Change of Heart	38 hymns
Of Patience and Perseverance	26 hymns
Of Human Misery and Great Wretchedness	26 hymns

[Facsimile of the title-page of the first edition of the *Psalter-Spiel*]

Davidisches Psalter-Spiel Der Kinder Zions/

Von
Alten und Neuen auserlesenen
Geistes-Gesängen;
Allen wahren Heyls-begierigen
Säuglingen der Weißheit/
Insonderheit aber
Denen Gemeinden des HErrn/ zum
Dienst und Gebrauch mit Fleiß zusammen
getragen/
Und in gegenwärtig-beliebiger Form
und Ordnung/
Nebst einem doppelten darzu nützlichen und der
Materien halber nöthigen
Register/
ans Licht gegeben.

Im Jahr Christi 1718.

The last one hundred and eleven pages of the *Psalter-Spiel* are music. The hymns themselves are printed as prose, two columns to a page, the verses being numbered consecutively. To add to their effectiveness certain hymns are written in the form of acrostics, the initial letters spelling out such admonition as: "Strive with fear and trembling that ye may be saved", or "To love Jesus is much better than to know everything."

The following hymn, which is based upon the Twenty-third Psalm is illustrative of the 1167 numbers which are included in the *Psalter-Spiel*:

The Lord is my faithful shepherd. He keeps me in his fold, where I shall not want for anything good. He gives me pasture without ceasing, where grows the succulent grass of his word.

To the pure waters he leads me that I may refresh myself, that is his joyous holy Spirit, which makes me of good cheer. He leads me without ceasing on the path of his commandments for his name's sake.

Though I wander through the dark valley, I fear neither misfortune, persecution, suffering and sorrow, nor the evil malice of this world. For Thou art ever with me, Thy staff and support console me, on Thy word I lean.

Thou dost spread a table for me before all mine enemies, and makest bold and glad my heart, annoint'st my head with Thy holy spirit, the oil of joy, and fillest my soul with Thy divine joys.

Kindness and compassion attend me in my life, I shall ever remain in the house of the Lord, on earth in his holy Community, and after death I shall be with Christ, my master. [219]

Here and there throughout the volume certain verses are marked with a star and are recommended to the members of the Community as prayers. The following verses illustrate the simple dignity and supreme faith pervading the *Psalter-Spiel*:

Oh be thou merciful to me, thou great God, according to thy great kindness. Free me from the distress of sin, which fills my heart, soul, and mind, that I am sad and despairing, as the sin gnaws at my being.

Hold and beckon when I am sinking, and help me in my weakness. Ward off whatever ensnares me and drags me down to earth. When I am about to fall let me hear thy word. Blessed he who flees from sin.

Oh Holy Trinity, lead me entirely away from earthly things, direct my whole physical and spiritual being toward the course of eternity. Unite me with thee, and let me be here one with thee that I may also be with thee there in eternal glory. Oh Holy Trinity.

Oh Jesus, thou alone shalt be my one and all; test and try my earnestness; rid me of all hypocrisy; see whether I am on an evil treacherous path, and lead me, thou on high, in thine eternal ways. Grant unto me the grace to regard all else for naught, but the winning of Jesus. [220]

Many of the Community hymns were written by the *Werkzeuge* and their Scribes. The appended initials "J. F. R.", "E. L. Gr.", and "J. A. Gr." are a constant reminder of the "heroes of faith" of the early part of the eighteenth century. In the New Community much hymn writing was done by Christian Metz. Some of his beautiful hymns are found in the *Psalter-Spiel* and many more in his *Tagebücher*. When some misfortune had befallen the Community, or some great good had been bestowed, Christian Metz was wont to point a moral in song. On one occasion, owing to the carelessness of the shepherd, a number of sheep were killed by dogs; whereupon Christian Metz recorded the following verses in his *Tagebuch*:

1. Ten of our sheep have been torn and a number of others have been wounded, the shepherd was not with his flock and slept in a lazy and secure manner. Is not this indeed the way of the hireling, if one does not guard the flock?

2. The dogs of hell are never asleep, they break forth in the dark of night and God permits us to be punished whenever we are not on our guard. The shepherd must not leave his charge and must ever watch over his sheep.[221]

On another occasion after a fearful storm lasting all night Christian Metz wrote a hymn of many stanzas which reads in part:

When the darkness of night has gone by and the morning red breaks forth, when I have gone through hours of anxiety, then I raise my song of thanks. When my God brought upon me terror and the danger has gone by, then I will bring offerings of thanks and sing with mighty voice.

[Facsimile of the title-page of an early volume of songs wherein the name Eberhard Ludwig Gruber is concealed in the line which reads: *E*wigen *L*iebe *G*efalle]

J. J. J.

JEſus-Lieder

Für

ſeine Glieder/

ſonderlich

Für

ſeine Kleine und Reine/

Die

mehr im Weſen haben als im

Scheine:

Und

ihre Freude und Weyde

an

ſeinem Nahmen und Saamen

den

ſie empfangen/

Und

nach deſſen Aufſchluß in ihnen

ſie immer weiter verlangen;

gelallet

Von einem

Der nur ſuchet

wie Er der

Ewigen Liebe Gefalle.

Gedruckt im Jahr 1720

God is terrible and yet glorious, man, beast, hill and valley tremble and fall. Oh Lord where was I when I saw thy thunderbolt? Thou art ruler of all the world, whosoever dares to resist thee, thou crushest to dust, blessed is he to whom thou art merciful. [222]

But the real Christian Metz, whose religious zeal and devotion made possible in so large a measure the Community of to-day and whose beautiful spirit still lives at Amana, is best reflected in such hymns (and there are many) as *The Evening Song*:

1. Oft I consider what I am — a fragile thing, an atom of dust. The best years of my life are gone. Oh grant me Lord what I have believed.

2. I believe that my Savior lives. He does not desert me at the hour of death, when I lift up my heart to Him and call upon Him in my distress.

3. This day, too, has passed away, darkness now breaks forth. Be thou, oh Christ, ever near me. Grant me the light of grace. [223]

XVIII

THE RELIGIOUS SERVICES OF THE COMMUNITY

The religious services of the Community of True Inspiration are numerous but extremely simple. There are prayer-meetings every evening by neighborhood groups in rooms set apart for the purpose; there is a meeting by orders (*Versammlungen*) on Wednesday and Sunday mornings, and sometimes in the afternoons; and there are general meetings from time to time on Saturday morning and on Sunday afternoon. Thus, there are in the Community eleven services a week exclusive of observances of special religious holidays.

The stranger in the Amana villages would have some difficulty in finding the church buildings, unless perhaps his attention were challenged by their inordinate length; for the Amana church is no "steeple house", but simply a series of rooms made necessary by the fact that in the larger villages the men and women of the third spiritual order meet separately on Sunday morning, when four services are conducted simultaneously. The general meetings on Saturday morning and Sunday afternoon are held in a large assembly room of the church.

Until they become of age the children meet for Sunday morning worship with the lowest spiritual order — the girls with the women, the boys with the men. On reaching their majority, if they possess the requisite piety, they may in time be advanced to the highest spiritual order. A few members there are who never get beyond the *Kinder-Versammlung*; and so fathers and mothers and little children are sometimes found in the same *Versammlung*. But if parents would possess the highest respect of their own children as well as that of their Brothers and Sisters in the Community, it behooves them to heed the admonition of Paul that reads: "Set your affections on things above, not on things on the earth."[224]

Formerly attendance upon all of the religious services was compulsory, and the failure to attend a single meeting without good cause was the occasion of reprimand or punishment. But time and proximity to the world have brought about many modifications of the old rules and regulations; and so to-day if the young people signify their continued loyalty to the Community by attending services a reasonable number of times during the week and once on Sunday "the Elders are content." The youth who distinguish themselves through too numerous absences from the common evening prayer are still summoned before the daily Council of the Brethren and admonished earnestly.

Prohibiting members from attending the regular Community prayer-meetings has always been a mode of punishing the unruly. The term of punishment varies from one week to one year according to the gravity of the offence. The worldly may smile at the penalty, but it is effective in the Community of True Inspiration.[225]

The interior of the Amana meeting-house is marked by its plainness. The whitewashed walls, the bare floors, and the long unpainted benches worn smooth with much use and frequent scrubbings, all bespeak the character of the service which is simple, sincere, and deeply impressive. There is a serious effort to eliminate everything that might tend to divert the mind from the fear of the Lord. It is the exhibition of pride and vanity in church architecture and church furniture in the world that, according to the Inspirationist, causes the loss of what he regards as the true spirit of religion.

There is no pulpit, but instead a plain table where the presiding Elder sits. On either side of him, facing the congregation, is seated a row of Elders who possess the necessary "measure of enlightenment and discrimination" to "fulfil the calling of the shepherd of souls."

In the general meeting the men sit on one side of the church and the women on the other, both groups according to age and spiritual ranks — the youngsters on the front benches under the watchful eye of the Elders, the older members behind. Each member of the congregation from little Wilhelm and Johanna to the presiding Elder comes armed with a Bible and a copy of the ponderous *Psalter-Spiel* in a pasteboard case.

The service begins with silent prayer. Away back in the seventeenth century a Pietist ancestor wrote: "Prayer is a state of feeling rather than an act, a sentiment rather than a request, a continued sense of submission, which breathes moment by moment from the serene depths of the soul." For this and similar heresies the devout Pietist was "severely denounced by the authorities of the orthodox church and banished by the Court." The "authorities" and the "court" were forgotten three centuries ago; but that simple definition of prayer still lives, and expresses most aptly the Inspirationist's idea of the prayerful attitude.

After the prayer "unhindered by words", the presiding Elder announces a hymn, of which the congregation usually sing five or six verses and the Elder reads the remaining eighteen or twenty. The singing is done in a rather melancholy minor key. It is wholly unlike the church music of the world, and is quite remarkable, in the absence of all accompaniment, for its unison. The music of the *Psalter-Spiel* seems to be a quaint and altogether charming blending of the Gregorian chant and the old Lutheran hymn tunes, in which the deep and often tremulous notes of the First Brethren seem to be as essential a part as the clear strong voices of the youth. Sometimes the hymn is droned out line by line following the reading thereof by the presiding Elder.

There is no instrumental accompaniment, for all musical instruments are regarded, if not as in the mind of the Mennonite as absolute inventions of the devil, at least as diverting the soul from the ways of the Lord and hence are forbidden — not only in the meeting-houses but in the homes as well. For the Inspirationists say: "We are a church all the time, even in our homes."

After the hymn the presiding Elder reads some passages from the *Bezeugungen* — sometimes from those of the blessed time of the Awakening, sometimes from the more recent *Aussprachen* of Christian Metz and Barbara Heinemann, and always those most appropriate to the time and season. Most of to-day's trials and vexations, problems, and policies have had their counterpart in the earlier history of the Community; and there is in consequence much helpful admonition and guidance in the "rebukes and punishments'', ''the affirmation and direction'', ''the decisive word'', and the ''severe testimony of the Lord'' as given through His chosen *Werkzeuge.*

Following the reading of a *Bezeugung* comes a prayer, which varies with the nature of the meeting. Sometimes the Elders pray extemporaneously in the manner of the minister of the world. More often they repeat a prayer, ''given through the spirit of God'' in some recorded *Aussprache.* Again the entire congregation takes part in the prayer in the manner of the evening prayer-meeting, when the members in the order of their spiritual rank — the men first, the women last — repeat a short prayer. In divided meetings all pray in the order in which they happen to be seated. The custom of using chosen supplicatory verses of the more devotional hymns of the *Psalter-Spiel* as prayers is beautiful in practice and obviates the lame and halting attempts at extemporaneous prayer. They are simple, dignified, deeply devotional in spirit, and are repeated with an impressive earnestness. After each in turn has repeated his little prayer, some Brother or Sister prays the *Glauben* and the presiding Elder responds with an extemporaneous prayer which always closes with the Lord's Prayer. During prayer the members kneel, resting their forearms on the benches.

Then the Bibles are drawn from their pasteboard cases and the presiding Elder announces the chapter for the morning's lesson, which is read verse by verse by the members of the congregation — the men first, and then the women. The Elders make brief explanations of the more difficult passages as well as instructive remarks appropriate to the time. Absolute faith in the letter of the Scriptures and positive obedience to the injunctions therein recorded are taken for granted. Into the minds of these people the question of the inspiration ad literatim of the Bible has not seemed to enter.

There is no sermon, but instead brief addresses or exhortations by all of the Elders present[226] upon the supreme necessity of being clothed with the spirit of meekness and humility, and the absolute requisition of thorough consecration to God. Sometimes the address is admonitory in the manner of the *Bezeugungen*, in which the Elder protests against the tendency of some of the Sisters to relax a little in their strictness as to dress. He gives a "word of solemn warning" to the Brothers who "think and strive more for material prosperity and success than for divine things" or "have not been led into the deep paths of spiritual life." He reminds them that "the true harmony of spirit can be obtained only through genuine humility of heart and subjection of one to the other." He beseeches the young people to offer their "young hearts wholly and undividedly to the Lord", to keep apart from the world and shun the ways of the unregenerate, and to remember that if one can get rid of wilfulness and selfishness in this world there is just so much done for heaven. He also admonishes them to be loyal and devoted members of the Community, and points out the advantages of the Community over the world as a school of preparation for the life to come.

The religious assemblies of the Community are not attended by excitement, as are the meetings of the Shakers, who dance "as David danced before the Lord." In truth the members are admonished to "sit quietly and with collected mind at the meeting." Nor is there any attempt at rhetorical effect or eloquence on the part of the Elders. The service is dignified and breathes throughout a reverent and devout spirit. There is a sincere effort to eliminate all that is formal and bound to the letter. "True Christianity", said Christian Metz in his *Tagebuch,* "will ever remain a secret to him who practices only the empty form. Genuine Christianity is so humble, so lowly, and so simple that the child's mind comprehends it."

So zealously has the Community guarded against perfunctory religious service that meetings were often suspended as late as 1879 because of "the grave indifference on the part of the growing girls", "the indolence and lethargy of the older Sisters", or the insincere manner in which the opening hymn was sung, "which caused a withdrawal of the divine grace and despoiled the Community of the blessing intended for it." Nor were the meetings resumed until a new repentance and self-finding came over the members of the Community.

A hymn is sung in closing; the presiding Elder pronounces a benediction; and the congregation quietly files out of the church. If it chances to be a general meeting the women all leave the church by one exit and the men by another. This no doubt is calculated to prevent "silly conversation and trifling conduct." There are no greetings, no goodbyes, no visiting on the steps of the church — nothing in fact that would tend to lessen the solemnity of the occasion.

The religious service which is held upon the death of a member is conducted in the church. The body, however, remains in the home. The service is the regular church service with the lesson drawn from the life and death of the departed Brother or Sister. The *Werkzeuge* often "fell into Inspiration" on such an occasion. After the service the entire congregation, including the children, are permitted to go to the home to view the remains. Then the plain casket is placed in a light open wagon and the little procession proceeds on foot down the flower-bordered street to the cemetery. At the side of the wagon or behind it are the pall-bearers, the family of the deceased, and the relatives, who are followed by the Elders, the school children accompanied by their teacher, and the members of the Community. There is no service at the grave save a silent prayer offered by the entire congregation with bowed heads as the body is lowered into the earth.

There is no outward mourning for the dead. Indeed, the faith of the Community teaches that death is but "the blessed release of the spirit" from the pain and suffering, the sorrow and trouble which is the lot of man during his "pilgrimage on earth." The unencumbered spirit passes beyond into "a blissful eternity" where other souls will join it as they in turn are "freed of their burdens."

XIX

BROTHERS ALL AS GOD'S CHILDREN

Amana's simple doctrine of "Brothers all as God's children" is maintained even in death. In the cemetery there are no family lots, no monuments. The departed members of each village are buried side by side in the order of their death in rows of military precision, regardless of birth, family, or spiritual rank. The graves are marked by a low stone or white painted head-board with only the name and *Todestag* on the side facing the grave.

"Behold how good and how pleasant it is for Brethren to dwell together in unity", quoted Gruber to his little congregation two centuries ago. Eloquently the simple, silent, clover-scented Amana cemetery with its incense-breathing hedge of cedar speaks of the many sacrifices of personal ambition, of material prosperity, and of individual pleasures dear to the human heart made and suffered by those who have endeavored *treu zu bleiben* and to live together in unity. In the center of that quiet solemn place the men whose wealth made possible the establishment of the new home in the West sleep beside their Brothers who had naught to give to the Community save the labor of their hands. And beyond, resting beside the least among them, lies the great-hearted Christian Metz, whose head-stone reads simply: CHRISTIAN METZ 24 JULI 1867. The rest — the loving tribute of his followers — is graven upon the heart of every member of the Community.

A generation has passed since "that mighty heart was stilled." And as the ranks of "the still living witnesses" are gradually being thinned the question arises: What of the future, with continued material prosperity and "no religious struggles and trials for freedom of conscience sake"? It would be almost too much to hope, at least to expect, that the distinctive life which has thus far characterized the Community of True Inspiration will be immutable and remain unaffected by the intense worldly influences from without. And yet the Inspirationist would say that the "Lord's holy purpose and will" are often "hidden for a long time." Three quarters of a century after the death of the "beloved sainted Bro. Joh. Fried. Rock" the "New Era" was brought about by the Lord "in a strange and unexpected manner."

There are in the Community to-day, in spite of the "peaceful external state", many exceptionally spiritual young men and women — worthy sons and daughters of True Inspiration — who are earnestly and sincerely striving to preserve the dignity, the simplicity, and withal the spiritual devotion of the

Urgrosseltern. Who knows but that even now the Lord has taken into his "immediate training and preparation" some recipient of His mercy who will in time announce His word as before "much to the wonder and surprise, but also for the assurance and strengthening of the faith" of a Newer Spiritual Economy.

Were Amana simply an experiment in communism one might venture an opinion as to its permanency. But the *real* Amana, be it remembered, is Amana the Church — Amana the Community of True Inspiration. The history of mankind teaches that "religion often makes practicable that which were else impossible, and divine love triumphs when human science is baffled."[227]

NOTES AND REFERENCES

ɩn Amana home with grape vines—1890s

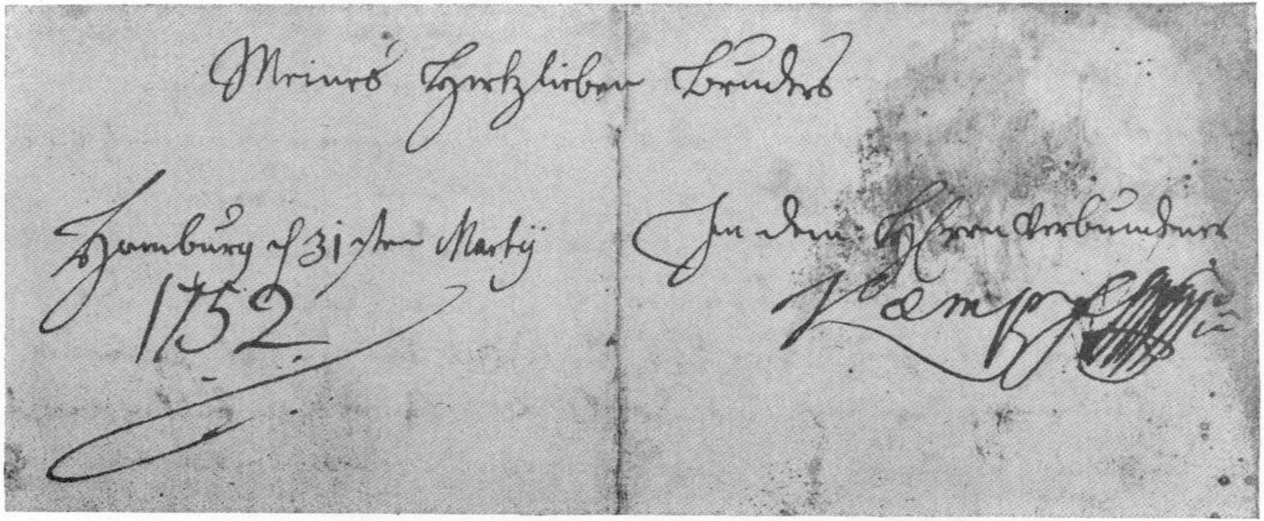

FAC SIMILE (WITHOUT REDUCTION) OF THE AUTOGRAPH OF JOHANN PHILIP KAMPF, FIRST INSPIRATIONIST EXILED FROM ZWEIBRUCKEN

NOTES AND REFERENCES

CHAPTER I

[1] German Mysticism had a very definite following as early as the time of Thomas á Kempis and Johannes Tauler in the fourteenth and fifteenth centuries. The most noted exponent of German Mysticism was, perhaps, Jacob Böhme, who preached the doctrine of the "inward light" at the beginning of the seventeenth century. — For a brief account of Mysticism and Pietism, see Perkins and Wick's *History of the Amana Society*, pp. 2-9.

[2] November 16, 1714, is regarded by the members as the birthday of the Community. On the evening of that day Eberhard Ludwig Gruber, Johann Adam Gruber, Johann Friedrich Rock, Johann Tobias Pott, Johanna Melchior, and Gottfried Neumann joined together for the organization of a new sect based upon a belief in the "Spirit of Prophecy" as "poured out through vessels of grace or *Werkzeuge* (Instruments) chosen and filled by the Lord." The duties and responsibilities of the *Werkzeuge* are discussed in the chapter on Religion. — See above Part III, p. 235.

Cf. Gottlieb Scheuner's *Historischer Bericht von der Gründung der Gebets-Versammlungen und Gemeinden*, p. 13.

[3] Philipp Jacob Spener was a German Lutheran clergyman who rebelled against the "cold faith of the seventeenth century" and organized and held weekly religious meetings at his own home which came to be known as "Collegia Pietatis." He gathered about him great numbers of pious

and enthusiastic followers. In 1675 he published a volume entitled *Pia Desideria,* which was a plea for simplicity in the church. He denounced "all mixture of philosophy and human science with divine wisdom" and urged "the perusal and study of the Holy Scriptures." Spener died in the year 1705, and the reform movement declined. Here and there, however, little groups of "outcasts from the church" continued their sitting-room meetings, and it was among these in the last quarter of the seventeenth century that "God in his mercy caused a spiritual wind to blow, soothed the troubled souls in their affliction, and raised up in their midst persons who were inspired." — See Gottlieb Scheuner's *Historischer Bericht von der Gründung der Gebets-Versammlungen und Gemeinden,* p. 7.

Cf. also Perkins and Wick's *History of the Amana Society,* p. 6.

[4] Eberhard Ludwig Gruber's *Kennzeichen der Göttlichkeit der Wahren Inspiration.* In this essay Gruber discusses at length the "divine origin of the old and the new revelations."

[5] Eberhard Ludwig Gruber's *Bericht von der Inspirations-Sache.* This work was published in February, 1715.

At the beginning of the year 1715 there were six *Werkzeuge* in the Community — four men and two women.

[6] The first false spirit "which made its appearance with false convulsions and false utterances" was a boy of fourteen who thought he was moved by the Spirit in 1715, but who was denounced by Johanna Melchior, one of the founders of the Community, "with great certainty and convincing power." — Eberhard Ludwig Gruber's *Bericht von der Inspirations-Sache.*

CHAPTER II

[7] The two names appearing oftenest with those of Rock and Gruber in the early accounts of these missionary journeys are "the Brothers Gleim" — Johann C. Gleim and H. S. Gleim. "The Brothers Pott," who were active in the organization of the new sect, seem to have lost their gift of Inspiration by the end of the year 1714.—*Joh. A. Grubers und H. S. Gleims Leiden zu Zürich.*

[8] Gottlieb Scheuner's *Historischer Bericht von der Gründung der Gebets-Versammlungen und Gemeinden*, pp. 50, 51.

These fundamental questions, it may be remarked, are recorded as the direct word of the Lord as revealed through the *Werkzeug.*

[9] It is not surprising that persecution followed these over zealous missionaries, since they made bold to interrupt the deliberations of rulers and magistrates in order to preach the wrath of God; and when the "power of the Spirit" arose they stood up during the church service and denounced the clergymen from their own pulpits. — See Perkins and Wick's *History of the Amana Society*, pp. 12-17.

[10] From *Joh. A. Grubers und H. S. Gleims Leiden zu Zürich.*

[11] *Cf. Joh. A. Grubers und H. S. Gleims Leiden zu Zürich.*

[12] One of the conspicuous and most learned leaders among the Separatists in the eighteenth century was Johann Philip Kämpf who, according to Gottlieb Scheuner's account, was the first to be banished from the country. "But our loving God", reads the account, "brought it

about that the *Landgraf* of Homburg [Hessen] not only granted him admission to his country but appointed him also his private physician. Thus Br. Kämpf's removal from Zweibrücken to Homburg vor der Höhe became the start and as it were the guiding post and pathbreaker to prepare for the other members in Zweibrücken a place where they might find a home and protection, when two years later they had to emigrate because of their assembling together." — *Historischer Bericht von der Gründung der Gebets-Versammlungen und Gemeinden,* p. 200.

CHAPTER III

[13] *Cf.* Gottlieb Scheuner's *Historischer Bericht von der Gründung der Gebets-Versammlungen und Gemeinden,* p. 146. Gruber held his first prayer meeting (*Gebets-Versammlung*) on November 16, 1714; and on November 21, 1728, he held his last meeting.

[14] Gottlieb Scheuner's *Historischer Bericht von der Gründung der Gebets-Versammlungen und Gemeinden,* p. 248.

Among the cherished memories of Johann Friedrich Rock are his last words which are recorded as follows:

> Der grosse Mann, der aus dem Himmel rufet, wird bald Odem machen. Er wird aus einer kleinen eine grosse Kraft machen. Jetzt schlaf ich ein in Jesu Namen, bald still und ruhig. Amen!

An examination of the manuscript archives of the Community reveals the fact that many of the *Zeugnisse* given through Rock have never been published.

Some mention should be made of Paul Giesbert Nagel who was one of the most prominent members of the Community in the eighteenth century. He had been the faithful Scribe of Johann Friedrich Rock, and was influential in keeping the Community together after the death of this notable *Werkzeug*. There is in the possession of the Noé family at Amana a valuable manuscript diary written by Nagel and covering the years 1745 to 1776.

[15] This lamentation occurs in the introductory paragraph of Christian Metz's *Historische Beschreibung der Wahren Inspirations-Gemeinschaft* which deals particularly with the history of the Community from the Reawakening in 1817-1818 to the year 1845.

[16] There existed between the Communities at this period "only an intercourse by means of letters, dealing moreover only with external and business matters; and of the work of the Lord little was recorded since there probably were only a few who possessed the necessary gift." — Gottlieb Scheuner's *Historischer Bericht von der Gründung der Gebets-Versammlungen und Gemeinden,* p. 387.

[17] Noé's *Brief History of the Amana Society,* p. 6.

[18] Gottlieb Scheuner's *Historischer Bericht von der Gründung der Gebets-Versammlungen und Gemeinden,* pp. 387, 388.

CHAPTER IV

[19] Noé's *Brief History of the Amana Society,* p. 7.

[20] "From his youth", says Gottlieb Scheuner, "he felt in his heart a strange inward liking for quiet seclusion; nay more there was in him a concealed longing and yearning for something which he himself could not comprehend." *Historischer Bericht von der Gründung der Gebets-Versammlungen und Gemeinden,* p. 429.

[21] Gottlieb Scheuner's *Historischer Bericht von der Gründung der Gebets-Versammlungen und Gemeinden,* p. 429.

[22] *Bezeugungen des Geistes des Herrn,* 1817.

[23] The opposition of the old Elders who "did not wish to be disturbed in their lukewarm form of worship which had become the custom" continued until "a separation soon resulted" — those who "looked askance and rejected the summons of the Lord" through Krausert forming one faction, and "those who bore within themselves a longing for renewal" forming the other and larger faction.

The records of the first five years of the Reawakening contain many accounts of trouble between the *Werkzeuge* and the "old hostile Elders." — See *Jahrbücher der Wahren Inspirations-Gemeinden,* 1819-1823.

[24] Gottlieb Scheuner's *Historischer Bericht von der Gründung der Gebets-Versammlungen und Gemeinden,* p. 432.

[25] The records during these times are quite complete. Besides the recorded testimonies there are accounts by Christian Metz, by various scribes, and by Barbara Heinemann in her *Kurze Erzählung von den Erweckungs-Umständen.*

[26] Gottlieb Scheuner's *Historischer Bericht von der Neuen Erweckung Sammlung und Gründung der Wahren Inspirations-Gemeinde,* p. 34.

[27] It is recorded that Christian Metz "suffered much inward anxiety and felt and fully recognized the backsliding and error of Krausert." The inspired passage (*Einsprache*) that he wrote upon the prompting of the

Spirit "as a warning and rebuke" to Krausert is given above in full.—See Part III on Religion, p. 253.

Barbara Heinemann "experienced great inward oppression and trouble and had to give a testimony concerning this difficult affair", i. e., the "errings" of Krausert. — See Barbara Heinemann's *Kurze Erzählung von den Erweckungs-Umständen.*

[28] It is recorded that even after several weighty and urgent testimonies occurred regarding the "sad erring and deception of His formerly faithful servant Krausert" the Lord evidently still attempted to retain him and win him back; "but he [Krausert] had lost his divine strength and had no longer sufficient grace to bow so deep as would have been necessary to be again raised after such submission and humiliation", and he was through a council of the Brethren expelled from the Community. — Gottlieb Scheuner's *Historischer Bericht von der Ueuen Erweckung Sammlung und Gründung der Wahren Inspirations-Gemeinde,* p. 42.

[29] Barbara Heinemann in her *Kurze Erzählung von den Erweckungs-Umständen* speaks of the "sad end" of Krausert in these words: "We were grieved deeply concerning this, especially I myself, since he was for me in my great ignorance and inexperience a guide and leader in these all important ways of faith and divine guidance."

It was likewise a sore trial for Christian Metz to feel compelled to testify against Krausert; for it was through Krausert that the Lord sent a "word of encouragement to persevere in the blessed service allotted to him by the Lord" when during the first year of his service "Satan assailed him with the spirit of doubt and unbelief."

[30] With the fall of Krausert "a great rent resulted in the Communities", and "many who still lacked the deeper conviction again withdrew and condemned and denounced the whole work." Barbara Heinemann seems to have been anything but a peacemaker, and so the work of rehabilitating the Community depended largely upon Christian Metz.

CHAPTER V

[31] In her *Kurze Erzählung von den Erweckungs-Umständen* Barbara Heinemann recounts numerous instances of how she resisted the Spirit before she understood its nature. On one occasion she felt commanded by the Lord to order for herself a pair of high lace boots. She tried to ignore the impulse, but it became so strong that she finally went to the shoemaker. He in turn tried to dissuade her, but the prompting was so persistent that she ordered the shoes made. When they were delivered she "put them in a corner without knowing what to do with them." But the hidden meaning of the whole matter became clear when a little later she "received an inward prompting to go to Bergzabern where Krausert just then was, which I however did not know."

[32] Barbara Heinemann's *Kurze Erzählung von den Erweckungs-Umständen.*

[33] Gottlieb Scheuner's *Historischer Bericht von der Neuen Erweckung Sammlung und Gründung der Wahren Inspirations-Gemeinde,* pp. 22, 23.

[34] A distinction is made between the oral and the written testimonies. The former are referred to as *Aussprache,* the latter as *Einsprache.*

[35] Barbara Heinemann's *Kurze Erzählung von den Erweckungs-Umständen.*

[36] The quoted passages are from a testimony given on July 31, 1819, and recorded in the *Jahrbücher* for 1819-1823.

Gottlieb Scheuner records these difficulties with great frankness and plainness of speech. — See *Historischer Bericht von der Neuen Erweckung Sammlung und Gründung der Wahren Inspirations-Gemeinde,* pp. 34-60.

The opposition to Barbara Heinemann from her point of view is clearly set forth in her testimonies for the years 1819-1823.

[37] "As long as she remained in her first state of mercy", writes Gottlieb Scheuner, "which had so powerfully seized her and uplifted her far above all human thought and desire, the Lord was her help and staff in all trials from within and from without. But when she began to listen to the arguments of reason which arose in her she found herself in the dark with regard to her inner and outer existence and future development. She could no longer see a way, for from within her the former guidance of the divine mercy had disappeared and from without temptations rushed upon her. . . . And above all", adds Gottlieb Scheuner by way of criticism of her treatment by the Elders, "the faithful brotherly support she should have received from Br. ———— she could no longer find." — *Historischer Bericht von der Neuen Erweckung Sammlung und Gründung der Wahren Inspirations-Gemeinde,* p. 59.

[38] The recalling of Barbara Heinemann to the "service of the Lord" was in response to a prayer of Christian Metz in which he pleads for assistance in his divine calling. This petition, recorded on page 112 of the *Auszüge aus den Tagebüchern von Br. Christian Metz,* is in rhyme and reads in part as follows:

HErr Du siehst die grosse Zahl, wann gehalten wird das Mahl; eine Stimme ist zu wenig, ja zu schwach und zu eintönig bei so vieler Gliederzahl, wanns soll kommen zu dem Mahl.

In response to this petition there came on December 2, 1849, the following testimony of the Lord:

Zu diesem Zweck und Beruf habe Ich dich auch, Meine Magd, aufgefordert, und dir beigeleget das Wort der Gnade zur Besserung in der Gemeine zu reden und zu zeugen.

[39] Two years after her marriage there came through Brother Christian Metz a testimony regarding her which contained "a most consoling promise of her restoration" (*Bezeugungen des Geistes des Herrn,* 1825). This promise had remained "hidden and concealed" for a quarter of a century, and no new *Werkzeug* had been called in the meantime. During the *Unterredungsarbeit* in 1849 there was an unusual amount of religious enthusiasm in the Community and "the expectation was indeed general that the Lord would call a new instrument. Brother Chr. Metz too cherished the wish." It was on the second day of December, 1849, during the progress of the *Unterredungsarbeit* at Middle Ebenezer that the gracious promise of 1825 was fulfilled, and Barbara Heinemann was again called into the service of the Lord.

CHAPTER VI

[40] Christian Metz had lost his gift for three and one half years because during the Krausert trouble he wished to "give in for the sake of peace and harmony, and questioned the validity of the word which had come [through Barbara Heinemann]". As the time of the marriage of Barbara Heinemann approached and she "became unfit for the service of the Lord and His work in the Community", the Lord did not wish the work to die out so He

"bestowed at the beginning of the year (1823) the grace again upon Br. Christian Metz to record his word through *Einsprachen.*" — Gottlieb Scheuner's *Historischer Bericht von der Neuen Erweckung Sammlung und Gründung der Wahren Inspirations-Gemeinde,* p. 58.

[41] Gottlieb Scheuner's account of the Reawakening as given in his *Historischer Bericht von der Gründung der Gebets-Versammlungen und Gemeinden,* p. 431.

[42] *Auszüge aus den Tagebüchern von Br. Christian Metz.* p. 90.

[43] Testimonies of both Christian Metz and Barbara Heinemann are given in whole or in part in Part III on Religion. — See above, p. 251.

[44] Gottlieb Scheuner's *Historischer Bericht von der Neuen Erweckung Sammlung und Gründung der Wahren Inspirations-Gemeinde,* p. 47. See also, Barbara Heinemann's *Kurze Erzählung von den Edweckungs-Umständen.*

[45] At this time there were eight congregations, namely: Ronneburg, Liebloos, Schwarzenau, Edenkoben, Bergzabern, Bischweiler, Strassburg, and Hambach. — See Christian Metz's *Historische Beschreibung der Wahren Inspirations-Gemeinschaft,* p. 44.

[46] Gottlieb Scheuner's *Historischer Bericht von der Neuen Erweckung Sammlung und Gründung der Wahren Inspirations-Gemeinde,* p. 67.

[47] *Bezeugungen des Geistes des Herrn,* 1819-1823. See also Barbara Heinemann's *Kurze Erzählung von den Erweckungs-Umständen.*

CHAPTER VII

[48] The Herrnhuter were a remnant of the Bohemian Brethren or Moravians who in order that they might worship in freedom settled by invitation from Count Zinzendorf on his estate in Saxony. They were soon joined by others and the little Community thus established was called Herrnhut (the Keep of God). The Community of True Inspiration in its beginnings and the early Herrnhuter had much in common. Both organizations were a protest against dogmatism and formality in the church, and both were firm believers in the Pietism of Spener. Neither Community in the eighteenth century practiced communism, but they held that the rich should give of their riches to the poor and that all Christians should live as nearly as possible in the fashion of the apostolic community at Jerusalem. Many Moravians joined the Community of True Inspiration during the time of Rock and Gruber. Count Zinzendorf was a Lutheran, and while he wished to form a Society distinct from national churches and devoted to good works he succeeded after long negotiation in establishing a sort of fellowship or union between the Lutheran Church and the Herrnhuter Society. The emigrants at Herrnhut attended the parish church and were simply a Christian society within the Lutheran Church — a church within a church. It was probably because of this "falling back" or concession that the curse mentioned in the text was pronounced.

[49] *Bezeugungen des Geistes des Herrn,* July 25, 1826, No. 31.

[50] *Cf. Bezeugungen des Geistes des Herrn,* 1828, No. 109. Christian Metz's *Historische Beschreibung der Wahren Inspirations-Gemeinschaft,* p. 44-74. See also *Histor-*

ischer Bericht von der Neuen Erweckung Sammlung und Gründung der Wahren Inspirations-Gemeinde, p. 75.

[51] The *Bezeugungen des Geistes des Herrn* for the years 1830-1837 are full of the "counsels", "approvals", and "decisions of the Lord" in regard to these estates.

[52] *Bezeugungen des Geistes des Herrn,* 1834, No. 105. The numerous testimonies of the year 1834 concerning the internal and external management of the Community were all given through Christian Metz.

[53] These estates with the exception of Armenburg, were located a little southeast of Büdingen in the southern part of what is now designated as the province of Oberhessen.

The castle at Ronneburg has within recent years been partly restored by the present owner. At Marienborn the main structure has been destroyed by fire. The large castle at Herrnhaag is no longer inhabited. At Armenburg the castle is in a very good state of preservation and partly inhabited.

[54] In a letter to one of the faithful Brothers at this time Christian Metz speaks of the refusal of "the Cabinet in Darmstadt" to grant "our petition for admission of families from neighboring states and the right of citizenship for those who according to certificate of residence already dwell here." The "divine order" to leave the country came "as a coincidence" on the same day as the reply of the Cabinet. "All this is, however", adds Christian Metz, "only of utmost importance to those who possess and feel the accompanying certainty [of the Lord's holy purpose] which no one but the only sure witness can give us." — See also Christian Metz's *Historische Beschreibung der Wahren Inspirations-Gemeinschaft.*

55 *Bezeugungen des Geistes des Herrn,* 1838, No. 64.

CHAPTER VIII

56 This Testimony was given through Christian Metz. —*Bezeugungen des Geistes des Herrn,* 1826, No. 23.

57 During one of these meetings at Armenburg (November 8, 1840) there came through Christian Metz *eine bedenkliche Aussprache* which reads: "About all these things and concerning all these things which are now pending my soul is oppressed, since the time is not yet fulfilled and because the delay is so great, in as much as I have not yet accomplished the holy purpose of My Love. Be watchful, rally yourselves, and keep yourselves in readiness for another time and hour is coming."—*Bezeugungen des Geistes des Herrn,* 1840, No. 101.

58 This testimony was given on July 27, 1842.—*Bezeugungen des Geistes des Herrn,* 1842.

59 Noé's *Brief History of the Amana Society,* p. 15.

60 Although the Inspirationists used the name Armenburg, it was never officially recognized outside of the Community. In atlases, geographies, and public documents the place is uniformly referred to as Arnsburg.

61 A full account of this *Liebes- und Abschiedsmahl* as recorded in the *Jahrbuch* for 1842 is given above in Part III, p. 292.

62 This letter was written to Abraham Noé, of Anweiler, great uncle of the present Secretary of the Amana Society.

CHAPTER IX

63 The members from Germany came as rapidly as they could be accomodated. At the end of the month of April, 1843, there were fifty-two persons in Ebenezer. Seventy-five more arrived June 3, forty-three on July 26, and sixty-seven on October 7 of the same year. Owing to the hardships of the ocean journey during the winter months there were no more arrivals until June 21, 1844, when two hundred and seventeen members came to Ebenezer. On August 2, 1845, one hundred more arrived; and on October 16 of the same year eighteen more came to the new settlement. These were only the larger groups; individuals arrived constantly.

64 I *Samuel*, 7:12.

65 In the Bible the word is written "Eben-ezer" (I *Samuel*, 7:12). In the records of the Community it is sometimes written "Eben-Ezer" but more often it appears as "Ebenezer".

66 It was some time before the negotiations with the Ogden Company were concluded. During the "period of waiting" the following testimony came through Christian Metz on December 4, 1842: "I bear witness that I shall keep the given promise [in regard to the land near Buffalo]. Therefore wait with patience in this affair for what I can and shall do with the other party . . . But if it should become impossible on your part because of their demands, well then in such case am I [the Lord] not bound."—*Bezeugungen des Geistes des Herrn*, 1842.

[67] *Bezeugungen des Geistes des Herrn,* 1842, No. 118. In the original lines read:

Ihr sollt ihn Ebenezer heissen,
Bis hieher half uns unser Gott!
Er half uns durch auf unsern Reisen,
Und rettete aus mancher Noth;
Sein Pfad und Weg ist wunderbar,
Das Ende macht den Anfang klar.

[68] Gottlieb Scheuner's *Historischer Bericht von der Neuen Erweckung Sammlung und Gründung der Wahren Inspirations-Gemeinde,* p. 314.

[69] The *Jahrbücher* for this period are made up for the most part of *Zeugnisse* "as a guidance for the Elders"; and are even more detailed than those recorded at the time of the renting of the estates in Europe. Not a step was taken nor a measure adopted without divine direction or approval. These directions were all given through Christian Metz.

CHAPTER X

[70] *Bezeugungen des Geistes des Herrn,* 1845.

[71] Gottlieb Scheuner's *Historischer Bericht von der Neuen Erweckung Sammlung und Gründung der Wahren Inspirations-Gemeinde,* p. 368. The testimony referred to is No. 4 in *Bezeugungen des Geistes des Herrn,* 1845.

[72] *Acts* 2:44, 45.

[73] *Bezeugungen des Geistes des Herrn,* 1854, No. 12.

[74] The removal of the Community from New York to Iowa extended over a period of ten years. This necessitated much letter writing between the leading Brethren at Ebenezer and at Amana. These letters, moreover, con-

stitute valuable sources of information for the history of this period.

CHAPTER XI

[75] In the midst of the trouble with the Ogden Land Company and the Seneca Indians there came to the Community one C. L. Meyer, a former resident of the Zoar Society in Ohio. He soon became "an important pillar of the Community." And because of his command of the English language and his experience in business affairs he was of the greatest service to the Community in "these different affairs."

[76] From the *Twenty-one Rules for the Examination of our Daily Lives.* These rules are given in full in Part III, p. 277.

CHAPTER XII

[77] *Bezeugungen des Geistes des Herrn,* 1854, No. 41.

[78] While Christian Metz helped in the upbuilding of the new home in Iowa, Barbara Heinemann was supposed to look after the spiritual condition of the Ebenezer Community. But one gathers from the records that "the work of grace was hampered" there, and "great worry to the Brethren was caused" by trouble between Barbara Heinemann and the Head Elder. "The Brethren in Amana, especially Br. Christian Metz, felt this, and therefore they offered to her the transfer to Amana or Homestead."— Gottlieb Scheuner's *Historischer Bericht von der Neuen Erweckung Sammlung und Gründung der Wahren Inspirations-Gemeinde,* p. 749.

79 From a letter dated June 22, 1864, from Brother Weber to whom much of the credit for the business-like disposal of the Ebenezer property is due.

CHAPTER XIII

80 The song *Bleibtreu* came to Christian Metz through the Spirit of Inspiration on the eighth day of August, 1855, and is recorded in the *Dreissigste Sammlung,* p. 162. It reads in full as follows:

1. Bleibtreu soll der Name sein Dort in Iowa, der Gemein. Bleib getreu bis in den Tod Deinem Gott in Angst und Noth!

2. B l e i b t r e u, hat Gott zugesagt, Wann Unglaub und Zweifel fragt, Ob deiss sei der rechte Nam', Ob er auch von innen kam.

3. Bleib treu, halt den Liebesbund, Stehe fest im Glaubensgrund, Nam' und That soll stimmen ein, Dass Gott segne die Gemein'.

4. Bleib treu, wann du müde bist, Gott ist, der das Leid (die Müh) versüsst! Bleib treu im Gehorsamsband, jedes Glied, in seinem Stand.

5. Bleib treu, denk was Gott gethan Schon von deiner Jugend an: Denk an deine Sündenschuld, Denk an Gottes Treu und Huld.

6. Bleib treu in dem Fortgangslauf, Häuf nicht Untreu, Sünden auf! Wann dein Alter kommt herbei, Du dann bist geblieben treu.

7. Bleib treu, ruft dir (mir) Jesus zu, Wahre Treu bringt Seelenruh! Wer ein Glied ist der Gemein, Präg sich diess ins Herz hinein.

8. Bleib treu im Verleugnungsstand, Bleib treu in dem Bruderband, Bleib treu, Wann dich lockt die Welt, Wann sie dir anbeut ihr (viel) Geld.

9. Ach bleib treu, du Jugendherz, Sonst kommt später Reu und Schmerz. Murre nicht bei deiner Last, Die du jetzt zu tragen hast.

10. Wann dirs wider Willen geht, Und sich die Gefahr erhöht, Denk zurücke, und bleib treu, Gottes Gnad wird wieder neu.

11. Wann es bei dir dunkel wird Und dich Fleisch und Blut verführt, Halte fest und bleib dabei: Ich bleib dennoch Gott getreu.

12. Bleib treu, leide, dringe ein Es gilt nicht ums Mein und Dein, Nein, es ist das beste Theil, Deiner Seelen Seelenheil.

13. Bisher half uns unser Gott Durch so manche Angst und Noth; Eben-Ezer, nun voran, Bleib treu, Gott bricht ferner Bahn!

[81] The resemblance between the bluff overlooking the site of the new village and "the top of Amana" described in the Song of Solomon (Chapter IV: 8) suggested the name Amana to the Werkzeug Christian Metz. The song in which the Lord gave his approval to the substitution of the name Amana or *glaub treu* for *Bleibtreu* is recorded in the *Dreissigste Sammlung,* p. 199. It contains eighteen verses, the 14th, 15th and 16th of which read:

14. Bis hieher hatte uns Die Gottesgnad geleitet, Ein Eben-Ezer ward Für uns allhier bereitet. Wohl dem, der dieses sich Allhier zu Nutz gemacht Und seinen Glaubenslauf Durch "blieb treu" hat vollbracht!

15. Gott, der von Alters her So weislich hat regieret, Und nun in letzter Zeit So wunderbar uns führet, Will auch also erkannt Und angenommen sein, Dass die gewisse Gnad', Amana, gründe ein!

16. Ach bete, bleibe treu! Der Name kann nicht krönen; Es wird der Spötter Zahl Dich sonst darüber höhnen. Geh' in die Einfalt ein Und in die Einsamkeit, Lern Unterthänigkeit, Sonst ist der Feind nicht weit!

A second *Lied von Amana* containing twenty-three verses was given through Christian Metz on December 18, 1855, and is recorded in the *Dreissigste Sammlung,* p. 280. The 21st verse reads:

21. HErr Jesu, komm, gebäre Dich In uns, hier und dort, gnädiglich! Mach A m a n a zum B e t h l e h e m, In Niedrigkeit, Dir angenehm.

[82] See Gottlieb Scheuner's *Historischer Bericht von der Neuen Erweckung Sammlung und Gründung der Wahren Inspirations-Gemeinde,* pp. 555, 556.

[83] This testimony was given on May 6, 1861.

[84] Although the Community does not hesitate to adopt the newest machinery and the newest methods in business, there seems to be little inclination to introduce modern improvements and conveniences in the homes.

[85] From the closing paragraphs of Gottlieb Scheuner's *Historischer Bericht von der Neuen Erweckung Sammlung und Gründung der Wahren Inspirations-Gemeinde,* p. 877.

CHAPTER XIV

[86] The following are the more important cases in which the legal aspects of the communistic societies referred to in the text are discussed and determined:

Gass *v.* Wilhite, 2 Dana 170, 26 Am. Dec. 446. (Relates to the Shaker Society.)

Waite *v.* Merrill, 4 Greenleaf 102, 16 Am. Dec. 238. (Relates to the Shaker Society.)

John G. Goesele et al *v.* Joseph M. Bimeler et al, 5 McLean Reports 223. (Relates to the Zoar Society.)

Goeselle et al *v.* Bimeler et al, 14 Howard 589. (Relates to the Zoar Society.)

Gaselys et al *v.* Separatists Society of Zoar et al, 13 Ohio State 144

Schriber *v.* Rapp, Watt 351, 30 Am. Dec. 327. (Relates to the Harmony Society.)

Schwartz *v.* Duss, 187 U. S. 8. (Relates to the Harmony Society.)

CHAPTER XV

[87] From an account of the last days of Christian Metz. — See *Anhang oder Ergänzung zu dem Tagebuch des Br. Christian Metz.*

PART II

CHAPTER I

[88] In 1875 the Shaker Communities numbered 2415 souls and owned real estate amounting to about 100,000 acres. This, in the words of Elder Evans, "comprised more than all the capital and couldn't be made to pay." — See Nordhoff's *The Communistic Societies of the United States,* pp. 161, 162; also Hinds's *American Communities,* p. 27.

The Amana Society at times during its residence in Iowa owned more land than at present; but finding additional lands an unprofitable investment sold where it could be done to advantage.

[89] A priest from one of the neighboring towns was in the habit of gathering the lotus seeds in great quantities every fall to use in making rosaries. The seeds when ripe are about the size of an ordinary bead, are perfectly round, and hard enough to admit of a high polish.

[90] The station agents at the several Amana railway stations and the four postmasters are all members of the Community who turn their earnings into the "Great Purse" of the Society. The grain elevators are likewise superintended by members of the Community.

At Homestead the business connected with the elevator has for many years been managed by Mr. Fred Moershel who is the Resident Trustee of that village. He was born at Marienborn, came to Ebenezer at the age of five, and removed to the new home in Iowa in 1859 where for the last half century he has been active in the temporal and spiritual affairs of the Community.

91 The Amana physicians are educated in the world at the expense of the Community. Dr. C. J. Winzenried of Amana—the President of the Great Council—is a graduate of Rush Medical College, class of 1866. Dr. C. H. Hermann of Middle Amana, Dr. William Moershel of Homestead, and Dr. Charles F. Noé of Amana are graduates of the College of Medicine of The State University of Iowa, of the classes of 1881, 1888, and 1898 respectively. Dr. Hermann and Dr. Moershel received supplementary training in New York hospitals, and Dr. Noé spent a year in graduate work in Europe.

The pharmacists of the Community are also educated in the world. The venerable *Apotheker* of Amana, Mr. Conrad Schadt received his training in Europe. Mr. August Koch of Middle Amana, and Mr. F. William Miller of Homestead (great grandson of Christian Metz) are graduates of the College of Pharmacy of The State University of Iowa of the classes 1897 and 1900 respectively.

92 From Charles M. Skinner's account of the Dunkard village of Ephrata, in Pennsylvania, in his series of *Studies in Applied Socialism* which appeared in the *Brooklyn Eagle* in 1900.

93 Randall's *History of the Zoar Society*, p. 50. Mr. Randall is the Secretary of the Ohio State Archaeological and Historical Society.

[94] Being "investigated" to the point of exasperation seems to have been one of the crosses borne by every American communistic organization.

[95] *Cf.* Hinds's *American Communities*, p. 81; Nordhoff's *The Communistic Societies of the United States*, pp. 66, 67, 395; and also Randall's *History of the Zoar Society*, p. 43.

[96] The hotel-keeper at Amana has been Marshal of the Colonies (as the Amana villages are sometimes called) for more than a quarter of a century. His naturally keen eye has been trained by years of observation and experience to distinguish between the professional tramp and the really unfortunate and worthy wayfarer. His ability as a detective and his fearless discharge of his duty are well known to the hobo fraternity. Recently a construction train was side-tracked at Old Amana. As the Marshal approached the train one of the "gang" mentioned him by name. "What", said the boss, "is that little feller the Dutch Marshal? Looks to me like he is a d—n small man to cause so much d—n trouble. I've heard of him many a time down on the Rio Grande. I tell ye, the fellers don't monkey wid him. He's a holy terror!"—*Cf.* Bertha M. Horack's *Amana Colony* in the *Midland Monthly* for July, 1896.

CHAPTER II

[97] This election is held in the school and assembly hall of the second school sub-district of the Township of Amana on the first Tuesday in December (See By-laws). In the practical workings of the Community the Board of Trustees has become a self-perpetuating body.

[98] *Cf. Bezeugungen des Geistes des Herrn,* 1844, No. 55.

[99] This account was written in 1891, almost half a century after the adoption of the Great Council system, and it reflects the spirit of the more conservative element in the Community. There is, as one might expect, a young aggressive element that would like to see an "intermingling of the spirit of the world" with the yearly election. In fact this element would not be averse to trying its own hand in the management of affairs.

[100] Christian Metz's *Historische Beschreibung der Wahren Inspirations-Gemeinshaft,* pp. 38, 48.

[101] *Auszüge aus den Tagebüchern von Br. Christian Metz,* p. 97.

[102] In this connection special mention should be made of the present officers of the Amana Society, namely: President C. J. Winzenried; Vice President George Heinemann; and Secretary Abraham Noé.

President C. J. Winzenried is the son of Jacob Winzenried, who was one of three brothers who dwelt at Liebloos in Germany. There the Winzenried family had been connected with the Community of True Inspiration as founded in the early part of the eighteenth century. When the revival occurred early in the nineteenth century, they accepted the new *Werkzeuge*; and later they came to America when the new home of the Community had been located. One of the three brothers, Charles M. Winzenried, an uncle of the present President of the Amana Society, was for many years intimately associated with Christian Metz in the management of the temporal affairs of the Society. He was, indeed, the first President of the Society, being succeeded in that office by John Beyer, Jacob Wittmer, Fred'k Moerschel, and by C. J. Winzenried, the present incumbent.

Vice President George Heinemann is the grandson of Johann Heinemann, who lived at Schwartzenau and who was one of the first to join the New Community from that place. This occurred in 1818 during a visit of Krausert, who was accompanied by C. Metz. The family originally came from Büdingen where some of their ancestors had belonged to the old Inspiration Community in Rock's time. When the little congregation at Schwarzenau had to make a choice between the renunciation of their faith and exile, the Heinemann family chose the latter and migrated to Marienborn, where they remained until the removal to America.

Secretary Abraham Noé is the son of William Noé, who was one of the committee of four sent to America for the purpose of securing a new home for the Community. The Noé family were members of the old Inspiration Community at Neuwied. They recognized the new *Werkzeuge* at the time of the revival in the early part of the nineteenth century. It is interesting to note that this family came originally from France as Huguenot exiles, having been banished by Louis XIV on account of their religion.

103 Both of these expressions are taken from the *Vierundzwanzig Regeln der Wahren Gottseligkeit* announced through Johann Adam Gruber and appended to the *Jahrbücher* for 1819-1823. These rules are given above in full. — See Part III, p. 267.

104 From Charles Lamb in "Mackery End in Hertfordshire" — See *Essays of Elia.*

105 This Lamentation was written on January 17, 1849. —See *Auszüge aus den Tagebüchern von Br. Christian Metz,* pp. 99, 100.

106 Constitution of the Amana Society, Article IV.

107 This testimony relates to matters in connection with the construction of a railroad through the Community.

108 *Hebrews,* 13:17.

109 From the *Kinder-Stimme* published originally in 1717 and still in daily use in the Community. Dr. Charles F. Noé of Amana has in his possession a copy of the first edition of this little book.

110 *Job,* 32:7.

111 These testimonies, which were given through Barbara Heinemann on January 26 and March 9, 1879, respectively, are found in the *Bezeugungen des Geistes des Herrn,* 1879.

112 From a testimony given through Barbara Heinemann appointing and outlining the duties of those "who should have supervision and oversight of the work." Practically the same qualifications "to fulfil the calling of a shepherd of souls" are given in the Catechism. — See above Part III, p. 297.

CHAPTER III

113 Constitution of the Amana Society, Article V.

114 Constitution of the Amana Society, Article VIII.

115 This was Brother C. L. Meyer, mentioned above in note 75. He was admitted to membership through Inspiration.

[116] There are a number of accounts of friendly visits of members from the *Rappischen Communisten-Gemeinde.* One of these accounts relates to a visit as late as August 5, 1875, of a Rappite Elder who in "a long discussion with the Brethren and Sister B. L. concerning matters of faith . . . . showed keen comprehension, great openness and sincere kindness . . . . and declared himself to be pleased and in agreement with all our internal and external institutions . . . . and expressed the opinion that in the course of time a closer mutual relationship between us and them might be brought about." — See Gottlieb Scheuner's *Beschreibung des Gnadenwerks des Herrn in den Gemeinden der Wahren Inspiration,* pp. 605, 606.

Christian Metz in his *Tagebuch* records visits from members of the Shaker Families and of the Mennonite Communities. It is interesting to note that while Christian Metz was sympathetic toward other communities and was ever ready to help them in time of need, he was usually of the opinion that in matters of religion "they had fallen into great error."

Christian Metz, it appears, was not favorably impressed with the form of worship of the Zoar Society. On April 19, 1843, with Brother Ackermann, he visited the Community of Separatists dwelling at Zoar. On the following Sunday they (Christian Metz and Brother Ackermann) attended the religious services of the Separatists, "but soon recognized through the mercy of God that the Community after a period of grace had begun to retrograde and decline. This was announced to them, especially concerning the Elder Baümler, through the word of the Lord, as Brother Christian Metz felt himself compelled from within to go to this Elder on the morning of April 22, where he also forthwith was compelled to give a testimony of truth concerning him and his Community which was left to them in writing."—Gottlieb Scheuner's *Historischer Bericht von der Neuen Erweckung Sammlung und Gründung der Wahren Inspirations-Gemeinde,* p. 321.

[117] The excommunication of one such Brother was, we are told by Gottlieb Scheuner, confirmed by the Lord in a testimony given through Barbara Heinemann in the year 1869.—See Gottlieb Scheuner's *Beschreibung des Gnadenwerks des Herrn in den Gemeinden der Wahren Inspiration,* p. 178.

[118] Being primarily a religious and not an industrial community the Amana Society has received new members with exceeding great care and only after thorough investigation of motives and religious faith. This has always been their great advantage over associations which admitted members too indiscriminately, thereby presently becoming asylums for the needy, sick, and disabled, if not a prey to the intrigues of a bogus Count Maxmilian de Leon as were the Rappites at Economy. Thus the Amana Society has also been saved the difficulties of organizing the heterogeneous assemblage so often found in those industrial communities which when in need of a blacksmith or a carpenter admitted to membership a man without other qualifications because he chanced to be a blacksmith or a carpenter.

[119] Instances of such public confession are given in the *Bezeugungen des Geistes des Herrn,* but being of a personal character specific references thereto are omitted.

[120] *Matthew,* 5:29.

[121] This letter was written on April 5, 1844, and was throughout a very frank account of a group of members then on their way to America.

CHAPTER IV

122 I *Corinthians*, 7:32, 33.

123 George Rapp (Father Rapp), founder and head of the Harmony Society, though not averse to the growth of asceticism evinced by the adoption of celibacy, warned his people not to act rashly in so serious a matter. — See Hinds's *American Communities*, p. 85; also Nordhoff's *The Communistic Societies of the United States*, p. 73.

124 Joseph Bäumler (or Bimeler as it is often spelled), the spiriual head of the Zoar Society, taught that God did not look with pleasure on marriage; that He only tolerated it; and that in the kingdom of heaven "husband, wife, and children will not know each other" and "there will be no distinction of sex there." Nevertheless, Bäumler married and had a family of children. — See Randall's *History of the Zoar Society*, p. 20; also Hinds's *American Communities*, p. 102; and Nordhoff's *The Communistic Societies of the United States*, p. 107.

125 This important testimony which was given through Eberhard Ludwig Gruber on November 19, 1727, is recorded in the *Bezeugungen des Geistes des Herrn*, 1727, No. 134.

126 *Cf.* Eberhard Ludwig Gruber's *Bericht von der Inspirations-Sache*. In this essay Gruber states twenty-six reasons (lettered from "a" to "z") for his belief in the divine origin of Inspiration. The last seven reasons deal with the son mentioned in the text who "was led into the ways of Inspiration contrary to inclination and habit of youth."

127 Gottlieb Scheuner's *Historischer Bericht von der Neuen Erweckung Sammlung und Gründung der Wahren Inspirations-Gemeinde*, pp. 74, 84.

The Brother to whom reference is made in the text was a "faithful friend" of Christian Metz. He was of great service to the Community, especially in financial matters.

128 It was not until about the year 1890 that the Community schoolmasters were allowed to marry.

129 *Auszüge aus den Tagebüchern von Br. Christian Metz,* p. 25.

There are other instances recorded by the Community historian, Gottlieb Scheuner, where Christian Metz was rebuked by "the more unbending Brothers" for his unwillingness to denounce the institution of marriage. Possibly he foresaw the effect of celibacy on the perpetuity of the Community.

130 Spiritually the Community of True Inspiration is divided into three grades or *Versammlungen.* These are discussed above under Religion. — See Part III, p. 280.

131 The Community has ever kept a watchful eye on those who have withdrawn or who have been "expelled because of sin or disobedience"; and it has always been made easy for those "who have repented of their sins" to return "in order that the wealth of Jesus Christ and his compassion for that which was lost and has been found again may become known."—See *Catechetischer Unterricht von der Lehre des Heils,* II, pp. 72, 73.

Gruber and Metz both preached the final redemption of all souls, and urged the Brethren to do all in their power to bring the "fallen spirit back to God."

132 This statement is taken from a monograph of eighty-eight pages on *Die Wahre Inspirations-Gemeinde in Iowa* written by Karl Knortz and published at Leipzig in 1896.

CHAPTER V

133 The social theory of the Oneida Community has been thoroughly aired by its founder and head, John Humphrey Noyes, in his *History of American Socialism* as well as by William A. Hinds, a former member of the Community, in his *American Communities.*

134 *Exodus,* 20:4.

"No picture-making" was also one of the fundamental principles of Shakerism. "We prohibit pictures of individual members", wrote one of the Shaker Elders to William A. Hinds, "because 1st of their tendency to idolatry; 2d the liability of causing personal vanity; 3rd the consequent disunity which might result from preferences given to individuals thus noticed." — See Hinds's *American Communities,* p. 41.

135 Amateur photography became so popular among some of the young people in the Community that within the past year these old testimonies have been reread and reinforced by resolutions of the Great Council of the Brethren restricting the activities of the kodak enthusiasts, thus making it necessary for the Amana photographer to be "more careful."

136 Gottleib Scheuner's *Beschreibung des Gnadenwerks des Herrn in den Gemeinden der Wahren Inspiration,* pp. 473, 474, 479, 480.

137 I *Corinthians,* 8:1; and *Ecclesiastes,* 1:18.

138 The Brethren were sometimes requested to abandon their investigations "in order that nothing should be mixed with the word."

139 The *Unterredung* or *Untersuchung* is the annual examination of the spiritual condition of the members of

the Community. — For a full discussion of this important ceremony, see above Part III, p. 283.

140 One gathers from the "still living witnesses" that these later ordinances of the "Old Sister" were a great cross to Christian Metz who was constantly called upon to "adjust the difficulties."

141 A little more sympathetic guidance on the part of the older members in the choice of "world literature" would not be amiss. All kinds of people and all kinds of books "visit" the Community, and unless a taste for that which is really good is encouraged and developed, that which is not so good will be found in the possession of the young people. The writer once discovered a sweet-faced *kleine Schwester* with a pile of novels of Bertha Clay in her lap, which had been sent to her by a friend from the world.

142 The outsider is sometimes surprised to hear a member of one village say of a member of another village: "I know him by name, but I have never met him." And it is still more surprising to learn that members of one village do not visit another village for perhaps years. It is even claimed that the home village of a member can be detected by his dialect.

143 Picnickers and excursionists are among the "problems" of the Community. During the summer-time they are often a real annoyance. They visit the school; go to prayer-meeting uninvited; pick the flowers in the gardens; peep in the windows; and wind up by insisting on being fed. The outsider who is not a "non-resistant" feels that the Community is over-patient in dealing with these "nuisances."

[144] The Shakers discouraged the eating of meat. Many of them used no animal food, even denying themselves milk, butter, and eggs. — *Cf.* Nordhoff's *The Communistic Societies of the United States,* p. 141.

[145] These *Sittenregeln* for the conduct of children are to be found in the *Catechetischer Unterricht von der Lehre des Heils (für die Jugend),* pp. 87-95.

[146] From Eberhard Ludwig Gruber's *Twenty-one Rules for the Examination of our Daily Lives.*

[147] *Sittenregeln* in the *Catechetischer Unterricht von der Lehre des Heils,* No. 65, p. 95.

[148] From the thirteenth of the *Vierundzwanzig Regeln der Wahren Gottseligkeit* given through Johann Adam Gruber.

[149] *Auszüge aus den Tagebüchern von Br. Christian Metz,* p. 107. This entry occurs under the date of March 8, 1849.

The *Jahrbuch* for 1852 records that on March 6 (1852) "the Lord gave through Br. C. M. important directions through the word with regard to the political elections in which the Community in accordance with the will of the Lord should not participate but which however from kindliness and yielding to the outside world had been neglected, but now the danger resulting from further mingling with the world was pointed out by the Lord, especially as a warning to posterity."

[150] The testimony referred to in the text was given through Barbara Heinemann (Christian Metz having died in 1867) on November 7, 1868, four days after election day. — *Bezeugungen des Geistes des Herrn,* 1868.

151 This memorial was drawn up by the Great Council "as a warning and rebuke" to those members of the Community who "had again succumbed to the spirit of partisanship and had also induced others to vote for or against certain parties and this in spite of the adverse testimony of two years ago." The memorial was circulated among the villages and read with emphasis in open meeting during the *Unterredung* following the election of 1868.

152 In the early seventies a German-Russian Mennonite Commune in Dakota *(Huterische Bruder-Gemeinde)* "came into difficulty through expensive purchase of land, and suffered want of nearly all necessities." A delegation came to Amana to appeal for aid. "They were kindly received", records Gottlieb Scheuner, "attended our worship and received two carloads of provisions as a gift, for which they later in a letter expressed their joy and gratitude. Somewhat later when two of them again came here they received from us a number of cattle and sheep . . . . and two came here from their community for a while to learn the milling trade and the handling of an engine." — Gottlieb Scheuner's *Beschreibung des Gnadenwerks des Herrn in den Gemeinden der Wahren Inspiration,* p. 602.

153 In a letter written from Amana under the date of December 6, 1863.

154 Charles Nordhoff in his account of the Shakers quotes an Elder as saying: "We have no scandal, no tea parties, no gossip." — See *The Communistic Societies of the United States,* p. 166.

155 A former member of the Community, who as a boy learned to play the violin "after night in the cellar", remarked recently in the hearing of the writer that al-

though he has lived in the world for a quarter of a century he still was conscious of a sense of guilt when he listened to instrumental music.

CHAPTER VI

[156] Charles Nordhoff in *The Communistic Societies of the United States* gives it as his opinion that "Communists are the most long-lived of our population", p. 402.

[157] Brother Rock seems to have been especially opposed to the *Handwerkszunft* and appealed without avail to the *Magistrat* in November, 1740, in behalf of the Inspirationists who could not join the trade guilds "for conscience sake." It was on account of the ordinance regarding the trade guilds that Rock removed from Himbach, the town in which he had lived since 1707.

[158] From John Humphrey Noyes's account of the Oneida Community in his *History of American Socialism.*

[159] One young Brother was granted a trip to the World's Fair at St. Louis "to study machinery." This was a very special privilege; for the young Brothers who went to St. Louis "for pleasure" without permission were promptly "excluded from the prayer-meetings" for two weeks.

[160] This was the slogan of the Hopedale Community founded at Mendon, Massachusetts, in 1841. The "industrious and well-disposed of all nations" were invited by Owen to participate in the "greatest revolution ever yet made in human society."

[161] Mr. Conrad Schadt, the *Apotheker* of Amana, is a chemist of more than local reputation. His services

have been sought in vain by wholesale drug houses of the world.

[162] There are in the *Jahrbücher* a number of severe testimonies of the Lord regarding the drinking of too much wine; and some of the offending Brothers are mentioned by name and warned that unless they mend their ways they are at liberty to "go and associate with the world and the ungodly."

[163] In his *History of the Zoar Society,* E. O. Randall tells of how that society continued to manufacture a grotesquely large and cumbersome stove long after the stoves of the world became light, graceful, and economical in the consumption of fuel. The same unprogressive spirit maintained in other kinds of manufacture until most naturally there was a general decline in its industries and a resulting shrinkage in values. With the decline in its business enterprise internal dissentions arose, and therein lies the beginning of the end.

CHAPTER VII

[164] The Amana school system requires an attendance of 364 weeks as opposed to 84 weeks required under the compulsory education law of the State.

PART III

CHAPTER I

[165] *Joel,* 2:28.

[166] Gottlieb Scheuner's brief account of the life-work of Christian Metz given at the close of his *Historischer Bericht von der Neuen Erweckung Sammlung und Gründung der Wahren Inspirations-Gemeinde.*

[167] From a letter by Christian Metz to Abraham Noé, of Anweiler, regarding the proposed removal to America, written in the summer of 1843.

CHAPTER II

[168] Johanna Melchior, it will be remembered, was one of the little group that founded the Community of True Inspiration under Rock and Gruber on the evening of November 16, 1714. She was the *Werkzeug* who discovered the first "false spirit" that made its appearance in the new Congregation.

[169] The elder Gruber doubted at first the genuineness of his own "inner promptings," attributing his sensations to a nervous temperament. However, when his son Johann Adam Gruber, to whom he devotes so much space in his *Bericht von der Inspirations-Sache* began to testify, Eberhard Ludwig Gruber became convinced of the divine origin of Inspiration.

From 1714 to 1717 Johann Adam Gruber made many "greater and lesser journeys" in the interests of True Inspiration. In 1726 he came to America and settled at Germantown, Pennsylvania. He kept up constant communication with the Congregations in Germany, but never established a branch of the faith in the New World.

There are hundreds of pages of manuscript in the *Archiv* of the Community in the handwriting of Johann Adam Gruber, including accounts of his early missionary journeys as well as many letters written from Germantown.

CHAPTER III

170 In her account of the Reawakening, Barbara Heinemann tells of falling into Inspiration in the courtroom where the *Werkzeuge* were to be tried for heresy, and of being forced by the Spirit in the presence of many spectators to give a powerful testimony of the truth whereby all those present including the magistrate were so smitten that the *Werkzeuge* were released without further examination.—Barbara Heinemann's *Kurze Erzählung von den Erweckungs-Umständen.*

171 Rock recounts in his *Erniedrigungs-Lauf Eines Sünders auf Erden* a number of instances of the sudden death of kings, magistrates, and ministers who "offended and persecuted the work of the Lord."

172 There are recorded in *Inspirations-Historie* many instances of the "bad end" of disloyal members of the early Congregations. One record will suffice as an illustration:

> "The Lord directed for the last time to him [the offender] His word; and mercy was once more offered to him if he wished to avail himself of it. But he did not accept it, for he had seated himself so high in his conceit that he neither could nor would find the grace for submission and humiliation. He is henceforth no more mentioned. His strength was broken. The Lord against whom he wished to contend was too powerful for him. He became physically and mentally ill and died in the following year." — Gottlieb Scheuner's *Historischer Bericht von der Neuen Erweckung Sammlung und Gründung der Wahren Inspirations-Gemeinde.*

173 Eberhard Ludwig Gruber's *Kennzeichen der Göttlichkeit der Wahren Inspiration.* See also, Johann Adam Gruber's *Kennzeichen und Gründe von der Göttlichkeit der Wahren Inspiration.* In this essay Johann Adam Gruber explains at length that he has been freed of phys-

ical fear and of respect of persons by the Spirit of Inspiration, and that the accompanying *Bewegungen* are not only not harmful but actually beneficial.

Johann Nicolaus Duill declares in his *Kurze Erzählung* that one of the proofs of the divine origin of Inspiration is "the lies and horrible blasphemies of the enemy [Satan], because he sees that his rule is at stake and that the Lord has given into the hands of his angels the chains with which he is to be bound."

174 Gottfried Neumann was one of the original band that joined in the establishment of the Community on November 16, 1714. He was a theological student and a graduate of the universities of Leipsic and Halle. He was about to enter upon his career as a minister in the established Lutheran Church when he became interested in True Inspiration.—See Gottfried Neumann's *Historische Erzählung von der Inspirations-Erweckung.*

Blasius Daniel Mackinet was a co-worker and warm friend of Johann Adam Gruber. He served as *Schreiber* during the early years of the Congregations in Germany, and in company with the younger Gleim joined Johann Adam Gruber in America. His *Schreiben von der Göttlichkeit der Wahren Inspiration* is a most interesting and valuable account of his own experiences and observations.

Georg Melber was a well-to-do merchant in Heilbronn, Hessen. He was not a preacher, although a devout believer in the doctrine of True Inspiration. He was of great service to the early Congregations as an organizer in temporal affairs.—See Georg Melber's *Zeugniss.*

Caspar Löw was a descendant of followers of John Huss, who had been compelled to flee from Austria on account of their religion. He became interested in the work of Rock and Gruber at the very beginning of the New Spiritual Economy but did not identify himself with the movement until 1717. He became inspired in 1728, and from that time until the day of his death in 1775 he devoted his energies to the cause of True Inspiration.—See Caspar Löw's *Erzählung.*

Johann Nicolaus Duill was a minister in the established Lutheran Church in Hessen who became interested in the *Neue Propheten* — the Brothers Pott — at the beginning of the eighteenth century. At the close of his *Kurze Erzählung* he gives seven reasons for, or rather proofs of, the divine origin of Inspiration (See above note 173).

CHAPTER IV

[175] It was because of her testimonies against Krausert that Barbara Heinemann was banished at this time; but after Krausert's expulsion she returned to the Community and was "strengthened and endowed anew by the Lord with special spiritual power." A little later during this "dark and troublesome period" she was again condemned and banished temporarily through the influence of the First Elder. Of this Gottlieb Scheuner says: "He [the Elder] had on his own responsibility gone much too far, and the other Brothers had also incurred guilt through their dumb submission to his despotic decree."

CHAPTER V

[176] From Blasius Daniel Mackinet's *Schreiben von der Göttlichkeit der Wahren Inspiration.*

[177] Johann Friedrich Rock's *Erniedrigungs-Lauf Eines Sünders auf Erden.*

CHAPTER VI

178 *Bezeugungen des Geistes des Herrn,* 1832. No. 55. This testimony was given on September 19, 1832, "not far from Bruchsal im Walde on the public highway."

179 The third period in Christian Metz's service lasted three times nine or twenty-seven years. Thus the number 9 seems to have had the same mystic significance in the life of Christian Metz that the number 7 had in the life of Johann Friedrich Rock. (See above Part I, p. 31).

180 *Bezeugungen des Geistes des Herrn,* 1841, No. 89. It was hoped that this new "grace and gift" would arouse religious fervor; and the Lord announced his mercy and forgiveness to all those "who had hitherto become unfaithful if they would be renewed through earnest repentance."

181 In 1824 Christian Metz was rebuked by the Overseer of the *Werkzeuge* for his humiliation and for more than half a year was without Inspiration. — See Christian Metz's *Historische Beschreibung der Wahren Inspirations-Gemeinschaft,* pp. 44, 45.

During the "violent contention" over the Krausert affair Christian Metz lost his gift for three and one half years "because he desired to give in for the sake of peace and harmony and questioned the validity of the word [as given through Barbara Heinemann]." — See Gottlieb Scheuner's *Historischer Bericht von der Neuen Erweckung, Sammlung und Gründung der Wahren Inspirations-Gemeinde,* p. 39.

CHAPTER VII

182 *Bezeugungen des Geistes des Herrn,* 1819, No. 17.

183 The testimony from which this expression was taken is described by Gottlieb Scheuner as "so powerful a message that a new conviction of the divine nature of the work through Barbara Heinemann came to the souls of the Community."

184 Barbara Heinemann was morbidly sensitive to and vigorously denounced all "marks of worldliness" in the "growing up youth." Her testimonies abound in "severe rebukes" and "warnings" regarding the "world and the ungodly." "He who does not leave behind everything that is worldly", reads one of her later testimonies, "cannot become and remain my disciple." "Thou shouldst erect a partition wall", reads another, "that the ungodly no longer may visit the Community."

185 The direct quotations in the paragraph in the text are all from the *Bezeugungen* — chiefly from those of Barbara Heinemann and Christian Metz.

186 From the first testimony given through Christian Metz which occurred at one o'clock at night on May 3, 1819. Midnight was not an unusual time for the "prompting of the Spirit."

187 This death occurred during the progress of the *Unterredung* at the beginning of the year 1868. The testimony mentioned was given through Barbara Heinemann (Christian Metz had died a few months before) and contains a threat that "sick-bed will follow sick-bed and death message meet death message on the way" unless the spiritual condition of the Community improve and the members cease "to criticise the work with unbelieving reason."

Gottlieb Scheuner records the fact that a certain Sister "who did not love the ways of humility and simplicity" took the message to herself, became ill, and died within two weeks. This illness was regarded as a "precious term of grace for the poor soul during which she came to comprehend the many sins of her youth and the time so illy spent and most sincerely repented." — See Gottlieb Scheuner's *Beschreibung des Gnadenwerks des Herrn in den Gemeinden der Wahren Inspiration.*

188 In 1871 the Amana Society received an anonymous prospectus of a book which contained much abusive material and "a number of malicious, horrible calumnies and false accusations" regarding the Society. The prospectus was accompanied by a letter which stated that the author had received an offer of $8000 for his manuscript; but if the Society should desire it and would pay him a larger sum he would not publish it. The matter was referred to Ex-Governor Samuel J. Kirkwood who very soon "unmasked the libelous spirit." "He wrote to the author", says Gottlieb Scheuner, "and denounced him at once as an evident swindler who was distorting the truth to extort money. And he warned him that this was a penitentiary offence." The Governor's letter had the proper effect upon the author of the prospectus, and nothing more was ever heard of or from him. The prospectus and the correspondence with Governor Kirkwood are in the possession of Mr. Arthur J. Cox, of Iowa City, through whose kindness the author has had the privilege of examining them.

189 In reviewing a certain stormy period in the history of the Community, Gottlieb Scheuner remarks: "It was however not a period of decline, on the contrary one of rallying and self-collecting and of a deeper founding after this storm that they [the Community] might have a firmer foundation and greater endurance in the new storms which

were to come.'' — See *Historischer Bericht von der Neuen Erweckung Sammlung und Gründung der Wahren Inspirations-Gemeinde*, pp. 42, 43.

[190] Gottlieb Scheuner's *Historischer Bericht von der Neuen Erweckung Sammlung und Gründung der Wahren Inspirations-Gemeinde,* p. 510. The testimony referred to was probably given through Christian Metz.

[191] See Georg Melber's *Ueberzeugung von der Göttlichkeit der Inspiration,* published at Ronneberg in 1715. In the *Bezeugungen des Geistes des Herrn* for 1834 there is recorded a similar testimony (No. 18) regarding an unfaithful member ''who no longer lived but whom they [some of the members of the Community] still greatly esteemed.'' It reads: ''Do not believe that such a soul which intentionally despised My Spirit and treated it mockingly has gone into rest and peace.''

CHAPTER VIII

[192] From a letter written by Christian Metz from Amana to the brethren at Ebenezer on July 15, 1859.

[193] The testimony referred to in the text was uttered on June 30, 1819, in the midst of the ''trouble and oppression'' of ''the Krausert affair.''

[194] *Bezeugungen des Geistes des Herrn,* 1819. This testimony was given on resuming the work after the ''fall'' of Krausert.

[195] *Bezeugungen des Geistes des Herrn,* 1819. This was an *Einsprache* written on June 27, 1819. The gift of *Aussprache* was not granted to Christian Metz until 1828.

CHAPTER IX

[196] These introductory paragraphs to the *Bezeugungen* constitute in themselves a fairly complete history of important events in the Community.

[197] The testimony referred to in the text in No. 19 in *Bezeugungen des Geistes des Herrn,* 1863.

This "most difficult and trying time" occurred during the summer of 1863. In addition to the spiritual troubles recorded the Community suffered at this time from "great heat and protracted drought."

[198] The earlier works of Dr. Johann W. Peterson were also burned at this time. Dr. Peterson was a "learned professor of Lüneburg" who espoused the cause of Inspiration in the seventeenth century — more than a quarter of a century before the time of Rock and Gruber. Under the Spirit of Inspiration "he saw many things which were to happen in the future." He wrote much concerning these visions. He had a gift for writing hymns; and there is in use in the Community at the present time a collection of Dr. Peterson's psalms. — For a sketch of Johann W. Peterson see Perkins and Wick's *History of the Amana Society,* p. 9.

[199] "The testimonies of Barbara Heinemann", says Gottlieb Scheuner, "furnished the groundwork for the historical account of this period."

[200] This entry was made on the second day of January, 1866. Owing to failing health the entries for the preceding year were few and brief. After the death of Christian Metz, Gottlieb Scheuner, who had been the constant companion and devoted Scribe of the *Werkzeug* for eleven years, wrote the *Anhang oder Ergänzung zu dem Tagebuch*

des l. sel. Br. Christian Metz. This supplement covers the period from 1865 to 1867 inclusive and deals particularly with the "circumstances of the illness and death of the beloved Brother."

[201] Gottlieb Scheuner was born in Engelthal, Hessen-Darmstadt, Germany. He was six and one-half years old when he came with his parents to the new home at Ebenezer. In a brief autobiography Gottlieb Scheuner relates that "Bro. Christian Metz exhibited a particular love and affection for me when I was a child; and after I grew up he often invited me to visit him, he gave me books, pictures, etc., as tokens of his good will, and sought ever to draw me toward him. He often said when I became more mature I should take up my abode entirely with him." This plan it appears was not at first pleasing to this gifted youth, and he was later earnestly admonished in a *Bezeugung* "not to lose the good intent, the good portion and lot to which I [the Lord] have called you from your earliest childhood." On October 15, 1852, he took up his residence with the *Werkzeug* Christian Metz, became his friend, companion, and faithful Scribe, and in 1853 he was called through Inspiration as a Community schoolmaster. To this service he devoted his talents until 1885 when he became the spiritual leader of the Community. His natural spirituality and his years of special training under Christian Metz well fitted him for his high calling. He was a fluent and convincing speaker and a pleasing writer; and his influence over the youth of the Community during the nearly half century of his service as schoolmaster and spiritual leader can not be over-estimated. It is the religious enthusiasm and unbounded devotion of such rare souls as Christian Metz and Gottlieb Scheuner that have done so

much to preserve in this materialistic age the ideals of the founders of the Community.

CHAPTER XI

[202] *Joh. A. Grubers und H. S. Gleims Leiden zu Zürich.*

[203] The *Vierundzwanzig Regeln der Wahren Gottseligkeit* are given in full as a preface to the *Jahrbücher* for 1819-1823. This volume, or *Sammlung*, contains the testimonies of Barbara Heinemann from the time of her "miraculous gift of Inspiration" to the date of her marriage.

[204] The *Bundesschliessung* of to-day is the renewing of this pledge according to the Twenty-four Rules for True Godliness. The young people "make their vow" and new members pledge their fidelity "with heart, mouth, and hand to the Elder and assistant Elders as witnesses of God, chosen by God and the congregation for this purpose . . . . according to the Twenty-four Rules for True Godliness [which were] given by the Spirit of the Lord through Inspiration."

CHAPTER XIII

[205] From the account of the *Liebes- und Gedächtnissmahl des Leidens und Sterbens unsers Herrn und Heilandes Jesu Christi* for 1855.

CHAPTER XIV

[206] William A. Hinds, who was a member of the Oneida Community, observes in his *American Communities* that "such a cleansing process [as the *Untersuchung*] might with advantage be adopted in every Community and every

church." The Shakers had its counterpart in the periodical confession of sin. "My son, give glory to the God of heaven", said Elder Evans, "confess unto Him and tell *me* what thou hast done." The system of "Mutual Criticism" of the Oneida and Perfectionist communities had the same underlying motive; while the Harmonists had their yearly reconciliation of all members of the Community.

This system of mutual criticism, personal confession of sin, or whatever form the "regulator" may take, bears the same relation to communism (according to John Humphrey Noyes, founder and President of the Oneida Community) which the system of judicature bears to ordinary society.

[207] *Bezeugungen des Geistes des Herrn,* 1851. This testimony occurred on July 7, 1851.

[208] *Bezeugungen des Geistes des Herrn,* 1858. It is a tendency to worldliness that is especially deplored in this testimony — a disinclination "to share the great and weighty inner and outer cares and burdens of the Community" and a growing desire "to choose and follow the broad way of the flesh."

[209] *Bezeugungen des Geistes des Herrn,* 1878.

[210] The quotations are part of a lengthy and rather elaborate *Zeugniss* given at a meeting of the Sisters at Nieder Ebenezer. It includes a general admonition, an appeal, thirteen individual admonitions, besides a "word to the children" and another to the "young Sisters."

[211] Christian Metz records in his *Tagebuch* the suspension of a meeting "because of grave indifference and desecration, especially on the part of the growing-up girls

and also because of the indolence and lethargy of the older Sisters, until a new repentance and self-finding shall come over them."

CHAPTER XV

212 *Catechetischer Unterricht von der Lehre des Heils,* Part II, p. 75.

213 At the present time the *Untersuchung* as well as the "arrangement and appointments" of the *Liebesmahl* itself are all decided through the Great Council of the Brethren. Even the selection of the testimonies to be read at the several meetings in each village is made by the Great Council.

214 This *Liebesmahl* of 1844-1845 was the first one celebrated in the New World. It was held under the direction of the *Werkzeug* Christian Metz.

215 Christian Metz had died in July of the preceding year.

216 Gottlieb Scheuner's *Beschreibung des Gnadenwerks des Herrn in den Gemeinden der Wahren Inspiration,* p. 57. In this account the appointees are all mentioned by name.

217 The two important testimonies referred to in this account are Nos. 105 and 107 in *Bezeugungen des Geistes des Herrn,* 1842. See also Gottlieb Scheuner's *Historischer Bericht von der Neuen Erweckung Sammlung und Gründung der Wahren Inspirations-Gemeinde,* pp. 293-295.

CHAPTER XVI

218 The title pages of the two Catechisms are almost identical and read:

> J. J. J. Catechetical Instruction of the Teachings of Salvation presented according to the statements of the Holy Scriptures and founded upon the evangelic-apostolic interpretation of the Spirit of God for the blessed use of the Youth [or members] of the Communities of True Inspiration.

All of the *Jahrbücher* and most of the books of a religious nature published by the Community have the mystic letters "J. J. J." prefixed to the title. They signify *Jesu Jehovah Immanuel.*

CHAPTER XVII

219 *Psalter-Spiel,* No. 152, p. 143. Many hymns in the *Psalter-Spiel* are based on the Psalms of the Bible.

220 These prayers are portions of Nos. 917, 159, 429, and 241 respectively of the *Psalter-Spiel.*

221 *Auszüge aus den Tagebüchern von Br. Christian Metz,* p. 45. The following prefatory paragraph to the hymn quoted in the text occurs under the date of August 21, 1847:

> Es waren des Nachts Hunde in unserer Schafheerde eingefallen und hatten mehrere zerrissen und die Heerde auseinander gesprengt. Dieses ist mir bedenklich.

222 *Auszüge aus den Tagebüchern von Br. Christian Metz,* p. 447. Den 4 Juli. Nach einer schrecklichen Gewitternacht mit fortwährendem Blitzen und Donnern.

223 *Auszüge aus den Tagebüchern von Br. Christian Metz,* p. 32. This *Abendlied* contains eleven verses.

CHAPTER XVIII

224 In the *Vierundzwanzig Regeln der Wahren Gottsel-*

igkeit "heads and fathers of households" are admonished to "see to this, that you prove truly heads and lights of your households . . . . that you may bring your help-mates . . . . to true conduct and fear of God." Again, "your children . . . . you shall endeavor with all your power to sacrifice to Me and to lead to Me."

225 The effectiveness of public opinion as a restraint in such a community as Amana can not be over-estimated. Even in the world it is perhaps true that "public opinion exercising a censorship over our actions is far more potent than all the laws which human wisdom can devise."

226 The Elders, being chosen with great care for their spirituality, are not educated for their office; nor do they give their time entirely to church work. Indeed, most of the religious communities of the past century have had no regular clergy. The Zoar Society particularly had a strong aversion to the ministers of the world who "do not get their knowledge from God but have learned it like a *trade* in the schools."

CHAPTER XIX

227 The concluding quotation in the text is from Horace Greeley's *Recollections of a Busy Life.* Horace Greeley was intensely interested in "association", and devoted time, influence and money to the promotion of Fourierism. In his retrospect of the "successes and failures of Socialism" he says: "With a firm and deep religious basis, any Socialistic scheme *may* succeed . . . . Without a basis of religious sympathy and religious aspiration, it will always be difficult."

Six young Inspirationists knitting—1890s

APPENDIX

THE CONSTITUTION AND BY-LAWS OF THE AMANA SOCIETY

Knitting lessons—1890s

Community kitchen hearth and utensils— 1890s

THE CONSTITUTION AND BY-LAWS OF THE AMANA SOCIETY

PREAMBLE

WHEREAS the Community of True Inspiration has in the year 1843, and in the years following, emigrated from Germany into the United States of America, for the sake of enjoying the noble civil and religious liberties of this country, and has settled at Ebenezer, in the County of Erie and State of New York, on the former Buffalo Creek Indian Reservation, where it has since existed, under the protection of God, in peace and prosperity; and whereas the said Community, in the year 1854, according to the known will of God, resolved unanimously, to sell the Ebenezer lands, and to undertake a new settlement in the western country, and has consequently, in the year 1855 and the years following, purchased a tract of land in the State of Iowa, and has paid for the same out of the funds of the Community; and whereas a beginning has since been made of this new settlement, with the purpose to continue and accomplish such resettlement by degrees, as the times and circumstances will permit.

NOW THEREFORE, we the undersigned members of the Community of True Inspiration, feeling thankful for the grace and beneficence of God, to be privileged under the liberal laws of this state to an incorporation as a religious Society, do hereby associate ourselves anew under the corporate name of in the County and State of Iowa, and have adopted and do herewith adopt the following Constitution and By-Laws.

CONSTITUTION

ARTICLE I

The foundation of our civil organization is and shall remain forever God, the Lord, and the faith, which He worked in us according to His free grace and mercy, and which is founded upon (1) the word of God as revealed in the old and new testament; (2) the testimony of Jesus through the Spirit of Prophecy; (3) the hidden spirit of grace and chastisement.

The purpose of our association as a religious Society is therefore no worldly or selfish one, but the purpose of the love of God in His vocation of grace received by us, to serve Him in the bond of union, inwardly and outwardly, according to His laws and His requirements in our own consciences, and thus to work out the salvation of our souls, through the redeeming grace of Jesus Christ, in self-denial, in the obedience to our faith, and in the demonstration of our faithfulness in the inward and outward service of the Community by the power of grace which God presents us with.

And to fulfill this duty we do hereby covenant and promise collectively and each to the other by the acceptance and signing of this present Constitution.

ARTICLE II

In this bond of union tied by God amongst ourselves, it is our unanimous will and resolution that the land purchased here and that may hereafter be purchased shall be and remain a common estate and property, with all improvements thereupon and all appurtenances thereto, as also with all the labor, cares, troubles and burdens, of which each member shall bear his allotted share with a willing heart.

And having obtained in pursuance of the act of the legislature of this State, Chapter 131, passed March 22d, 1858, an incorporation as a religious society, it is hereby agreed on that the present and future titles to our common lands shall be conveyed to and vested in the Amana Society, as our corporate name by which we are known in law.

ARTICLE III

Agriculture and the raising of cattle and other domestic animals, in connection with some manufactures and trades shall under the blessing of God form the means of sustenance for this Society. Out of the income of the land and the other branches of industry the common expenses of the Society shall be defrayed.

The surplus, if any, shall from time to time be applied to the improvement of the common estate of the Society, to the building and maintaining of meeting and school houses, printing establishments, to the support and care of the old, sick and infirm members of the Society, to the founding of a business and safety fund, and to benevolent purposes in general.

ARTICLE IV

The control and management of all the affairs of this Society shall be vested in a Board of Trustees consisting of thirteen members, to be annually elected out of the number of Elders in the Community, by the members of the

Society entitled to vote. The time, place, and manner of holding all elections for officers in this corporation and the qualifications of voters shall be regulated by by-laws to be adopted by the Community.

In the Trustees, so elected, we the undersigned members do hereby vest all the powers, rights of action and privileges granted to corporations by the laws of this State, and also all requisite power and authority to arrange, control, and manage, in brotherly concurrence according to our order of grace, or by a majority of votes, all the affairs and concerns of this corporation whatsoever; to receive new members under this Constitution; to assign to the members their work, labor and employment; to fix the amounts of the yearly allowances for the support of the members; to exclude, order away, and remove such members who are unruly and resisting, and who will not mend themselves after repeated admonition; to settle and liquidate the accounts of those members withdrawing from the Society, either by their own choice or by expulsion; to receive and to administrate all the active and passive property of the Society; to keep books and accounts of everything; to buy and to sell; to make, fulfill, and revoke contracts, to carry on agriculture, the rearing of cattle, manufactures, mills and trades of any kind, to erect buildings, to improve and take down the same; to make inventories; to appoint attorneys, agents, and managers; to borrow, lend and safely invest funds and moneys; also in the corporate name of the Society, or in the name of the Trustees, or of any member thereof to ask, demand, levy, recover and receive all kinds of goods, moneys, principal and interest, effects, debts, demands, inheritances and legacies, wheresoever and whatsoever; to receive, execute and deliver all deeds, mortgages, notes, powers of attorney, receipts, and all other documents and accounts whatsoever; and to do, transact and carry out all needful, beneficial, legal, proper, just and equitable acts, matters and things in general of all and every kind whatsoever, all for and in the name, behalf and benefit of this corporation.

In the event however of matters of great importance and responsibility it shall be the duty of the Trustees to hold special meetings and to decide therein either by unanimous concurrence or by a majority of votes whether or not such matters shall be submitted for counsel and decision by vote to all the Elders of the Community and to the members entitled to vote.

All resolutions of the Board of Trustees relating to the sale of the Society's lands situate within the township of Amana require the consent of two-thirds of all the Trustees and of two-thirds of all the Elders in the Community, as also the consent of a majority of the members entitled to vote.

The lands now owned by the Society lying beyond the township of Amana shall be under the administration of the Trustees with power to sell, exchange, or rent the same, as they shall find best in the interest of the Society.

Vacancies in the Board of Trustees occasioned by withdrawal, sickness or death of any of its members, may be filled for the intervening time until the next annual election by the remaining Trustees themselves, out of the number of the Elders in the Community.

The Trustees shall annually elect out of their number one President, one Vice President, and one Secretary, and shall procure a seal, which shall be the corporate seal of the Society.

All public and legal documents and instruments emanating from the Society by a resolution of the Trustees, in conformity with this Constitution, shall be signed by the President, countersigned by the Secretary, and the corporate seal of the Society affixed thereto.

In the month of June in each year the Trustees shall exhibit to the voting members of the Society a full statement of the real and personal estate of the Society.

ARTICLE V

Every member of this Society is in duty bound to hand over his or her personal and real property to the Trustees for the common fund, at the time of his or her acceptance as a member, and before the signing of this Constitution.

For such payments into the common fund each member is entitled to the credit thereof in the books of the Society, and to a receipt signed by the President and Secretary of the Board of Trustees, and is moreover secured for such payments by the pledge of the common property of the Society.

ARTICLE VI

Every member of this Society is, besides the free board and dwelling, and the support and care secured to him in old age, sickness and infirmity, further entitled out of the common fund to an annual sum of maintenance for him or herself, children and relatives in the Society; and these annual allowances shall be fixed by the Trustees for each member single or in families, according to justice and equity, and shall be from time to time revised and fixed anew, in accordance with a list to be kept thereof.

And we, the undersigned members of this corporation in consideration of the enjoyment of these blessings in the bond of our Communion, do hereby release, grant and quit-claim to the said corporation, for ourselves, our children, heirs, and administrators all claims for wages and interest of the capital paid into the common fund, also all claims for any part of the income and profits, and of any share in the estate and property of the Society separate from the whole and common stock.

ARTICLE VII

All children and minors in the Society, after the death of their parents or relatives, shall as orphans be under the special guardianship of the Trustees of the Society, during the time of their minority. In case of such parents or relatives deceased having a credit on the books of the Society, without their leaving a will or testament for the disposition of the same; or in case such parents or relatives are indebted to the Society for advances made them, then the children or minors of such parents and relatives shall at the time of their majority, in regard to such credits or debts, enter into the rights and into the liabilities of their deceased parents and relatives, as their natural and lawful heirs, and the credits and debts of members so deceased shall then be transferred on the books of the Society to such heirs, according to the proper share of each, under the direction of the Trustees. Such personal estates or credits as may be left by members, dying in the Society, without having made any will or testament for the disposition of the same, and without leaving any lawful heirs, shall revert to and invest in said corporation.

ARTICLE VIII

Such members as may recede from the Society, either by their own choice or by expulsion, shall be entitled to receive back the moneys paid by them into the common fund, and to interest thereon at the rate not exceeding five per cent per annum, from the time of the adjustment of their accounts until the repayment of their credits, which rate is to be fixed by the Board of Trustees.

Such receding members shall, however, not be entitled to any other allowance for any services rendered to the Society during their membership, except such as may be granted them by the Board of Trustees, on the settlement of their accounts, as a gratuity and not as a legal claim.

To enable however the Society to make such repayments to receding members, as also eventual payments of legacies and inheritances of members deceased in the Society, to relatives or heirs thereto entitled beyond the Society, without loss and oppression, it has been agreed on between ourselves, that such payments shall be made in the following manner, viz: of all sums up to $500, one-fourth part on the adjustment of the claim, and the remainder within four months thereafter; of all sums over $500 up to $20,000, and over, the sums of from $200 to $600 at the time of settlement, and the remainder in three, four, six, nine, twelve, fifteen, eighteen and twenty-one equal four-monthly installments, in proportion to the amounts to be paid.

Our purpose is not to withhold from any one his due without necessity, but also to secure the Society in all cases against distress and trouble; the authority shall therefore be left with our Trustees to act herein according to the times and circumstances, and to effect a compromise with the claimants in question according to justice and equity.

ARTICLE IX

Amendments to this Constitution may at any time be proposed by any member of this Society to the Board of Trustees for counsel and examination. Any amendments however to be received and accepted as a part of the present Constitution, require the consent of two-thirds of the Board of Trustees, of two-thirds of the remaining Elders, and of a majority of the members entitled to vote.

ARTICLE X

This Constitution shall take effect on the first of January, 1860, and shall be signed by all members of lawful age, male and female, in a separate book to be appropriated hereto and to be left in the safe keeping of the Board of Trustees. A copy of this Constitution shall upon request be handed to any voting member of the Society for perusal and reference.

Done in public meeting. Witness our signatures.

Amana, in the County and State of Iowa, in the Month of December, A. D. 1859.

BY-LAWS*

Concerning the Election

The election shall be held annually on the first Tuesday in the month of December.

Each male member who has signed the Constitution, as also the widows and such female members over thirty years of age, who are not represented by a male member shall be entitled to vote.

*These By-Laws were adopted in 1859.

On said day of election thirteen (13) Trustees shall be chosen by the ballot of the qualified voters for the term of one year, beginning on the second Tuesday in the month of December of the same year.

The election of Trustees shall be held at Amana at the polling place. Any change of place or time of election shall be made known to the voters fourteen days before election. The Township Trustees and Clerk shall constitute the board of this election.

These thirteen (13) Trustees thus elected shall meet on the second Tuesday in the month of December and shall elect out of their own number one President, one Vice President, and one Secretary. Vacancies by withdrawal or decease may be filled by the Trustees during the year in like manner.

Schoolgirls at play—1890

ɔp: *A young girl, Homestead—1890s.* *Below:* *Schoolgirls*

Kitchen gardens, cabbage for sauerkraut, Amanas—1890s

INDEX

Amana girls holding their sunbonnets—1890s